Secured Transactions

BY DOUGLAS J. WHALEY
Ohio State University

Twelfth Edition

THOMSON
BAR/BRI

EDITORIAL OFFICES: 111 W. Jackson Blvd., 7th Floor, Chicago, IL 60604
REGIONAL OFFICES: Chicago, Dallas, Los Angeles, New York, Washington, D.C.

PROJECT EDITOR
Erin Johnson Remotigue, B.A., J.D.
Attorney At Law

SERIES EDITOR
Elizabeth L. Snyder, B.A., J.D.
Attorney At Law

QUALITY CONTROL EDITOR
Sanetta M. Hister

Summary of Contents

SECURED TRANSACTIONS TEXT CORRELATION CHART   i
SECURED TRANSACTIONS CAPSULE SUMMARY   I
APPROACH TO EXAMS   (i)

I.	**INTRODUCTION**	
	Chapter Approach	1
A.	Goals of the Debtor and the Creditor	1
	CHART: **Rights of Secured vs. Unsecured Creditors**	**2**
B.	Pre-Code Security Devices	3
C.	Uniform Commercial Code	9
D.	Liens	10
II.	**COVERAGE OF ARTICLE 9**	
	Chapter Approach	11
A.	Terminology	11
B.	Scope of Article 9 Coverage	13
	CHART: **Summary of Types of Collateral**	**19**
	CHART: **True Lease vs. Disguised Secured Transaction—An Approach**	**21**
	CHART: **Article 9 Consignments—An Approach**	**24**
C.	Transactions Excluded from Article 9	25
	CHART: **Transactions Excluded from Article 9**	**28**
III.	**CREATION OF A SECURITY INTEREST**	
	Chapter Approach	31
A.	Introduction	31
	CHART: **A Typical Secured Transaction Scenario**	**32**
B.	Attachment of a Security Interest—In General	33
	CHART: **Has the Security Interest Attached?**	**35**
C.	Security Agreement	36
	CHART: **Sufficiency of Description of Collateral in Security Agreement**	**39**
D.	Value	42
E.	Debtor's Rights in the Collateral	43
IV.	**PERFECTION**	
	Chapter Approach	45
A.	Methods of Perfection	46
	CHART: **Comparison of Attachment vs. Perfection**	**46**

		CHART: Summary of Methods of Perfection	**63**
	B.	Time of Perfection	63
	C.	Place of Perfection—Multistate Transactions	64

V. FILING

		Chapter Approach	73
	A.	The Financing Statement	73
		CHART: Authenticated Security Agreement vs. Financing Statement	**79**
	B.	Where to File	80
	C.	Mechanics of Filing	81
		CHART: Summary of Types of Filed Records	**84**
	D.	Request for Statement of Account or List of Collateral	84

VI. PRIORITIES

		Chapter Approach	87
	A.	Competing Interests in Collateral—The Claimants	87
	B.	Priority—Unperfected Creditors	89
	C.	Priority Among Perfected Creditors—General Rule	90
		CHART: Example of "First to File or Perfect" Rule	**92**
	D.	Priority Among Perfected Creditors—Special Rules for Purchase Money Security Interests	94
		CHART: PMSI Super-Priority—Examples	**98**
		CHART: How to Gain PMSI Super-Priority	**99**
	E.	Priority Among Perfected Creditors—Special Rules for Certain Types of Collateral	100
	F.	Priority Among Perfected Creditors—Perfection by Control	113
	G.	Priority Among Perfected Creditors—As Affected by Terms of Security Agreement	115
	H.	Priority Among Perfected Creditors and Other Claimants	119
		CHART: Requirements for Buyer in Ordinary Course of Business Status	**122**

VII. BANKRUPTCY PROCEEDINGS AND ARTICLE 9

		Chapter Approach	133
	A.	Debtor's Bankruptcy	133
		CHART: Rights of Perfected Creditor vs. Unperfected Creditor upon Debtor's Bankruptcy	**135**
		CHART: Was Transfer of Debtor's Property a Voidable Preference?	**138**
	B.	After-Acquired Property in Bankruptcy	143

VIII. DEFAULT PROCEEDINGS

		Chapter Approach	145
	A.	Introduction	145
	B.	Occurrence of Default	146
	C.	Remedies—In General	149
	D.	Right of Possession upon Default	150
	E.	Realizing on the Collateral	153
		CHART: Notice of Disposition of Collateral by Sale—A Summary	**160**
		CHART: Order of Application of Proceeds of Sale	**162**
		CHART: Seller's Retention vs. Sale of Collateral—A Comparison	**165**

F.	Debtor's Right of Redemption	168
G.	Effect of Failure to Comply with Default Provisions	169
H.	Nonwaivable Rights Under the Security Agreement	170
I.	Special Default Rules for Intangibles and Fixtures	172

REVIEW QUESTIONS AND ANSWERS	**175**
EXAM QUESTIONS AND ANSWERS	**195**
TABLE OF CITATIONS TO UNIFORM COMMERCIAL CODE	**205**
TABLE OF CASES	**209**
INDEX	**211**

Text Correlation Chart

Gilbert Law Summary SECURED TRANSACTIONS	Schwartz & Scott *Commercial Transactions: Principles and Policies* 1991 (2nd ed.)	Warren & Walt *Commercial Law* 2004 (6th ed.)	Whaley *Problems and Materials on Commercial Law* 2005 (8th ed.)	Whaley *Problems and Materials on Secured Transactions* 2003 (6th ed.)	White *Secured Transactions— Teaching Materials* 2006 (3rd ed.)
I. INTRODUCTION					
A. Goals of the Debtor and the Creditor	545-548	2-17	865-868	1-4	
B. Pre-Code Security Devices	791-814	17-18	870-880	6-15	
C. Uniform Commercial Code	2-3, 565-566	18-20	865-866		
D. Liens		3-4	866-867	2-3	
II. COVERAGE OF ARTICLE 9					
A. Terminology	566-567	20-21	881-882, 921-926	2, 17-18	
B. Scope of Article 9 Coverage	566-567, 701-713, 735-756	19, 148-157, 179-181, 297-338	882-900, 911-921	18-34, 45-55	235-254, 274-332
C. Transactions Excluded from Article 9	566, 735-745, 756-761	339	900-909	35-43	
III. CREATION OF A SECURITY INTEREST					
A. Introduction	565-566	20-21	921-924		
B. Attachment of a Security Interest—In General	567-568, 628-636, 659-660	21-22	934-944	63-73	2-18, 41-46
C. Security Agreement	567-568, 659-660	21-44	922-923	55-63	
D. Value	567	44	934	63	
E. Debtor's Rights in the Collateral	567	45-49	934-944	63	
IV. PERFECTION					
A. Methods of Perfection	568-591, 669-680, 773-826	50-52, 82-92	945-980	75-108	18-28, 204-229, 344-359, 434-454
B. Time of Perfection			945-946	75	
C. Place of Perfection— Multistate Transactions	591-598	92-107	981-986	109-114	28-41
V. FILING					
A. The Financing Statement	570-591	52-76	923-934	11, 55-63	19-28
B. Where to File	569	76-77	976	105	20-22
C. Mechanics of Filing		77-82	976-979	105-108	20-28
D. Request for Statement of Account or List of Collateral					
VI. PRIORITIES					
A. Competing Interests in Collateral—The Claimants	608	108	987	2-3	

Gilbert Law Summary **SECURED TRANSACTIONS**	Schwartz & Scott *Commercial Transactions: Principles and Policies* 1991 (2nd ed.)	Warren & Walt *Commercial Law* 2004 (6th ed.)	Whaley *Problems and Materials on Commercial Law* 2005 (8th ed.)	Whaley *Problems and Materials on Secured Transactions* 2003 (6th ed.)	White *Secured Transactions— Teaching Materials* 2006 (3rd ed.)
B. Priority— Unperfected Creditors			988-989	115-119	41-42
C. Priority Among Perfected Creditors— General Rule		109-118	925-926, 1148-1149	116-117	43-46
D. Priority Among Perfected Creditors— Special Rules for Purchase Money Security Interests	672-677	119-135	998-1017	18-23, 126-144	209-229
E. Priority Among Perfected Creditors— Special Rules for Certain Types of Collateral	685-699, 713-735	168-205, 418-437	1068-1086, 1131-1150	191-208, 251-268	229-235, 268-270, 333-343
F. Priority Among Perfected Creditors— Perfection by Control		179-188, 565-568	1017-1021	144-148	
G. Priority Among Perfected Creditors— As Affected by Terms of Security Agreement	628-637, 659-660	110-112	990-998, 1037-1047	117-126, 163-171	202
H. Priority Among Perfected Creditors and Other Claimants	616-659	135-148, 205-223	1021-1068, 1086-1109	148-191, 208-230	254-270
VII. BANKRUPTCY PROCEEDINGS AND ARTICLE 9					
A. Debtor's Bankruptcy	827-928	438-503	1111-1119, 1129-1130	231-238, 247-249	71-183, 392-412
B. After-Acquired Property in Bankruptcy	882-886	488-489	1119-1120	238-247	149-152
VIII. DEFAULT PROCEEDINGS					
A. Introduction	929-930	224-225	923, 1157-1158	271-275	
B. Occurrence of Default	930-950	225-243	1158-1164	283-284, 289	
C. Remedies—In General		243-246			67-70, 309-312
D. Right of Possession upon Default	950-961	246-254	1164-1179	284-309	363-392
E. Realizing on the Collateral	952-955, 961-983	254-295	1179-1184	305-314	
F. Debtor's Right of Redemption		295-296	1184-1189	310-314	
G. Effect of Failure to Comply with Default Provisions	962-971	247-248, 271-274	1180-1189	283, 309	
H. Nonwaivable Rights Under the Security Agreement		276, 279, 282	1183	308-309	
I. Special Default Rules for Intangibles and Fixtures	698, 713-715, 731-735	286-295, 430-437	1179	191-207	

Capsule Summary

I.	**INTRODUCTION**		
A.	**GOALS OF DEBTOR AND CREDITOR**		
	1.	**Debtor's Goal**	§1
		To get as much credit as needed *without* giving any more security (collateral or a surety) than necessary.	
	2.	**Creditor's Goal**	§2
		To get *repayment plus a profit.* Creditor also wants *priority* over other creditors as against debtor's collateral or surety.	
	3.	**Goal of Security Interest Legislation**	§3
		To regulate a *balance* between goals of creditor and debtor.	
B.	**PRE-CODE SECURITY DEVICES**		
	1.	**Seller's Fraudulent Retention of Goods After Sale Not Allowed**	
		a. **Statute of Elizabeth**	§5
		Seller's possession of goods after sale was *void and fraudulent* as against seller's creditors.	
		b. **Early U.S. law**	§6
		U.S. law generally retains the policy against "sham" sales, *presuming fraud* if the seller retains possession.	
		c. **U.C.C.**	§7
		The U.C.C. incorporates existing law *except* that the seller's retention "in good faith and current course of trade" for a "commercially reasonable time" is *not* deemed fraudulent.	
		(1) **Sale and leaseback**	§8
		Although in a sale and leaseback arrangement the seller retains possession of the goods, such an arrangement is allowed under the U.C.C.	
	2.	**Pledge**	§10
		A pledge occurs when the creditor takes *possession* of the debtor's property (collateral) during the debt period. Note that the pledge is still a widely used security device.	

3. Chattel Mortgage §13
A chattel mortgage is a mortgage on the debtor's personal property *filed in the appropriate place* to give notice of the creditor's interest.

4. Conditional Sale §16
A conditional sale occurred when the seller of property retained *title* (but not *possession*) until the buyer completely paid for the goods.

5. Trust Receipt §21
The trust receipt was a form of *inventory financing* in which a bank purchased goods from a manufacturer, keeping *title* thereto, and then released them "in trust" to the retailer, after filing a notice that it was engaged in such financing.

6. Field Warehousing §24
Field warehousing was and is a means of pledging collateral of great bulk. The warehouse is created around the goods and the *warehouse receipt* is issued to the creditor, who then lends the debtor money.

7. Factor's Acts §25
State statutes allowing financers ("factors") to perfect their interests in inventory goods that their extensions of credit had helped to produce.

8. Assignment of Accounts Receivable §28
This method of financing was accomplished in most states by filing notice of the creditor's interest in the outstanding accounts of the debtor-business. The debtor's customers (the obligors) may or may not have been notified that their obligations were assigned to the creditor.

C. Uniform Commercial Code

1. In General §35
Adoption of U.C.C. Article 9 (Secured Transactions) eliminated most of the above pre-Code security devices.

2. Revisions of Article 9 §36
The original version of Article 9 was substantially rewritten in 1971, and again in 1999. The 1999 version has been adopted in *all 50 states*. It became effective in most of those states on July 1, 2001. This Summary contains the rules of the 1999 revision.

3. Revision of Articles 1 and 2 §37
Article 1, which includes a larger definition section and a command that good faith is imposed in all U.C.C. transactions, was revised in 2001, but has not been widely adopted. Similarly, 2003 revisions to Article 2 have not been adopted in most states. Citations in this outline are to the *prerevision U.C.C. versions* unless designated by the letter "R."

D. LIENS

1. In General §38
A lien is a creditor's interest in the debtor's property.

2. Types of Liens

a. **Judicial liens** §39
These are acquired in judicial proceedings.

b. **"Statutory" liens** §40
Statutes and the common law have created certain liens for specific unsecured creditors (*e.g.,* landlords, attorneys, artisans, and the I.R.S.).

c. **Consensual liens** §41
These are created by agreement by the debtor and creditor and include *Article 9* security interests.

II. **COVERAGE OF ARTICLE 9**

A. **TERMINOLOGY**

1. **Introduction** §42
The Code simplified financing arrangements by introducing standard terminology.

2. **"Security Interest"** §43
This is every interest in the debtor's *personal property or fixtures* given to the creditor to *secure payment or performance* of the debtor's obligation.

a. **Note** §45
The term also includes the outright sale of accounts, chattel paper, payment intangibles, or promissory notes.

3. **"Security Agreement"** §46
This is the agreement (contract) by which the security interest is created.

4. **"Secured Party"** §47
This refers to the creditor having a security interest, or the buyer in the sale of accounts, chattel paper, payment intangibles, or promissory notes.

5. **"Debtor" and "Obligor"** §48
The *debtor* is the *owner* of the collateral. The *obligor* is the person who *owes the debt* to the creditor. They often are one and the same person.

B. **SCOPE OF ARTICLE 9 COVERAGE**

1. **In General** §49
Article 9 applies to: (i) *any transaction intended to create a security interest in personal property or fixtures*; (ii) any *sale of accounts, chattel paper, payment intangibles, or promissory notes*; (iii) *consignments*; (iv) *agricultural liens*; and (v) security interests arising under *other U.C.C. articles*.

2. **Types of Collateral** §50
Proper classification of the *type* of collateral involved is necessary for application of the appropriate Article 9 rule.

a. **Tangible collateral—goods** §51
"Goods" include things that are *moveable* and includes unborn young of animals, crops, timber to be cut, fixtures, and computer software embedded in goods.

(1) Four types of goods

(a) *"Consumer goods"* are goods used or bought primarily for *personal, family, or household purposes*. §55

(b) *"Inventory"* includes goods held for *sale or lease* to others *in the ordinary course of business*. It also includes *raw materials* and materials *used up or consumed* in a business (*e.g.*, pencils). §56

(c) *"Farm products"* are goods that are *used or produced in farming operations* and that are in the possession of a farmer-debtor. §57

(d) *"Equipment"* includes goods that *do not fit into any of the other three categories*. §58

b. Quasi-tangible collateral §60

These are legal rights often represented by a *writing*. There are four types:

(1) *"Instruments"* include U.C.C. Article 3 *negotiable and nonnegotiable instruments* (checks, promissory notes, etc.). §61

(2) *"Document"* means a U.C.C. Article 7 *"document of title"* (*e.g.*, a warehouse receipt or a bill of lading). §63

(3) *"Chattel paper"* refers to a record (*i.e.*, written or electronically stored information) or a combination of records that contain *both a promise to pay money and a security interest in or lease of* specific goods. Electronically stored chattel paper is *"electronic chattel paper,"* and written chattel paper is *"tangible chattel paper."* §64

(4) *"Investment property"* includes stocks and bonds (*"certificated securities"*), and commodity contracts and accounts in which stocks and bonds are held (*"uncertificated securities"*), and are given special treatment in Article 9. §66

c. Intangible collateral §67

Intangible collateral has *no physical form*. There are five types:

(1) Accounts §68

Account refers to a *right to payment* for goods or services sold or leased, which is not contained in an instrument or chattel paper. *Health care insurance receivables* are a *subcategory* of accounts.

(2) Letter of credit rights §70

In a typical letter of credit transaction, a seller of goods requires the buyer to get a letter of credit from a bank in favor of the seller, so that the bank makes payment to the seller. The *seller's rights against the bank issuing the letter of credit*, when used as collateral, are governed by Article 9.

(3) Deposit accounts §71

Deposit accounts include checking, savings, and passbook accounts. *Note: Article 9 does not cover consumer deposit accounts* (those used for personal, family, or household use), **except** to the extent they include **proceeds**.

(4) Commercial tort claims §72
These are claims filed by **organizations** (e.g., corporations and partnerships), and **business-related, nonpersonal injury claims** filed by individuals.

(5) General intangibles §73
This term refers to personal property used as collateral that does not fit into any other category, e.g., literary rights, good will. Many courts have held that a security interest can be perfected in a **liquor license**. **Software** not embedded in goods is also a general intangible. **"Payment intangibles"** are general intangibles under which the account debtor's principal obligation is the payment of money, e.g., oral promise to repay loan.

3. Types of Transactions §76
Any **financing** transaction may be subject to Article 9 if the purpose is to create a security interest in collateral.

a. Leases §77
Leases are **not** covered by Article 9 unless the so-called lease is actually a disguised attempt to create a security interest in leased property that is being sold to the "lessee."

(1) True lease compared with security interest §78
Whether the transaction is a true lease or a disguised sale on credit depends on the facts of each case, but a sale on credit will be presumed if: (i) the lessee has **no right to terminate** the lease, **and** (ii) either the lessee has an **option to purchase for no or nominal consideration** or the goods will have **no economic value** at the **end** of the lease term.

(2) Protective filing §87
A lessor who is unsure whether the transaction is a true lease or a disguised sale may file a financing statement to **guarantee priority** if appropriate, without conceding that Article 9 applies.

b. Consignments §88
As is the case with leases, security interests disguised as consignments (i.e., consignments in which the consignee cannot return unsold goods to the consignor) are governed by Article 9. In addition, unlike leases, some true consignments are covered by Article 9.

(1) True consignments that are covered by Article 9 §89
A true consignment is covered by Article 9 if (i) the goods, which are **not consumer goods** in the hands of the consignor, have a value of at least **$1,000** at the time of delivery to a consignee; (ii) the consignee is a **merchant** not generally known by its creditors to be substantially engaged in the selling of goods of others; and (iii) the consignee's professional name is different than that of the consignor. Such consignments are treated

as *purchase money security interests ("PMSIs") in inventory* (*see infra*). True consignments not covered by Article 9 are governed by the common law. As with leases, an unsure consignor can make an Article 9 *protective filing*.

C. TRANSACTIONS EXCLUDED FROM ARTICLE 9

1. Federal Statutes   §94

Federal law *supersedes* state statutes (*including Article 9*) to the extent it governs rights of parties to the security agreement or rights of third persons.

    a. Exception—federal loans   §95

    Federal loans are governed by the U.C.C.

2. Landlord's Liens and Liens on Real Property Interests   §97

Such liens are excluded from Article 9. Article 9 applies *only to personal property*.

3. Mechanic's and Artisan's Liens   §98

These statutory liens are excluded from Article 9's coverage.

    a. Agricultural liens covered   §99

    Article 9 does, however, govern agricultural liens (*i.e.*, statutory nonpossessory liens on farm products created in favor of unpaid furnishers of goods, services, etc., to a farmer).

4. Claims Arising Out of Judicial Proceedings   §100

These are also excluded (except for commercial tort claims and settled tort claims).

5. Wage or Salary Claims   §102

These are also exempt.

6. Insurance Policies and Consumer Deposit Accounts   §103

These are also excluded from Article 9.

7. Assignments Not for Financing Purposes   §104

These assignments (such as assignments for *collection*, coupled with a performance obligation, or as part of a *sale of a business*) are isolated "one shot" transactions and so are not part of Article 9.

8. Surety's Subrogation Rights   §109

These rights, entitling the surety to amounts still due the debtor, are not Article 9 security interests.

9. Subordination Agreements   §110

Where creditors agree to change their priorities in collateral, these agreements are not within Code coverage.

10. Underlying Transactions Not Within the Code   §111

If the underlying transaction does not fall within the Code, this does not necessarily make subsequent transactions involving the same interest exempt.

11. Consumer Protection Statutes   §112

The federal government or the states may provide special rules for security interests in consumer goods. Those rules override Article 9 provisions.

III. CREATION OF A SECURITY INTEREST

A. INTRODUCTION

1. Basic Policies §114
The Code guarantees protection to lenders complying with the U.C.C. and prevents lenders from creating private systems outside the framework of the Code.

2. Creation of Security Interest—Overview

a. Attachment and perfection §116
Attachment is the process by which the debtor and creditor *create* a security interest in the debtor's property *effective between these two* parties. *Perfection* is the process by which this security interest is made *effective against most of the rest of the world*.

b. Security agreement and financing statement §117
The *security agreement* is the *contract* between the debtor and creditor that creates the security interest. The *financing statement* is the document filed in the place mandated by section 9-501 that *notifies* the world of the creditor's interest in the debtor's property.

B. ATTACHMENT OF A SECURITY INTEREST—IN GENERAL

1. Three Requirements §119
The parties must have (i) a *security agreement*; (ii) the secured party *must give value*; and (iii) the debtor *must have rights in the collateral*.

a. Coexistence required §120
Attachment occurs the moment *all three* requirements are met (*regardless* of their order).

C. SECURITY AGREEMENT

1. Necessity of a Record §122
In most cases the debtor must *"authenticate"* a *"record"* of a security agreement (which includes electronic authentication and electronically stored information). However, sometimes an oral understanding is sufficient.

a. Collateral in possession or control of secured party—oral agreement sufficient §123
If the secured party has possession (a pledge) of the collateral, no authenticated record is required; an *oral* agreement is sufficient. Similarly, a secured party who has control of investment property, letter of credit rights, deposit accounts, or electronic chattel paper pursuant to agreement need not acquire an authenticated record.

b. Collateral not in secured party's possession or control—authenticated record required §125
Where the secured party does not have possession or control of the collateral, an *authenticated* (*i.e.*, signed by the debtor in writing or by electronic means) *record* (a writing or electronically stored and retrievable information) that *describes the collateral* is required.

(1) **Description of Collateral**

(a) **Sufficiency of description** §128
The description is sufficient if it **reasonably identifies** what collateral the parties intended the security interest to cover. If the collateral is timber to be cut, the **related land** must also be described.

1) **Exception—collateral that cannot be described by type alone** §131
While most kinds of collateral can be described by their type in a security agreement (*e.g.,* "debtor's equipment"), **commercial tort claims, consumer goods, consumer securities accounts, and consumer commodity accounts** must be described more specifically.

2) **Supergeneric descriptions not allowed in security agreement** §132
Supergeneric descriptions (*e.g.,* "all the debtor's property") are not sufficient to describe the collateral in a security agreement. *But note:* **Financing statements can** contain supergeneric descriptions of collateral (*see infra*).

3) **Errors in description** §134
Errors are **not** fatal if other proof shows the parties intended particular collateral to be covered.

(b) **"After-acquired property"** §135
Collateral that the debtor may **acquire in the future** may be covered by a security agreement. *Note:* A security interest in such collateral automatically attaches when the debtor acquires rights in it.

1) **Exceptions—consumer goods** §136
Consumer goods are not subject to after-acquired property clauses unless the debtor gets rights in the goods **within 10 days** after the creditor gives value. Also, under the Credit Practices Rule, a non-purchase money, nonpossessory security interest **cannot** be created in **household goods**.

2) **Exception—commercial tort claims** §137
Future commercial tort claims are not subject to after-acquired property clauses.

3) **Specificity required** §138
Express mention of after-acquired property is necessary **except for inventory** ("inventory" implies coverage of future inventory), **accounts receivable**, and **farm equipment**.

(c) "Floating liens" §141
Such liens attach to an aggregation of collateral (*e.g.,* inventory) so that *individual items* may change (due to sales or purchases by debtor), but the collateral *as a whole* remains subject to the lien.

2. **Other Terms of Agreement** §144
The security agreement usually states the parties' rights, duties, etc., and may specify circumstances constituting *default*.

D. VALUE

1. **Value Must Be Given** §146
For attachment the creditor *must give value* for rights in the collateral. Value can be in the form of *consideration* that would support a contract (*e.g.,* the payment of money or delivery of goods), an *antecedent debt* owed the creditor, a buyer's *acceptance of delivery* under a contract of sale, or a binding *commitment* by the creditor to give future value.

E. DEBTOR'S RIGHTS IN THE COLLATERAL

1. **Rights in Collateral** §147
Attachment requires the debtor to have rights in the collateral (*i.e.,* some ownership interest, right to possession, etc.).

   a. **Title irrelevant** §149
   Full title to collateral is *not* required.

2. **Effect of Restriction on Debtor's Right to Transfer Collateral** §152
Any purported restriction on the debtor's right to transfer collateral is *void and unenforceable*. However, a provision *accelerating* the creditor's right to payment in the event of the debtor's transfer of the collateral may be valid.

IV. PERFECTION

A. METHODS OF PERFECTION

1. **Four Methods of Perfection** §155
The Code provides the following four methods of perfecting a security interest.

2. **Filing a Financing Statement** §156
The *most common* method of perfection is by *filing* a financing statement indicating the security interest and generally describing the type of collateral covered in the place provided by U.C.C. section 9-501 (usually the secretary of state's office). (*Note:* This is the *only* method for *accounts and general intangibles.*)

3. **Perfection by Possession** §158
Possession of the collateral by the creditor (a pledge) perfects the creditor's security interest in the collateral as soon as all requirements for attachment have been met.

   a. **Types of property covered** §160
   Security interests in goods, money, negotiable documents, instruments,

certificated securities, or tangible chattel paper are perfected by possession.

b. Means of taking "possession" §162
The creditor must have physical control sufficient to put third parties on notice but the means of acquiring control vary according to the type or location of the collateral.

(1) Inventory §163
The common method for possessing inventory is by field warehousing (*supra*, §24).

(2) Goods in possession of bailee §164
If goods are in the possession of a bailee, a creditor can indirectly take possession through the bailee using the following methods:

(a) Goods covered by negotiable document of title §165
In this case, *possession of the document* perfects a security interest in **both** the document and the goods covered by the negotiable document.

(b) Goods covered by nonnegotiable document of title §166
In this case, a secured party can perfect a security interest in the *goods* covered by the nonnegotiable document by having the document *issued directly to the secured party* or by *sending the bailee a notice* of the secured party's interest in the goods.

(c) Bailment with no document of title §167
The secured party can perfect a security interest in such goods by getting the bailee to *authenticate a record* acknowledging that the bailee holds the goods for the benefit of the secured party.

c. Duration of perfection §168
Perfection by possession lasts only as long as the secured party has possession.

d. Rights and duties of secured party in possession §169
A secured party in possession must take *reasonable care* to store and protect the collateral.

(1) *Exculpatory clauses* totally absolving the secured party from liability are void. §173

(2) *The secured party is entitled to reimbursement* for expenses incurred in storing and protecting the collateral (including the cost of insurance). §174

(3) *Rents, issues, profits* (*i.e.*, money received from the collateral) must be returned to the debtor or applied against the secured obligation. §175

(4) **_Risk of loss_** is on the debtor, but only to the extent of any deficiency in the creditor's insurance coverage. The secured party has a duty to insure collateral in her possession. §176

(5) **_The secured party can repledge the collateral_** to a third party if this action does not impair the debtor's ability to redeem. §179

(6) **_The secured party cannot use the collateral_** unless: (i) the use is necessary to **_preserve_** the collateral; (ii) the use is pursuant to a **_court order_**; or (iii) (if the collateral is not consumer goods) their use is **_agreed to by the debtor_**. §180

4. Perfection with Neither Possession Nor Filing—"Automatic Perfection" §181
The third method of perfection is "automatic"; *i.e.,* perfection occurs in some situations without filing once attachment of the security interest has happened. Automatic perfection is present in the following situations:

a. Purchase money security interest in consumer goods §182
A purchase money security interest in **_consumer goods_** is automatically perfected on attachment of the security interest.

(1) "Purchase money" transactions §184
A purchase money security interest ("PMSI") arises when the secured party **_sells the goods_** to the purchaser **_on credit_** or **_advances_** the purchaser the **_money used to purchase the goods_**. Note that the creditor must have an **_authenticated security agreement_** with the debtor to have a valid security interest.

(2) "Consumer goods" §187
In determining whether the goods are truly to be used for consumer purposes (and hence qualify for automatic perfection), the debtor's **_primary use_** of the collateral determines its type.

(3) Exceptions—motor vehicles and fixtures §190
There can be no automatic perfection for the following types of collateral, even if they are used for consumer purposes: (i) motor vehicles covered by a certificate of title (a **_notation on the certificate of title_** is required), and (ii) fixtures (a **_fixture filing_** is required).

(4) Combining PMSI with other security interests §194
A PMSI in **_nonconsumer goods_** does not lose its status as a PMSI if it is refinanced or consolidated with other loans (this is the **_"dual status" rule_**). The effectiveness of such PMSIs in **_consumer goods_** is left for the courts to decide.

b. Beneficial interest in decedent's estate §197
Perfection is also automatic in the **_assignment_** of a beneficial interest in a decedent's estate.

c. Certain accounts and payment intangibles §198
Automatic perfection occurs in the **_assignment_** of an **_insignificant portion_** of the debtor's outstanding accounts or payment intangibles.

d.   Sale of promissory notes and payment intangibles   §204
A buyer of promissory notes and payment intangibles is automatically perfected (sales of such collateral are covered by Article 9; *see supra*).

e.   Supporting obligations   §205
Supporting obligations (*i.e.*, rights against sureties and issuers of letters of credit) are automatically perfected if the security interest in the **underlying obligation** is perfected.

f.   Temporary perfection   §206
Temporary "automatic" perfection is allowed in certain situations:

(1)   New value given   §207
A creditor as to **negotiable documents, instruments, or certificated securities** who advances **new value** to the debtor obtains a **20-day** perfection period from the moment of attachment.

(2)   Other twenty-day extensions   §208
If a secured party gives the debtor instruments, certificated securities, negotiable documents, or goods that were in the hands of a bailee and not covered by a negotiable document for the purpose of ultimate sale, shipping, etc., the security interest in the collateral is perfected for **20 days** after the secured party relinquishes possession.

5.   Control Over Investment Property   §211
A security interest in investment property can be perfected by **filing** or taking **control**.

a   Priority   §212
A **creditor with control** has priority over a creditor who perfected by filing. If two creditors have control, the **first** creditor to gain control prevails.

b.   Methods of obtaining control

(1)   Certificated securities   §214
A creditor gains control over certificated securities by taking **delivery** of them with any necessary **indorsements**.

(2)   Uncertificated securities   §215
A creditor gets control over uncertificated securities by becoming the **registered owner** of the securities or by having the issuer of the securities **agree to comply with the creditor's instructions without the debtor's consent.**

(3)   Securities or commodity accounts   §216
If the collateral is a securities or commodity account, the creditor can obtain control by either **changing the name** on the account to that of the creditor or by having the broker or clearing corporation **agree that it will act according to the instructions of the creditor without the debtor's consent.**

6.   Control over Deposit Accounts   §218
A security interest in a deposit account may be perfected **only by control**.

There are three different ways to get control over a deposit account: The **bank** in which the deposit account is maintained **automatically has control** over the deposit account if it makes a loan to the debtor using the deposit account as collateral. If **creditors other than the bank** in which the deposit account is maintained want control, they must either (i) **change the account name** to the name of the creditor or (ii) have the bank **agree in an authenticated record that it will follow the instructions of the creditor without further consent of the debtor.**

7. Control over Letter of Credit Rights §220

A security interest in letter of credit rights may be perfected **only by control**. A creditor gets control by having the issuer of the letter of credit **consent to an assignment to the creditor** of the proceeds of the letter of credit.

8. Control over Electronic Chattel Paper §222

A security interest in electronic chattel paper can be perfected by **filing** or taking **control**. A creditor can obtain control over electronic chattel paper if: (i) it obtains a **single authoritative copy** of the electronic chattel paper that is marked to indicate that the creditor is the assignee of record, and (ii) the creditor makes sure the chattel paper can be changed only with the agreement of the creditor.

9. Rights and Duties of Secured Party in Control §223

A secured party in control must account for rents, issues, and profits of collateral, and has the right to repledge the collateral.

B. TIME OF PERFECTION

1. Completion of Necessary Requirements §224

Perfection occurs when (i) the interest has **attached and** (ii) **all required steps for** the particular method of **perfection** (e.g., filing, possession, or control) have been taken. If the steps for perfection are taken **before attachment** (e.g., the financing statement is filed before the security agreement is signed), perfection occurs when attachment finally occurs—i.e., when **both requirements are met**.

2. Effect of Secondary Perfections §225

Perfection first by one means and then another **relates back** to the time of the first perfection as long as there was never a period in which the security interest was unperfected.

C. PLACE OF PERFECTION—MULTISTATE TRANSACTIONS

1. Introduction §226

U.C.C. section 9-301 deals with the problems of multistate transactions and removal of collateral from one state to another.

2. General Rule—Debtor's Location Governs Perfection §227

The law of the state where the **debtor is located** generally governs perfection.

a. Debtor's location §228

A **corporation** is located in the place of its **incorporation**. An **organization** *other than a corporation* (e.g., a partnership) is located at its *place of business* (*i.e.,* the place where the organization conducts its affairs) if it only has one place of business and at its chief executive office if it has more than one place of business. An *individual* is located in the place of her *primary residence*.

    (1) Foreign debtors   §234
        If a debtor is located in a foreign country, that country's laws govern perfection if its laws are similar to the relevant Article 9 provisions. Otherwise, the District of Columbia is considered the debtor's location.

3. Exceptions

    a. Possessory security interests and security interests in fixtures and timber to be cut   §235
      The perfection of these types of security interests is governed by the law of the state in which the *collateral is located.*

    b. Minerals   §236
      The law of the state in which the *wellhead or minehead* is located governs the perfection of a security interest in minerals.

    c. Goods covered by certificate of title   §237
      The perfection of a security interest in such goods (*e.g.,* cars) is governed by the *state issuing the certificate of title.*

    d. Deposit accounts, investment property perfected by control, and letter of credit rights   §238
      The law governing such collateral is generally determined by *agreement* between the debtor and the bank, securities intermediary, etc. *Exception:* The perfection of a security interest in a *certificated security* is governed by the law of the state in which the certificated security is located.

    e. Agricultural liens   §241
      The perfection of an agricultural lien is governed by the law of the state in which the *farm product covered by the lien* is located.

4. Location of Collateral Governs Issues Other than Perfection   §242
The law of the state where the *collateral* is located governs the *effect of perfection and issues of priority.*

5. Change of Debtor's Location   §243
If perfection is governed by the law of the state in which the debtor is located and the debtor moves to a new state, the secured party must reperfect under the laws of the new state within *four months* after the move.

    a. New perfection "relates back"   §245
      A new perfection within the four months relates back to the date of the original perfection.

    b. Effect of failure to reperfect   §246
      If the secured party fails to reperfect within the four months, the interest

becomes unperfected as against **any** purchaser and any later perfection does **not** relate back.

(1) Judicial lien creditors §247
Under the Code a "purchase" or "purchaser" requires a **voluntary transaction**. Since a judicial lien is not voluntary, its attachment **during** the four-month grace period makes it junior to the original security interest even if that interest is never reperfected.

c. Effect of lapsing perfection §249
Where the financing statement lapses before the four-month period ends, the grace period for reperfection also ends.

d. Exception to four-month rule §250
The four-month rule is inapplicable where the security interest is **perfected automatically**.

e. Change in identity of debtor §251
When a debtor changes its identity and becomes a **"new debtor"** (e.g., if a corporate debtor merges with another company or sells the collateral to a buyer who assumes the debt) and the new debtor is located in a different state than the old debtor, the original perfection against the old debtor lasts for **one year.**

6. Movement of Collateral Covered by Possessory Security Interest §252
If a security interest is perfected by possession and the collateral (whose location governs perfection) is moved to a new state, the security interest will remain perfected **without any further action** as long as the security interest is also perfected by possession under the laws of the new state.

7. Protective Filings §253
When there is doubt as to whether or where to file, a wise attorney will file a financing statement in **every place** arguably relevant to the transaction.

8. Interstate Transfers of Motor Vehicles

a. General rule—no action needed §254
A security interest noted on a certificate of title generally remains perfected after the vehicle is moved to a new state, even if the vehicle is reregistered in the new state.

(1) New certificate obtained—four-month grace period §255
If the new state issues a certificate of title that does not note a prior perfected security interest in the vehicle, the prior security interest remains perfected only for **four months** after the issuance of the new certificate. After the four-month period, the secured party will lose to later purchasers for value (which include Article 9 secured parties). *Exception:* There is **no grace period** if the vehicle is sold to an **innocent buyer or used as collateral** in favor of a creditor that does **not know** of the security interest. A prior perfected security interest will lose to these parties once the new certificate is issued.

V. FILING

A. THE FINANCING STATEMENT

1. **Notice Filing** §258

   Parties may file a copy of the security agreement **or** a financing statement. The financing statement is **less detailed** but it gives **notice** that a security agreement is in effect. It is **filed under the debtor's name**.

2. **Required Contents of Financing Statement** §261

   The financing statement must contain the **names and addresses** of both parties and a **description of the collateral**.

   a. **Debtor's authorization required** §266

   Although the financing statement does not need to be signed, it must be **"authorized by an authenticated record."** The authenticated security agreement **meets** this requirement.

3. **Sufficiency of Financing Statement**

   a. **Financing statement without seriously misleading errors generally effective** §267

   A financing statement **substantially complying** with the contents requirements is effective even though it contains minor errors that are not seriously misleading. The test for determining whether a **debtor's** name is seriously misleading hinges on whether the financing statement (which is usually indexed under the debtor's name) can be found using the filing office's **search logic**.

   b. **Name and address of secured party** §269

   This information **must** be included on the financing statement to give sufficient notice of where to go for more information. Although a complete street address is not always required, the address must be **reasonable under the circumstances**.

   c. **Name and address of debtor** §271

   This information **must** be included on the financing statement to give notice to other creditors of the debtor.

   (1) **Trade names** §272

   The debtor must be listed under her **real name** and not under any trade name.

   (2) **Partnership** §273

   A partnership debtor **may** be listed under the partnership name.

   (3) **"Seriously misleading" rule** §274

   A change in the debtor's name or form of identity that is **seriously misleading** requires a refiling within four months or the creditor's perfection ceases as to **new** collateral acquired after the four-month period has lapsed.

   d. **Description of collateral** §275

   The description of the collateral in the financing statement is sufficient if **reasonable identification** is given.

(1) Supergeneric description allowed　　　　　§276

Unlike authenticated security agreements, financing statements allow a supergeneric description of the collateral (*e.g.,* "all the debtor's assets").

(2) After-acquired property　　　　　§277

The financing statement may cover after-acquired property. Express mention is *not* necessary if the *types* of collateral are sufficiently described.

(3) Fixtures, timber to be cut, and minerals　　　　　§278

Financing statements covering such real property-related collateral must also state that the collateral *will be affixed* to realty, *describe* the realty, provide the *name of the record owner* of the realty (if not the debtor), and recite that the *financing statement is being recorded* in the real estate records.

4. Amendments　　　　　§279

Amendments to the financing statement that add collateral are *effective* only from the date the amendment is filed. Distinguish amendments from *floating liens*, which are covered from the date of filing, regardless of when they were added to inventory.

B.　WHERE TO FILE

1. General Rules　　　　　§281

Generally, a filing statement should be filed in one *central* state office (usually the *secretary of state's office*). *Exception:* Financing statements covering *real property-related collateral* (*i.e.,* minerals, timber to be cut, and fixtures) must be filed in the office where a *real estate mortgage* would be filed (usually the *county recorder's office* in the county where the realty is located).

2. Federal Filing Acts　　　　　§282

Federal acts supersede state filing requirements for certain security interests (*e.g.,* railroad equipment filing, aircraft, etc.).

3. Transmitting Utilities　　　　　§283

Transmitting utilities (*e.g.*, phone, gas, and railroad companies) have lines or tracks across many counties and such assets are usually classified as fixtures. To avoid multiple filings, companies using such assets as collateral need only file a *single* financing statement in the usual *central filing office* of the state.

C.　MECHANICS OF FILING

1. When Effective　　　　　§284

A financing statement becomes effective upon *tender* of the statement and fee to the filing officer. The filing officer *indexes* the statement by the *debtor's* name, and any *errors* in the officer's filing or indexing do *not* affect the validity of the security interest.

2. Duration of Filing §287

The financing statement generally *lapses after five years* unless renewed by the filing of a new statement or a continuation statement. In a *public finance transaction*, government-issued debt securities have a maturity of 20 years or longer. Financing statements for *manufactured homes* are effective for 30 years.

3. Continuation Statement §291

A continuation statement adds *five more years* to the effectiveness of the financing statement. The statement must identify the original statement by file number and must indicate that it is a continuation statement. The continuation statement may be filed in the six-month period before lapse of the original.

4. Termination Statement and Release of Collateral §292

Where the debt is paid, the debtor may make an *authenticated demand* for a termination statement, and the creditor *must* send such within 20 days or be liable for the debtor's actual damages plus $500.

a. Necessity of demand §293

For *consumer goods*, the secured party *must* file a termination statement within one month of repayment *regardless* of the debtor's demand. In all other cases, the *debtor must make the written demand*.

b. Who can demand §294

Only the *debtor* can force the secured party to give such a statement.

c. Releases §295

The secured party may also release collateral by making an amendment to the financing statement.

d. Bogus filings §296

If a bogus filing is filed against the debtor, the debtor may remedy the situation by filing a termination statement, filing a correction statement, or suing the offender for conversion. The debtor can recover actual damages plus punitive damages of $500.

5. Assignment §297

The secured party may assign rights under a financing statement by filing an amendment to the financing statement. The secured party may, but *need not, file* to preserve the assignee's perfected status.

D. REQUEST FOR STATEMENT OF ACCOUNT OR LIST OF COLLATERAL

1. Request by Debtor §299

The debtor may send the creditor a statement of the amount owed or collateral covered and request the creditor's approval. The debtor may also request an accounting of the amount still due. The creditor must send an accounting, correction, or approval within 14 days or be liable for any loss caused and a $500 penalty.

2. Protection of Secured Party §302

The creditor may impose up to a $25 charge for requests made more often than once every six months.

3. **Third Party Problems**   §303
    Third parties **cannot** compel the secured party to disclose information. How-
    ever, the secured party may be **estopped to deny misstatements** made to
    third parties.

VI. PRIORITIES

A. COMPETING INTERESTS IN COLLATERAL—THE CLAIMANTS

1. **Introduction**   §306
    When more than one person claims a security interest in the same piece of
    collateral, the Code decides who has priority on the basis of each person's
    status.

2. **Obligor and Debtor**   §307
    The person **owing payment or other performance** of the secured obligations
    is the **"obligor,"** and the **owner of the collateral** is the **"debtor."** Often the
    obligor and debtor are the same person.

3. **Unsecured (General) Creditor**   §308
    An unsecured creditor is one who has **no security interest** in the collateral
    but only a personal claim against the debtor.

4. **Judicial "Lien Creditor"**   §309
    A creditor who has acquired a lien on the debtor's property through the **ju-**
    dicial process is a judicial "lien creditor." In most states, the lien arises at
    the time of levy (*e.g.,* when the sheriff seizes the property). Under the U.C.C.,
    "lien creditor" also includes a trustee in bankruptcy, and the lien arises the
    moment the **bankruptcy petition is filed**.

5. **Secured Creditor**   §312
    A creditor **with an attached security interest** in the debtor's collateral is a
    secured creditor.

6. **Perfected and Secured Creditor**   §313
    A creditor who has taken the steps necessary to **perfect** the security interest
    is both perfected and secured.

7. **Statutory Lien Creditor**   §314
    This is a creditor who has an **automatic** statutory or common law lien (*e.g.,*
    landlord, mechanic, etc.).

8. **Buyers of Property**   §316
    Note that a **good faith buyer** of the collateral is often favored over the debtor's
    creditors.

B. PRIORITY—UNPERFECTED CREDITORS

1. **Unperfected Creditor vs. Other Unperfected Creditor—First to Attach**   §317
    Where there are two conflicting security interests in collateral, **neither** of
    which has been perfected, the **order of attachment** determines priority.

2. **Unperfected Creditor vs. Perfected Creditor**   §318
    A perfected creditor has **priority over an unperfected creditor**. This rule ap-
    plies **regardless** of which creditor's interest attached first and **regardless** of
    the perfected creditor's knowledge of the other's interest.

3. **Unperfected Creditor vs. Judicial Lien Creditor** §320
A judicial lien creditor who levies before the unperfected creditor perfects his interest has *priority* over an unperfected creditor.

4. **Unperfected Creditor vs. Statutory Lien Holder** §321
Unless the statute creating the lien states otherwise, the statutory lien holder has *priority* over the unperfected creditor.

5. **Unperfected Creditor vs. Buyer** §322
A purchaser who pays value and receives delivery *without knowledge* of the unperfected interest takes *free* of such interest.

   a. **Purchase of inventory** §323
   The purchaser of *inventory* in the ordinary course of business takes *free of all* security interests *regardless* of knowledge.

C. **PRIORITY AMONG PERFECTED CREDITORS—GENERAL RULE**

1. **General Rule—First to File or Perfect** §325
As between two *perfected* security interests, priority goes to the creditor who either *filed first or perfected first* (except as modified by the special rules below). Knowledge of another creditor's interest and time of attachment is irrelevant.

2. **New Debtors** §327
If two different debtors, each of whom have given creditors security interests in their collateral, merge into a "new debtor," the original security interests continue in the new debtor without the need for a new security agreement or financing statement, and the usual rules of priority apply.

D. **PRIORITY AMONG PERFECTED CREDITORS—SPECIAL RULES FOR PURCHASE MONEY SECURITY INTERESTS**

1. **Introduction** §330
A purchase money security interest ("PMSI") may have "super-priority" status.

2. **Non-Inventory, Non-Livestock PMSIs** §331
A PMSI in such collateral has *priority* over conflicting security interests in the collateral and its identifiable proceeds if the PMSI is perfected when the debtor takes possession of the collateral *or within 20 days* thereafter.

   a. **Effect on general rule of priority** §333
   This priority supersedes the general rule of first to file or perfect both as to time and manner of perfection.

   b. **Knowledge of prior interest immaterial** §334
   Knowledge of the conflicting security interest is irrelevant.

   c. **Limitation to "purchase money"** §335
   Priority is limited to the *extent* of the purchase money used to acquire the collateral.

3. **PMSIs in Inventory** §336
The rule of super-priority of a PMSI is modified where the PMSI is in inventory. To have priority in the inventory, the purchase money creditor must send

notice of the transaction to the other perfected creditors *before the debtor receives possession* and *perfect before the debtor receives possession* (no 20-day grace period). The notice lasts for *five years* and must describe the inventory.

a.	**Proceeds covered**	§343

PMSI super-priority also extends to the following types of proceeds of the inventory: cash proceeds (*i.e.*, the amount given to the debtor/seller by a retail buyer of the collateral) received on or before the buyer receives the inventory, chattel paper proceeds, and instrument proceeds.

b.	**Livestock purchase money priority**	§345

Creditors with PMSIs in livestock can gain PMSI super-priority by taking the same steps as those required for PMSI super-priority in inventory. This super-priority also extends to identifiable proceeds and unmanufactured products (*e.g.*, milk) of the livestock.

c.	**Article 9 consignments**	§346

Consignments covered by Article 9 are treated as **PMSIs in inventory**; thus, consignors can attain PMSI super-priority if they meet the requirements for attaining a PMSI in inventory.

4.	**Conflicting PMSIs in Same Collateral**	§347

If more than one creditor has PMSI super-priority in the debtor's goods, a **seller** taking a partial security interest in the goods sold has **priority** over a **lender** who lends money to the debtor for a down payment on the goods.

E. PRIORITY AMONG PERFECTED CREDITORS—SPECIAL RULES FOR CERTAIN TYPES OF COLLATERAL

1. **Fixtures**

a.	**"Fixtures defined"**	§349

Fixtures are goods **permanently attached to real property**. This generally does **not** include materials incorporated into a building (*e.g.*, bricks, lumber, etc.), mobile homes on leased land, or readily removable factory equipment, office machines, or domestic consumer appliances. Local (non-U.C.C.) law determines which goods become fixtures.

b. **Priority rules**

(1)	**PMSI—fixture filing required**	§351

A PMSI in goods that will be attached to realty must be perfected by a **fixture filing in the real estate records** prior to affixation, or **within 20 days** thereafter, to be perfected against all future and prior perfected interests. The debtor must be the **owner** or someone in possession of the real estate. The filing must contain a description of the related real estate and, if not the owner, identify the record owner so it can be indexed also under that name.

(a) Limitation—construction mortgages	§355	

A recorded construction mortgage (*i.e.,* one that finances the construction of the building) takes *priority* over a perfected PMSI in fixtures.

(2) Non-PMSI §357

In a contest between a non-PMSI in fixtures and most recorded real estate interests, the *first party to file a fixture filing or record its interest* has priority. However, a non-PMSI in fixtures prevails over subsequent parties (*e.g.,* later mortgages or buyers) by recording a fixture filing before the subsequent parties obtain rights in the realty.

2. Accessions §360

Accessions are goods *attached to other goods* (*e.g.,* a telephone installed in a car).

a. Perfection continues in accession §361

As long as a security interest in an accession is perfected *before* it is affixed to other goods, the perfection continues in the accession after affixation.

b. Priority determined by other rules §362

There are no special priority rules for accessions, so the usual Code priority rules apply. *Exception:* If the accession is affixed to a motor vehicle covered by a certificate of title, a security interest in the vehicle *perfected by notation on the certificate prevails* over a security interest in the accession.

3. Commingled Goods §364

A perfected security interest in commingled goods (*i.e.,* goods that are so physically united with other goods that their identity is lost in a product or mass) *extends to the ultimate product or mass*.

a. Competing interests in ultimate product §366

Perfected security interests in the commingled goods take priority over unperfected security interests. Where there are competing perfected security interests, each creditor takes a *pro rata share* in the total product or mass.

4. Proceeds

a. Introduction §369

"Proceeds" includes anything received by the debtor *on the sale, lease, exchange, or other disposition* of the collateral, whether or not the disposition violates the security agreement. Proceeds include second generation proceeds (*i.e.,* proceeds of proceeds).

(1) Insurance and tort claim proceeds §375

Insurance claims and tort claims *received as proceeds* of collateral are included in the definition of "proceeds" and are covered by Article 9.

(2) Express reference to "proceeds" not required §376

The security agreement or the financing statement need *not* expressly mention proceeds for the secured party's rights to arise.

(3) Secured party's option between proceeds or collateral §377

The secured party has the option of asserting her interest in the proceeds, the collateral, or both (but is limited to one satisfaction of the debt).

b. Rules regarding attachment and perfection of security interest in proceeds

(1) Same filing office—no new perfection required §380

If a financing statement covering the original collateral was filed in the *same office* that a financing statement covering the proceeds would be filed, the creditor need do *nothing more* to continue its perfection. However, this rule does not apply when *cash proceeds* intervene in the creation of the new proceeds.

(a) Proceeds of cash proceeds §381

If cash proceeds intervene in the creation of new proceeds, a secured party has *temporary perfection for 20 days* in the second generation proceeds, after which a new financing statement describing the new proceeds must be filed.

(2) Cash proceeds—tracing rules §382

Perfection of a security interest in original collateral *continues* in cash proceeds as long as the proceeds are still *identifiable* using common law rules for tracing money. However, if the cash proceeds are money in a *bank account*, the bank handling the account has a superior setoff right in the account.

(3) All other instances—creditor must perfect within 20 days §384

If neither of the above rules applies, the creditor must obtain a perfected security interest in the proceeds within *20 days* after the debtor receives the proceeds to retain its perfected security interest.

c. Rules of priority §385

The general rule (*first to file or perfect*) governs most disputes. *Special rules* are the following:

(1) Accounts as "proceeds" of inventory §386

Priority between a secured party with a perfected interest in accounts and a perfected inventory financer claiming the accounts as proceeds is generally determined by the usual *first-to-file-or-perfect rule.* But as to *chattel paper, instrument, and cash proceeds* of the inventory, an *inventory purchase money secured party* who complies with section 9-324(b) (*see supra,* §336) has *priority* over the accounts financer.

(2) Chattel paper as proceeds   §389
The purchaser of chattel paper giving **new value** and taking **possession** in the ordinary course of business has priority over a perfected security interest in the chattel paper as the proceeds of inventory—even if the chattel paper purchaser knew of the prior interest.

    (a) Distinguish—chattel paper subject to security interest other than as inventory "proceeds"   §391
    If the prior security interest is in something other than inventory, a chattel paper financer must buy **without knowledge** that the purchase violated the rights of the secured party to have priority.

d. Returned goods   §395
If goods sold by the debtor are returned to the debtor, the **original security interests reattach**, as long as the goods are **returned to the debtor's inventory**. If not perfected, the creditor must **file or take possession to perfect**.

    (1) Repossessed goods   §396
    If the debtor repossesses goods that it sold, its creditors' rights do not attach **until it again becomes the debtor's property** (e.g., foreclosure sale).

    (2) Rights of third parties   §397
    A purchaser of chattel paper or account receivables deriving from a sale of goods has a security interest in the returned goods. However, **perfection** within 20 days by filing or taking possession is necessary for protection against creditors of the transferor as well as purchasers of the returned or repossessed goods.

    (3) Conflicting security interests   §399
    As to returned goods, a perfected inventory financer is junior to a purchaser of chattel paper claiming the returned goods as proceeds of the chattel paper.

F. PRIORITY AMONG PERFECTED CREDITORS—PERFECTION BY CONTROL

1. Priority in Investment Property, Deposit Accounts, and Letter of Credit Rights   §401
A **creditor with control** prevails over creditors who do not have control. If more than one creditor has control, the **first creditor to gain control** has priority. *Exceptions: **A securities intermediary has super-priority** over all other creditors with an interest in a securities account, even those who have control. A **depositary bank** holding a deposit account has a superior right of setoff in the deposit account for debts owed to it by the depositor, and prevails over another creditor having control over the deposit account, **unless** the creditor obtained control by putting the account in its own name, in which case it prevails over the bank's right of setoff.*

G. PRIORITY AMONG PERFECTED CREDITORS—AS AFFECTED BY TERMS OF SECURITY AGREEMENT

1. Future Advances §404
The original security agreement can create a security interest in *future loans* by the creditor to the debtor as well as in the current loan. A new security agreement is not needed when the future loan is made. The original filed financing statement will perfect the later advances to the debtor.

    a. Advances under later agreements §405
The secured party's original priority will also extend to loans under later security agreements where the *original interest was perfected by filing or possession.* Intervening creditors lose out on the theory that the original perfection put them on notice of the secured party's claim.

2. Dragnet Clauses §410
The security agreement may provide that the collateral secures the current loan and *all other debts* owed by the debtor to the creditor, now or in the future. These clauses are *valid except* possibly where the future debt is totally unrelated to the original loan. A number of state consumer protection statutes prohibit or regulate dragnet clauses.

3. Consent Clauses and Waiver of Security Interests §413
Priority can be lost where the secured party's failure to enforce the security agreement is found to constitute a waiver (*e.g.,* permitting the debtor to sell the collateral without obtaining the consent of the secured party).

H. PRIORITY AMONG PERFECTED CREDITORS AND OTHER CLAIMANTS

1. Buyers of the Collateral—General Rule §419
A buyer of collateral covered by a *perfected* security interest generally takes the collateral *subject to* the security interest.

    a. Exceptions

        (1) Buyers in ordinary course of business §420
Buyers of *inventory* in the ordinary course of business take *free of perfected nonpossessory security interests* created by the seller unless they know that the *sale violates* the security agreement.

            (a) Buyer of farm products §421
Under federal law, such buyers must comply with notices received from the secured party in order to take free of perfected interests in the farm products.

        (2) Buyers not in the ordinary course of business—future advances §430
A purchaser of non-inventory takes free of increases in the security interest due to future advances, *unless* the advances are: (i) made *within 45 days* following sale, and (ii) made or committed to *without knowledge* of the sale.

(3) Buyers of consumer goods from other consumers §433
These buyers take *free* of security interests unless the interests
are *known or perfected by filing*.

(4) Buyers of quasi-tangible collateral §434
Certain buyers of instruments, documents, or chattel paper (*e.g.,*
holders in due course) take *free of unknown* perfected security
interests.

2. Statutory Lien Holders §436
Possessory statutory liens for materials or services furnished *prevail* over
perfected security interests *unless* the statute creating the lien provides otherwise.

    a. Only possessory liens covered §437
Only the *priority* of *possessory* liens is governed by Article 9. When
the statute does not require the lien claimant to keep possession of
the collateral, priority is governed by non-U.C.C. law.

3. Federal Tax Lien §443
Once filed, a federal tax lien *prevails* over most security interests except security interests perfected before the tax lien was filed. It also prevails over
security interests in after-acquired property unless they arose within *45
days after the filing*, and security interests enlarged by advances made after the filing, unless the advances were made without knowledge of the tax
lien filing in the 45-day period following the filing.

4. Judicial "Lien Creditors" §452
A judicial lien creditor (defined to include a trustee in bankruptcy or an assignee for the benefit of creditors) is *junior* to prior perfected security interest holders and to future advances as long as such advances were made
within 45 days after the lien attached or were made thereafter *without
knowledge* of the lien creditor's interest or pursuant to a commitment made
without such knowledge.

5. Article 2 Claimants—Buyers and Sellers

    a. Automatic Article 2 security interests §454
Under certain circumstances, Article 2 creates possessory "security
interests" in favor of buyers and sellers of goods (*e.g.,* when buyer rejects defective goods tendered by the seller). *Possession* alone is the
means of perfection for such interests. (No security agreement or financing statement is required).

    b. Priorities between Article 2 claimants and Article 9 creditors §458
When the same goods are subject to conflicting claims under Article 2
and Article 9, the Article 2 claimant wins if it has *possession* of the
goods.

        (1) Special rule where buyer insolvent §459
Under Article 2, the buyer's trustee in bankruptcy is subject to
the seller's written demand for return of the goods within 10 days

of delivery. However, a secured party with a perfected security interest in the goods prevails over the seller.

VII. BANKRUPTCY PROCEEDINGS AND ARTICLE 9

A. DEBTOR'S BANKRUPTCY

1. Introduction   §466
The acid test of the validity of a security interest is its ability to withstand attack by a trustee in bankruptcy, because a trustee in bankruptcy can assert the rights of *almost everyone* who can challenge the validity of a security interest.

2. Bankruptcy Proceedings   §467
Bankruptcy is a federal procedure initiated by filing a petition in bankruptcy and tried before a bankruptcy judge. A trustee takes *title to all of the debtor's property* and investigates the claims to the property.

a. Distribution of debtor's assets   §472
Property *exempt under state law* is released; property subject to *liens and perfected security interests* is generally released to the lien creditors; and the remaining property is *sold* and the proceeds are applied to pay the Code's designated creditors and finally the unsecured creditors.

b. Discharge   §478
In return for surrendering all nonexempt property, the debtor is usually granted a discharge of further personal liability for most debts.

3. Effect of Bankruptcy on Secured Party's Rights—the Automatic Stay   §479
Even when the secured interest is *fully perfected*, the bankruptcy of the debtor may interfere with the secured party's rights: Possession of the debtor's property passes to the trustee and a secured creditor must seek permission of the court or trustee to enforce his rights. The filing of the bankruptcy petition creates an *automatic stay* against any creditor collection activity.

4. Trustee's Powers   §480
The trustee in bankruptcy has the following powers:

a. *All rights and powers of the debtor;*

b. *Power to set aside any transfer* (including the creation of a security interest) that is *fraudulent* as to *any* existing unsecured creditor; and

c. *Under the "strong arm clause,"* all rights of a *judicial lien creditor (real or hypothetical)* who has levied on the debtor's property.

5. Preferences   §490
A security interest that is neither fraudulent nor attackable by the trustee asserting the powers under the strong arm clause may still be vulnerable if perfection of the interest constitutes a preference.

a. What constitutes a "preference"   §491
Security interests first perfected while the debtor was *insolvent* and

within the **90 days prior to filing** of the debtor's bankruptcy petition on account of an **antecedent debt** that allow the creditor to obtain a greater percentage of the debt than the creditor otherwise would have received in the bankruptcy proceeding may be **voided** by the trustee in bankruptcy as preference. *Note:* In a **consumer** case, the aggregate value of the affected property must be **greater than $600** for a preference to exist.

(1) Result of finding preference §492
If the trustee **voids** the transaction, the creditor must repay the money to the trustee, or in the case of preferential perfection of a secured transaction, the interest is invalid and the secured creditor becomes a **general creditor**.

(2) Nonpreferential payments §493
Payments in exchange for **new value** or those to a **fully secured creditor** are **not** voidable as preferences.

(3) Insolvency required §494
A transfer is preferential **only** if it was made while the debtor was insolvent (more debts than assets). There is a **presumption** that the debtor was insolvent within 90 days of the filing of the bankruptcy petition.

(4) Certain preferences excused §497
Substantially contemporaneous exchanges and **routine payments** are not preferences.

(5) Special rules for transfers to "insiders" §500
If the preferred creditor is an "insider" (*e.g.*, relative, partner, etc.), the preference period can extend to a **year** before the petition was filed, but the trustee must show that there was reasonable cause to believe that the debtor was insolvent at the time of the transfer if the transfer was made more than 90 days before the petition was filed.

b. When "transfer" complete §502
A preferential transfer is complete when a general creditor of the debtor (or a bona fide purchaser of real property) **could no longer have secured an interest in the collateral superior** to that of the transferring creditor (*i.e.*, when the transferring creditor **perfects**).

(1) Grace periods §504
If a purchase money secured creditor perfects within 30 days after the debtor receives possession of the property, no preference occurs. The Bankruptcy Code gives other creditors a 30-day grace period.

C. AFTER-ACQUIRED PROPERTY IN BANKRUPTCY

1. No Preference §508
Under Bankruptcy Code section 547(c)(5), security interests in accounts receivable or inventory falling under a perfected floating lien are **not** preferential

even though first acquired in the 90 days (or one year for insiders) prior to the bankruptcy petition.

<table>
<tr><td>a.</td><td>**Exception**</td><td>**§509**</td></tr>
</table>

a. **Exception** §509
If the secured party has the debtor "build up" (*i.e.,* acquire more inventory or accounts receivable than were present at the start), a preference occurs if unsecured creditors are harmed due to the buildup.

VIII. DEFAULT PROCEEDINGS

A. INTRODUCTION

1. Default §510
When the debtor is unable to meet the obligations set under the security agreement, there is a default. Thus, default is defined by the **terms of the parties' security agreement**.

B. OCCURRENCE OF DEFAULT

1. In General §512
Within limits, the parties are free to establish any conditions they like in the security agreements. The following are clauses frequently used in agreements.

2. Acceleration and Insecurity Clauses §513
Clauses permitting acceleration of the entire debt on the happening of an event or "at will" or when the creditor feels "insecure" are permitted if exercised in **good faith**.

3. Waiver of Defenses Against Assignees §518
A clause waiving defenses against an assignee is generally **valid** in the hands of an assignee who purchases in **good faith** and **without notice** of any defenses the buyer has against the seller.

    a. "Real defenses" not affected §521
    The waiver does **not** cut off **real defenses** (*i.e.,* those good against a holder in due course of a negotiable instrument).

    b. Consumer goods limitation §522
    The waiver is not valid in consumer transactions if prohibited by other statutes.

4. Time Is of the Essence Clauses §526
A security agreement can state that "time is of the essence" in the making of debt payments, meaning that a debtor's late payment could result in **default**. However, if a creditor routinely accepts late payments in spite of the clause, the creditor **waives** its right to declare a default due to a late payment, even if there is an "anti-waiver clause" in the security agreement.

C. REMEDIES—IN GENERAL

1. Cumulative Remedies §527
Remedies under Article 9 are cumulative; thus, the creditor is not forced to make an election of remedies.

2. Three Basic Remedies   §528
These are (i) *retention* of the collateral, (ii) *sale* of the collateral, and (iii) an *action for the debt*.

3. Documents as Collateral   §529
In this case, the secured party may proceed against the documents or underlying collateral.

4. Collateral Involving Real Property   §530
If the collateral involves both real and personal property interests, the secured party may use the procedure governing real property as to all of the collateral or may use U.C.C. remedies as to the personal property.

D. RIGHT OF POSSESSION UPON DEFAULT

1. In General   §531
Upon default, the creditor may use *court proceedings* to collect the debt or *"self-help"* to repossess the collateral.

2. Is Judicial Process Necessary?

   a. No breach of peace   §532
Self-help is permitted if it can be done *without a breach of the peace* (meaning any disturbance, threat of disturbance, constructive force, or breaking and entering). However, *trickery is permitted*. If a creditor breaches the peace, the debtor can sue for *conversion* and recover actual and/or punitive damages.

   b. Requirement of notice   §541
Unless required by the security agreement, the creditor need *not* give notice of repossession to the debtor.

   c. Unconscionability   §544
Debtors may attack repossession provisions on grounds of unconscionability if they involve an unreasonable forfeiture of the debtor's equity.

3. Right of Assemblage   §545
If the collateral is scattered, the security agreement may require the debtor to assemble it.

4. Disabling Equipment   §546
Bulky equipment may be constructively repossessed by disabling it, subject to a standard of commercial reasonableness.

5. Duties of Secured Party in Possession   §548
The possessor must take *reasonable care* of the collateral and must return all personal items seized with it.

E. REALIZING ON THE COLLATERAL

1. Strict Foreclosure   §550
After repossession, the creditor may elect to *keep* the goods in *full or partial satisfaction* of the debt ("strict foreclosure").

a. Exception for consumer goods   §551

Where the collateral is consumer goods and the debtor has repaid at least **60%** of the principal debt, the creditor **must** resell the collateral within 90 days of repossession (or within a longer period agreed to by the debtor) and turn over any excess to the debtor. This debtor's right to resale may be waived only *after* default.

b. General notice requirement   §554

A creditor electing strict foreclosure must send an **authenticated notice** to the debtor and other creditors with interests in the collateral who have sent an authenticated notice of their interests to the repossessing creditor or who have filed a financing statement. Those notified have **20 days** in which to **object** and force the creditor to sell the collateral.

c. Strict foreclosure in partial satisfaction of the debt   §558

A creditor wishing to retain collateral in partial satisfaction of the debt must also acquire the debtor's **consent** in an authenticated record. This remedy is only available for collateral that is **not consumer goods.**

2. Disposition of Collateral by Sale   §559

The creditor may sell, lease, license, or otherwise dispose of the collateral. Sale is the most common method because sale can be by **public or private sale,** and after the sale, the creditor may pursue the debtor for any **deficiency**.

a. Commercial reasonableness standard   §560

The creditor may sell the collateral in any **commercially reasonable manner** and must act in **good faith**.

b. Notice requirement   §563

Authenticated notice of the sale must be given to the debtor, sureties, and other creditors who have filed a financing statement within 10 days before notice was required to be sent or from whom the creditor sending notice has received an authenticated notice of a claim of interest in the collateral. *Exception:* This notice need not be sent if the collateral is **perishable** or of a **type sold in a recognized market** (e.g., stocks and bonds).

(1) Contents of notice   §564

The notice must contain: (i) **descriptions of the debtor, the secured party, and the collateral;** (ii) the **method** of sale; (iii) the **time and place of a public sale** or the **time after which a private sale will be held;** and (iv) a statement that the debtor is **entitled to an accounting** for the unpaid indebtedness and the **charge** for performing the accounting.

(a) Additional requirements for consumer goods   §565

Notice of the sale of consumer goods must *also*: (i) describe the debtor's **liability for a deficiency** after sale; (ii) give a phone number to find out how much must be paid to **redeem** the collateral; and (iii) give a phone number or address from which **additional information** can be requested.

(b) Improper notice   §567
Reasonable steps must be taken to ensure the notice is **actually received** by the debtor.

(2) Timing of notice   §576
The notice must be sent **after default** and a **reasonable time** before the date of disposition of the collateral (**safe harbor rule**). In a **nonconsumer transaction,** the notice will be presumed to be timely sent if it is sent at least **10 days** before the earliest possible disposition of the collateral. The safe harbor rule does **not** apply if the collateral is **consumer goods**. In these cases, courts decide reasonableness on a case-by-case basis.

c. Secured party's right to bid for collateral   §579
The creditor may buy at a **public** (auction) sale. Bidding at a **private** sale is permitted only if the goods are of the type sold in a **recognized market** or are subject to a **standard price quotation**.

d. Application of proceeds   §581
Proceeds of the sale first pay the **expenses** of the sale, then pay the **debt owed** to the selling secured party, and then pay any **junior secured parties** who sent an authenticated demand for payment to the repossessing secured party.

e. Surplus and deficiency   §586
The debtor is entitled to any surplus proceeds. Any deficiency (except where the collateral was accounts, chattel paper, payment intangibles, or promissory notes) is the responsibility of the debtor.

(1) Computing surplus or deficiency   §587
The amount received on the sale of the collateral is usually the basis for determining whether there is a surplus or deficiency.

(a) Low price not determinative   §588
The mere fact that a low price was received at the sale is **not enough** to make a sale commercially unreasonable (commercial unreasonableness could prevent recovery of a deficiency; see infra).

(b) Collusive sales—Rapson rule   §589
If the buyer at a resale is the **creditor,** a person **related** to the creditor, or a party owing a **supporting obligation,** and the amount of the proceeds of the resale is **significantly below** what an **independent person would have paid**, there is a **presumption** that the surplus should be determined based on what the **independent person would have paid**, rather than what was actually paid.

(c) Accounting to consumers §591

In a *consumer transaction*, a creditor must send a debtor an *explanation* of how a deficiency or surplus was calculated before the creditor pays a surplus or makes a demand for a deficiency (and in any event within *14 days* after a debtor's demand). If a consumer owes a deficiency but the creditor decides not to collect it, the creditor must send the consumer a statement *waiving* its right to a deficiency within *14 days* of the debtor's request. If the creditor does not meet the above requirements, it will be liable for *actual damages plus $500 in punitive damages.*

(2) Possible loss of deficiency in noncomplying resale §592

In a *nonconsumer transaction,* if a resale is not commercially reasonable, there is a *rebuttable presumption* that a foreclosure sale following the Code default rules would have brought the amount still due (*i.e., it is rebuttably presumed that the debtor does not owe a deficiency*).

(3) Consumer cases §593

The statutory rebuttable presumption rule does *not* apply in consumer cases. Some courts find that a noncomplying creditor forfeits any right to a deficiency, while many courts apply the rebuttable presumption rule. In any event, a consumer may recover *punitive damages* for creditor noncompliance.

f. Rights of purchaser of collateral §596

The purchaser of the collateral takes all the debtor's rights and those of the secured party/seller and any junior secured parties. A sale by a repossessing creditor gives rise to *all the usual warranties*.

3. Allowing Debtor to Retain Collateral and Suing on Debt §601

The secured party may allow the debtor to keep the collateral and sue on the debt. The secured party's judgment lien *dates back* to the perfection of the original security interest.

F. DEBTOR'S RIGHT OF REDEMPTION

1. In General §603

Prior to resale, the debtor may *redeem the collateral* by *tendering the debt owed at the time of redemption plus expenses* of repossession.

2. No Waiver Prior to Default §606

A debtor cannot waive the right of redemption *prior to default*.

G. EFFECT OF FAILURE TO COMPLY WITH DEFAULT PROVISIONS

1. In General §607

If the secured party does not comply with the default provisions of the Code, the debtor may seek *judicial direction* as to disposition of the collateral, or may wait until the goods have been disposed of and proceed against the secured party for *damages*.

2. Penalty for Secured Party's Noncompliance   §608
If the creditor fails to comply with the default rules of Article 9, the creditor will be liable for *actual damages* (and, in certain cases, $500 in punitive damages). In *consumer goods* cases, minimum damages are 10% of the finance charge or the time-price differential plus 10% of the cash price.

H. NONWAIVABLE RIGHTS UNDER THE SECURITY AGREEMENT

1. In General   §615
Debtors may *not* waive the following rights *in advance of default,* although the parties may agree on standards for performance of these rights.

2. Accounting for Surplus   §616
The parties may not dispense with the obligation to account for any surplus.

3. Notice Requirements   §617
The secured party must comply with notice requirements; these cannot be waived. *Exception: After default*, the debtor may waive notice of *sale* of the collateral.

4. Discharge Upon Retention   §618
The debtor is entitled to a discharge of the obligation to the extent it is satisfied if the creditor retains the collateral in full or partial satisfaction of the debt.

5. Right of Redemption   §619
The agreement may not eliminate the debtor's right to redeem the collateral. This right may be waived *only after default*.

6. Liability for Failure to Comply   §621
The secured party may not disclaim or limit liability for failing to comply with U.C.C. default provisions.

7. Waiver of Rights by Guarantor   §622
Sureties, guarantors, and co-signers have the same nonwaivable rights as the debtor.

I. SPECIAL DEFAULT RULES FOR INTANGIBLES AND FIXTURES

1. Intangibles   §623
If the collateral is accounts or chattel paper, the creditor may give notice to and collect directly from the account or chattel paper obligors.

2. Fixtures and Related Interests   §626
A creditor *with priority* may remove the fixture or accession but must pay the parties *other than the debtor* for any damage caused to their interests by the removal.

Approach to Exams

Common to all transactions under Article 9 of the U.C.C. is the fact that there is an advance of value—whether by loan or by outright sale of accounts or other rights—made against some future performance that is guaranteed or *secured by collateral*. In analyzing a secured transactions problem, ask yourself the following questions. (For a more detailed approach to a topic, refer to the chapter approach at the beginning of the appropriate chapter.)

1. **Does the Transaction Fall Within Article 9?**

   Look for an intent to create a security interest, whether the type of collateral or transaction is covered by Article 9, and whether any exclusions apply.

2. **Has a Valid Security Interest Arisen (Attached to the Collateral)?**

   Without attachment, there is no security interest.

3. **Is the Security Interest Perfected?**

   Check for one of the four types of perfection: filing a financing statement, the secured party's taking possession of the collateral, the secured party getting "control" over the collateral, or automatic perfection (*e.g.*, purchase money security interest in consumer goods).

4. **Against Whom Will the Secured Party Prevail?**

   Creditors with perfected security interests prevail over creditors with unperfected security interests. When determining whether a creditor with a perfected security interest will prevail over another creditor with a perfected security interest, use rules such as the "first-to-file-or-perfect" rule, the purchase money super-priority rules, and the control rules. However, even if a creditor with a perfected security interest prevails under the above rules, the creditor still may lose to buyers in the ordinary course of business and certain others.

5. **Is the Secured Party's Interest Valid in Bankruptcy?**

   Be sure there was perfection, but also note that the trustee may attack the interest as a fraudulent conveyance or a preference.

6. **What Are the Rights of the Secured Party Upon Default?**

   Consider the rights *and duties* of *each party* upon default. For these, look to the terms of the security agreement and the provisions of the U.C.C.

Chapter One:
Introduction

CONTENTS

Chapter Approach

A.	Goals of the Debtor and the Creditor	§1
B.	Pre-Code Security Devices	§4
C.	Uniform Commercial Code	§35
D.	Liens	§38

Chapter Approach

In this chapter, you are introduced to the basic concepts underlying the law of secured transactions, which is codified in Article 9 of the Uniform Commercial Code ("U.C.C."). The rules of Article 9 do not float in a vacuum, and are best understood against a background of the commercial pressures that led to the adoption of legislation and an explanation of the historical solutions that preceded the Code.

Also important to an appreciation of the law of secured lending is mastery of the strange language used in Article 9; some of the key words are introduced in this chapter.

A. Goals of the Debtor and the Creditor

1. Debtor's Goals [§1]

A person needing to borrow money or obtain goods or services on credit (the debtor) wishes to persuade the person extending credit (the creditor) to trust the debtor to repay the debt without requiring the debtor to give the creditor any kind of security other than the debtor's promise of payment. Such a trusting creditor is said to be "*unsecured*"; *i.e.,* in the event of default (nonpayment), the creditor will have to go to court, win a judgment, and send out the sheriff to realize on any of the debtor's property. A creditor may, of course, refuse to extend credit on an "unsecured" basis. In this event, the debtor will be required either to get a *surety* (guarantor) to back up the debtor's promise or to furnish *collateral* (the debtor's own property, or property borrowed from a friend) that can be seized without court action in the event of default. Some creditors want *both* a surety and collateral. The debtor's goal is to get as much credit as is needed without tying up any more property than is absolutely necessary. After all, the debtor plans to repay the debt out of income and not by forfeiting property.

2. Creditor's Goals [§2]

The creditor extends credit and wants repayment plus a profit on the transaction. A surety and collateral are back-up devices to insure collection of at least some of the debt if the debtor fails to repay as promised. If the debtor goes bankrupt, the right to go against the surety or the collateral ahead of other creditors is a must, because in bankruptcy proceedings there are rarely enough assets to satisfy debts owed to the unsecured creditors after the "*secured*" creditors (creditors with rights in collateral) take their property and the bankruptcy expenses are paid. Nonetheless, a creditor's insistence on a *security interest* (a right to seize the property on the debtor's default) is only a hedge against the debtor's potential failure to repay. The creditor must prepare for the worst, but cannot tie the debtor's hands to the point where the debtor cannot earn enough income to repay the debt.

RIGHTS OF SECURED VS. UNSECURED CREDITORS

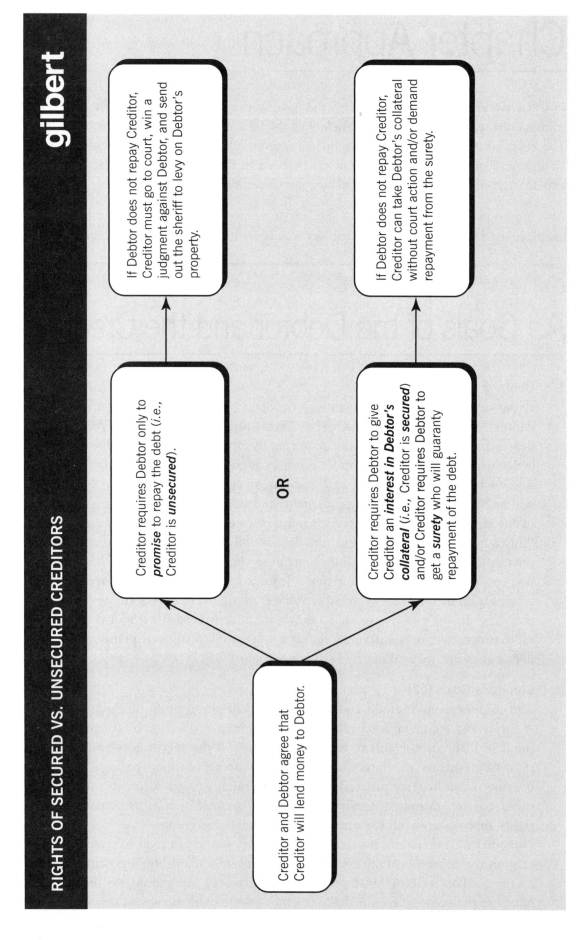

Creditor and Debtor agree that Creditor will lend money to Debtor.

Creditor requires Debtor only to *promise* to repay the debt (*i.e.,* Creditor is *unsecured*).

If Debtor does not repay Creditor, Creditor must go to court, win a judgment against Debtor, and send out the sheriff to levy on Debtor's property.

OR

Creditor requires Debtor to give Creditor an *interest in Debtor's collateral* (*i.e.,* Creditor is *secured*) and/or Creditor requires Debtor to get a *surety* who will guaranty repayment of the debt.

If Debtor does not repay Creditor, Creditor can take Debtor's collateral without court action and/or demand repayment from the surety.

3. Goals of Security Interest Legislation [§3]

Laws designed to regulate the balance between the goals of the parties must protect the debtor from creditors who want too much collateral, from creditors seizing the debtor's property at will and doing with it as they like, and from excessive regulation of the debtor's affairs. On the other side, the creditor who has taken proper steps to secure the debt must be protected from debtor misbehavior, from other creditors, and from loss of the collateral in the event of default. Article 9 of the U.C.C. focuses on the creditor's rights in the collateral. It does not, however, regulate the creditor's recourse against the debtor's surety, which is left to the common law, special statutes [*see, e.g.,* Cal. Civ. Code §§2787 *et seq.*], and other parts of the U.C.C. [*see, e.g.,* U.C.C. §§3-116, 3-419, 3-605].

B. Pre-Code Security Devices

1. Introduction [§4]

Before the U.C.C. was enacted, creditors used a variety of complex security devices, which are described below. The U.C.C. did not abolish these security devices, but instead imposed its requirements on them, thus effectively eliminating many of them.

2. Seller's Fraudulent Retention of Goods After Sale Not Allowed

a. "Statute of Elizabeth" [§5]

The English Statute of 13 Elizabeth (1570) was designed to prevent "fraudulent conveyances" (*i.e.,* any transfer of the debtor's property that interfered with the legitimate rights of the debtor's creditors). An early reading of the statute interpreted it to mean that a sale of goods in which the buyer had permitted the seller to retain possession of the goods after the sale was *void and fraudulent as against the seller's creditors.* The purpose was to prevent such a transaction from being used to cheat the seller's creditors. [**Twyne's Case,** 76 Eng. Rep. 809 (1601)]

Example: A creditor might have loaned money to a merchant on the appearance of the merchant's equipment or other goods, and then, upon trying to collect, the creditor would suddenly learn that the merchant had no money and had secretly "sold" the equipment or goods to an obliging confederate, who had allowed the merchant to retain possession.

(1) Effect

Thus, under the English Act, the buyer had to take *possession* of the merchandise purchased. Otherwise, the sale could be set aside to protect the seller's creditors, and the buyer's interest in the goods cut off.

b. Early U.S. law [§6]

This policy against "sham" sales was carried over to the United States in early decisions and statutes and is generally retained in the law today. In most cases where the seller retains possession of the goods, fraud is presumed.

(1) Majority view

In most states, the seller's retention of possession creates only a *rebuttable presumption* of fraud, allowing the buyer to show that there was a bona fide reason for allowing the seller to retain possession (*e.g.*, goods too bulky to move immediately, etc.). [**Robertson v. Andrus,** 266 P. 53 (Kan. 1928)]

(2) Minority view

In other states, however, such a transaction is *conclusively presumed* fraudulent against the seller's creditors. [*See* Cal. Civ. Code §3440]

c. U.C.C. [§7]

The U.C.C. basically incorporates existing law. It provides that the seller's retention of the goods following sale is fraudulent against the seller's creditors "if fraudulent under any rule of law of the state where the goods are situated." [U.C.C. §2-402(2)]

(1) But note

The Code carves out one *exception:* A merchant-seller's retention of possession "in good faith and current course of trade" for a "commercially reasonable time" is *not* deemed fraudulent. [U.C.C. §2-402(2)]

(2) Sale and leaseback [§8]

It is common in the leasing industry for the owner of goods (such as a computer) to sell them to a financing entity (*e.g.*, a bank) and then lease them back from the bank (thus turning the original owner of the goods into a lessee, which may be advantageous for both tax and accounting purposes). Such a "sale and leaseback" arrangement does have the problem of the possible false appearance of assets (someone in possession of a computer appears to be the owner thereof but is really only a lessee), but this transaction is saved from attack as fraudulent because it is specifically blessed by Article 2A of the U.C.C., which regulates leasing of goods. [U.C.C. §2A-308(3)]

d. Risks if seller retains goods [§9]

In any event, retention of the goods by the seller is not a good idea for either party. The seller runs the risk of having the "security interest" in the goods voided as a fraudulent transaction, and the buyer hazards a court holding that the seller's creditors or other buyers are entitled to the goods.

3. Pledge [§10]

In most situations in which the creditor gets a security interest in the debtor's property (the collateral), the property itself remains in the debtor's control. In the case of a "pledge," however, the property is kept in the *creditor's* ("pledgee's") physical control until the loan is repaid by the debtor ("pledgor"). A pledge is sometimes called a "hypothecation."

a. Possession as notice [§11]

Transfer of the pledged collateral acts as *notice* to the world that the pledgee has rights in the property. However, it does not render the transaction fraudulent, because the property still *belongs* to the pledgor.

b. Status today [§12]

Because of the notice inherent in such transactions, the pledge is still a *widely used* security device and is given special recognition throughout Article 9. (*See infra,* §123.)

4. Chattel Mortgage [§13]

A chattel mortgage is a mortgage on the debtor's personal property filed in the appropriate place to give notice of the creditor's interest.

a. Background [§14]

Before the 19th century, the only effective security devices were the mortgage of real property and the pledge of chattels. However, the pledge of chattels (which required that the creditor take *possession* of the chattels to avoid invalidity as a fraudulent conveyance) was obviously not suited to the needs of an industrial economy in which the debtor invariably needed the goods to use as equipment or inventory.

b. Chattel mortgage acts [§15]

To meet these needs, chattel mortgage acts were enacted by state legislatures. Generally, these acts allowed the debtor to *retain* the property, but required the debtor to *record or file* the mortgage in a specified manner. Without the filing, the acts provided that conveyances intended as mortgages of chattels were *void* against creditors.

5. Conditional Sales [§16]

To avoid the filing requirements of the chattel mortgage acts, sellers developed the "conditional sale." The basic idea of the conditional sale was that *possession* of the goods would go to the buyer, but *title* would remain in the seller until the buyer had *paid the entire purchase price* (the "condition").

a. Varying views on conditional sales [§17]

Some courts held that the seller had avoided the language of the chattel mortgage acts since no lien was created. By retaining title, the seller's rights were protected against subsequent lienors and against purchasers from the buyer, even without filing or recording the sale. *Other courts* were bothered by the "secret lien" interest the seller had in the buyer's goods and refused to recognize the seller's unrecorded interest.

b. Conditional sales filing statutes [§18]

Eventually, most states enacted conditional sales filing statutes similar to the chattel mortgage filing laws. Even so, the two doctrines maintained a separate existence—sometimes to the embarrassment of creditors who followed the wrong form.

c. U.C.C. [§19]

The U.C.C. rejects the whole concept of "title" as being relevant to a seller's rights in goods sold. [U.C.C. §9-202] Under the Code, a seller's retention of title is converted into an "unperfected" security interest— *i.e.,* one that is not good against other parties claiming the goods—unless the seller takes the further steps called for by Article 9 (*see infra,* §§154 *et seq.*). [U.C.C. §§1-201(37), 2-401(1), second sentence in each]

(1) Seller cannot reclaim goods [§20]

Contrary to popular belief, an unpaid seller who has not complied with Article 9 has no right to reclaim the specific goods sold to the buyer unless the buyer received the goods while insolvent and the seller demanded their return within 10 days after delivery. [U.C.C. §2-702; *and see infra,* §459]

6. Trust Receipt [§21]

The trust receipt was a form of inventory financing that sought to adapt the principles of trust law so as to keep *title* to a dealer's inventory in the financing bank while allowing the debtor/dealer to have *possession.*

a. Background [§22]

The trust receipt device was originally developed by banks that financed imported goods. It was later extended to domestic transactions—chiefly the financing of the inventories of retail automobile dealers.

b. Procedure [§23]

The Uniform Trust Receipts Act first required the bank (the "entruster") to file a *notice* that it was engaging in trust receipt financing with the dealer. Then, the bank would buy the goods (*e.g.,* vehicles) from the manufacturer and turn them over to the dealer (the "trustee") for resale. The bank would *retain title* until the dealer/trustee returned the proceeds of the resale to the bank.

(1) Note

One difficulty with this financing system was that it was adapted only to goods that could be *specifically identified,* such as automobiles, and could not be used for a store selling many small items.

(2) And note

Another difficulty was that the Uniform Trust Receipts Act was very complicated, and failure to comply with all its technicalities often invalidated the bank's security interest.

7. Field Warehousing [§24]

If the collateral is physically awkward to pledge but the creditor requires possession, the goods (typically inventory, sometimes equipment) are physically segregated at their usual location (*e.g.*, the manufacturer's plant), and a negotiable warehouse receipt for them is issued. This *warehouse receipt* (a "document of title"), which must be surrendered to retrieve the goods, is then *pledged* to the creditor. [U.C.C. §7-403]

a. Effect

Since a pledge is accomplished—*i.e.*, the warehouse receipt is the pledged collateral over which the creditor maintains control—the debtor cannot (at least in theory) get to the warehoused goods without going through the creditor. For this reason, field warehousing is *still a popular means of financing*.

8. Factor's Acts [§25]

Originally, "factors" were sellers who helped finance the operations of their suppliers. Eventually, the selling aspect of factoring dropped off, and only the financing function remained. Thereafter, "factors" were creditors who loaned money used to produce inventory and who acquired a statutory lien in the inventory that attached to the goods from the time of manufacture to the time of retail sale.

a. Statutory requirements [§26]

Factor's acts were not uniform, but three formalities were generally required: (i) the borrower and lender had to execute a written agreement describing which goods were to be subject to the lien; (ii) a notice of lien had to be filed (designating the names and addresses of the parties and containing a general description of goods covered); and (iii) the borrower had to submit periodic designation statements to the lender listing the inventory subject to the lien.

b. Only inventory subject to lien [§27]

The use of the factor's lien was limited to assets acquired by the borrower for sale in the ordinary course of business. Therefore, only inventory could be covered; equipment and machinery were excluded. The borrower was free to sell the inventory, and a purchaser who bought goods in the ordinary course of business would take free of the factor's lien, whether or not the purchaser knew of it.

9. Assignment of Accounts Receivable [§28]

Nonnotification assignment of accounts receivable was also a widely used financing device. The lender took an assignment of the borrower's accounts but did not notify the account-debtors of the assignment. They would continue to pay the account-creditor who had assigned the account, who would then pay the proceeds to the lender.

a. Priorities [§29]

When a borrower wrongly assigned the same account receivable to two different lenders, a problem of priority between the claimants arose:

(1) Majority rule

The majority view was a *"first in time is first in right"* rule. The first assignee took everything the assignor had to assign, so there was nothing that could be assigned to the second assignee. The first assignee would always prevail. [**Salem Trust Co. v. Manufacturer's Financial Co.**, 264 U.S. 182 (1924)]

(2) Minority rule

The minority (English) rule protected the first assignee *if* that assignee gave *notice* of the assignment to the account-debtor. The second assignee could win only if she (i) was a *bona fide purchaser* for value of the account *and* (ii) gave the account-debtor *notice* of the assignment before the first assignee did so. [110 A.L.R. 774]

b. Notice filing statutes [§30]

The interest in allowing lenders to feel secure in lending on accounts receivable led many states to enact notice filing statutes that provided other creditors of the assignee with the information they needed to protect themselves.

c. Bankruptcy proceedings [§31]

The most serious problem with nonnotification financing as a security device was encountered where the borrower went bankrupt and the trustee in bankruptcy attacked the financing arrangement as a fraudulent conveyance or a *voidable preference* (see infra, §§490 et seq.).

(1) Former law—no valid lien [§32]

The early rule was that a nonnotification assignment of accounts receivable did *not* create a valid lien on the accounts.

(a) Rationale—borrower retained control

Because the borrower was allowed to maintain dominion over the security, payments made to the lender in the months before the borrower's filing a petition in bankruptcy could be attacked by the trustee as either a fraudulent conveyance or as a preference. And this was true whether the payments were turned over voluntarily by the borrower or whether the lender had, during the period, notified the account-debtors of the lender's interest and seized collections of the account. [**Benedict v. Ratner**, 268 U.S. 353 (1925)]

1) This was a direct blow at nonnotification financing because the operation of the system requires that the borrower maintain the assigned accounts and collect the proceeds from the account-debtors, who have no notice of the assignment.

2) The effect of *Benedict* was to force lenders to exercise more formal dominion over the accounts—by giving more careful

scrutiny to the operations of the borrower and by requiring immediate accounting for all proceeds from the accounts.

(b) Problem of notice [§33]

An additional difficulty for nonnotification accounts receivable financing under the Bankruptcy Act was created in states following the minority (English) rule (which protects the first assignee to give *notice*; *see* above). In such states, a hypothetical bona fide purchaser for value could acquire a better right to the account than the lender because notice to the account-debtor was the controlling factor. This failure to have a perfected security interest was also held to constitute a voidable preference within the months before bankruptcy. [**Corn Exchange National Bank & Trust Co. v. Klauder,** 318 U.S. 434 (1943)]

(2) Present law [§34]

Today, the U.C.C. provisions allow the lender to perfect a security interest in accounts or contract rights without notification and without creating a voidable preference. [U.C.C. §§9-205, 9-607(a)(1)]

C. Uniform Commercial Code

1. Article 9—In General [§35]

The U.C.C. was originally promulgated in 1951 and has been adopted in every state. Article 9 of the U.C.C. sets forth a comprehensive statutory framework covering *all types* of secured transactions in personal property. Thus, as stated above, the Code has eliminated most of the pre-Code security devices and swept away the unnecessary distinctions in form and effect of those remaining viable.

2. Revisions of Article 9 [§36]

The very fact that the original Article 9 was the first basic statute in this complex field led to some imperfections and uncertainties and an unexpected number of variations from state to state in enacting it. This prompted a new in-depth study of the field of secured transactions, and certain revisions to Article 9 were approved by the Permanent Editorial Board in 1972 and, most recently, in 1999 (effective July 1, 2001, in most states). This Summary contains the rules of the 1999 revision.

3. Revision of Articles 1 and 2 [§37]

Article 1 of the Uniform Commercial Code is a general Article whose rules are applicable to all the Articles that follow (unless they state otherwise). It contains general principles such as a section explaining how the Code is to be construed [§1-102], a section preserving the common law unless obviously changed by the Code [§1-103], a command that *good faith* be imposed in all U.C.C. transactions

[§1-203], and, most importantly, a huge definition section [§1-201] explaining the meaning of terms used throughout the rest of the statute. Article 1 itself was rewritten in 2001, and it has so far failed to be widely adopted. Consequently, unless otherwise noted, citations in this Summary are to the *original* numbering of Article 1 (and those containing the letter "R" are to the revised version). Likewise, Article 2 was rewritten in 2003, but has similarly failed to be adopted by most jurisdictions. As such, the citations to Article 2 also refer to the original version, unless designated with the letter "R."

D. Liens

1. In General [§38]

A "lien" is a property interest given to the creditor in the debtor's property.

2. Types of Liens

a. Judicial liens [§39]

Judicial liens are those liens acquired in judicial proceedings. They are typically created when the winning party in a lawsuit has the sheriff or other court official "levy" on (seize) the property.

b. "Statutory" liens [§40]

Statutory liens are liens created by statute (or common law) in favor of certain unsecured creditors. Examples of creditors accorded this special legislative protection are landlords, attorneys, artisans (*i.e.,* those who perform work on personal property, such as TV repairers and automobile mechanics), and the I.R.S.

c. Consensual liens [§41]

Unlike the two types of liens above, consensual liens arise by agreement between the debtor and creditor. *Article 9* security interests (and those created by real estate mortgages) are examples of consensual liens.

EXAM TIP   gilbert

Although many types of liens on personal property are **not created** by Article 9 (e.g., judicial and statutory liens), their **priority** over Article 9 security interests in the same property is often governed by the rules of Article 9. (See *infra*, Chapter VI.)

Chapter Two:
Coverage of Article 9

CONTENTS

Chapter Approach

A. Terminology   §42

B. Scope of Article 9 Coverage   §49

C. Transactions Excluded from Article 9   §93

Chapter Approach

This chapter describes the scope of Article 9. A lawyer must be sensitive to the possibility that the Uniform Commercial Code may apply to a problem because the possible application of the Code to an excluded transaction, or vice versa, could amount to malpractice.

For exam purposes, you also must determine whether Article 9 applies. Ask yourself whether:

1. The parties *intended to create a security interest* in personal property or fixtures.

2. The *collateral* is of a type covered by Article 9; look for:

    a. *"Goods"*—consumer goods, inventory, farm products, or equipment (keep in mind that "equipment" is a catchall for goods not falling in the other three categories);

    b. *"Quasi-intangibles"*—pieces of paper used as collateral: stocks and bonds, negotiable and nonnegotiable instruments, documents of title, or chattel paper; and

    c. *"Intangibles"*—accounts receivable, letter of credit rights, deposit accounts, or general intangibles.

3. The *transaction* is of a type covered by Article 9.

If the facts of your question seem to show that Article 9 applies, be sure to consider whether there are any applicable exclusions. Although the Code's coverage is quite broad, there are some exceptions.

A. Terminology

1. Introduction [§42]

Under pre-Code law, different types of financing arrangements had their own terminology, procedures, and substantive law, although the essence of the underlying transactions—an advance of credit secured by collateral—was often identical. The Code's efforts at simplifying the preexisting maze begin with the introduction of a set of standard terms to describe the parties in secured transactions, their agreement, and their rights.

2. "Security Interest" [§43]

The Code definition of "security interest" expands prior law in two respects:

a. Interests in personal property [§44]

First, the Code lays down a blanket definition that includes *every interest* "in personal property or fixtures that *secures payment or performance* of an obligation." Pledges, chattel mortgages, conditional sales, and trust receipts all fall under this broad definition. [U.C.C. §1-201(37)]

b. Certain sales [§45]

Second, the Code *expands the definition* to include rights and interests not previously considered security interests and makes them subject to Article 9. For example, an outright *sale* of accounts, chattel paper, payment intangibles, or promissory notes (all defined below) is covered by Article 9 because it is generally too difficult as a factual matter to distinguish the sale of such interests from their transfer as collateral in a financing transaction. [U.C.C. §1-201(37)]

Example: Ed's Roofing Co. does a lot of home repairs under oral agreements, generating promises of repayment (accounts). When the company needs money, it *sells* these outstanding accounts to Octopus National Bank for immediate cash. Even though this is a true sale and not a use of the accounts as collateral for a loan, Article 9 is triggered. The parties are treated legally as if the transaction were a loan, with Ed's being the "debtor" and the bank being the "creditor." Of course, Article 9 would also be triggered by the use of Ed's accounts as collateral for a loan.

---

3. "Security Agreement" [§46]

A "security agreement" is an agreement that creates or provides for a security interest, no matter what it calls itself (*e.g.,* "conditional sale") and regardless of its form. [U.C.C. §9-102(a)(73) and Comment 3b]

4. "Secured Party" [§47]

A lender, seller, or person in whose favor there is a security interest is called a "secured party." In the case of a sale of accounts, chattel paper, payment intangibles, or promissory notes, the purchaser is the secured party.

5. "Debtor" and "Obligor" [§48]

In a change from prior versions of Article 9, the 1999 revision draws a distinction between a "debtor" and an "obligor." A *debtor* is the *owner, lessee, etc.,* of the goods being used as collateral. On the other hand, an *obligor* is the person who *owes the debt* to the creditor. [U.C.C. §9-102(a)(28), (59) and Comment 2a] Normally the same borrower would fit both definitions, but this may not be the case if, as in the first example below, the person who borrows the money also uses someone else's property as collateral.

e.g. **Example:** Needing to borrow money to start his law practice, a young lawyer asked his parents if he could use their yacht as collateral. They signed the security agreement in favor of the lender, giving the lender a security interest in the yacht, and the young lawyer signed the promissory note in favor of the lender, thereby promising to repay the debt so his parents would not lose their yacht. Under the U.C.C. definitions, the lawyer's parents are the "debtors" and the lawyer is the "obligor."

e.g. **Example:** If a piano company borrows money from Bank A, giving the bank a security interest in the pianos (its inventory) as collateral, the piano company is both the "debtor" and the "obligor," and the bank is the "secured party." If the piano company sells a piano on credit to a musician, reserving a security interest in the piano until it is paid for, the piano company is now the "secured party" and the musician is the "debtor" and "obligor." If the piano company then *sells* the musician's promise to pay the debt (an "account," commonly called an "account receivable") to Bank A, the piano company is, as to this transaction, the "debtor" and Bank A would be the "secured party."

EXAM TIP	gilbert

Make sure you understand how all the new terminology you have just learned works together: A *debtor* (the owner, lessee, etc., of goods) grants a *security interest* in collateral to a *secured party* by executing a *security agreement*. The *obligor owes the debt* secured by the security interest. Notice that the definitions of "debtor" and "obligor" deviate dramatically from the normal meanings of these words (*i.e.,* the party who owes the debt is called the "obligor," while the party who *does not* owe the debt is called the "debtor"). Happily, the debtor and obligor are usually the same person (*i.e.,* the person granting a security interest is the same person who owes the debt to the creditor).

a. **Note**

The distinction between the debtor and the obligor is chiefly important for rights on default (*see infra,* Chapter VIII). In this Summary, the term "debtor" will be used to identify *both debtors and obligors.*

B. Scope of Article 9 Coverage

1. **In General [§49]**

Article 9 of the U.C.C. applies to (i) "*any transaction* (regardless of its form) which is *intended to create a security interest in personal property or fixtures,*" (ii) any *sale of accounts, chattel paper, payment intangibles, or promissory notes,* (iii) *consignments,* (iv) *agricultural liens,* and (v) security interests arising under *other U.C.C. articles.* [U.C.C. §9-109(a)]

2. Types of Collateral [§50]

Because many of the rules in Article 9 turn on the *type* of collateral involved, it is important to classify the property under its proper Article 9 label. Article 9 types of collateral can be divided into the following manageable groups: (i) *tangible collateral* (*i.e.,* "goods"); (ii) *quasi-tangible collateral* (*i.e.,* writings having legal significance, such as promissory notes); and (iii) *intangible collateral* (*i.e.,* collateral having no physical form, such as accounts receivable).

a. Tangible collateral—goods [§51]

Collateral having a tangible physical form is called "goods" in the U.C.C. The Article 9 definition of "goods" is virtually identical to the definition under Article 2 (the Sales Article). [U.C.C. §§2-105, 9-102(a)(44); *and see* Sale & Lease of Goods Summary]

(1) Definition [§52]

Included in the term "goods" are "all things that are movable when a security interest attaches." The term also includes unborn young of animals, crops, timber to be cut under a contract or conveyance, and fixtures. [U.C.C. §9-102(a)(44)]

(a) Computer software embedded in goods [§53]

Normally, computer software is a "general intangible" (*see infra,* §73), even if sold in a box by a computer store, but if the software is *embedded* in goods, it is included in the definition of "goods." [U.C.C. §9-102(a)(44)]

 Example: Software that is contained in a talking doll is goods, not a general intangible, because it is embedded in the doll.

(2) Four types of "goods" [§54]

"Goods" as a category is further broken down into four subgroups. Categorization here depends not on the nature of the goods, but rather on the *principal use* to which the debtor puts the property. The subcategories are mutually exclusive; *i.e.,* a particular piece of property can fit into *only one* of the following categories with regard to any particular secured transaction: "consumer goods," "inventory," "farm products," or "equipment." [U.C.C. §9-102, Comment 4a]

(a) "Consumer goods" [§55]

Goods are "consumer goods" if they are used or bought primarily for *"personal, family, or household purposes."* [U.C.C. §9-102(a)(23)]

(b) "Inventory" [§56]

Goods are "inventory" if they are held for *sale or lease to others in the ordinary course of business.* This category also includes raw materials and materials used up or consumed in a business (*e.g.,* pencils and stationery). [U.C.C. §9-102(a)(48)]

(c) "Farm products" [§57]

Goods are "farm products" if they are used or produced in farming operations and are in the possession of the farmer/debtor. The term includes: (i) *crop*s; (ii) *livestock* (horses, cattle, chickens, fish, etc.); (iii) *products* of crops and livestock (*e.g.,* maple syrup, milk, eggs, and manure) as long as the products are still in their *unmanufactured* state; and (iv) *supplies used or produced in farming operations* (*e.g.,* cattle feed). Once the products have gone through a manufacturing process (such as canning), they cease to be farm products, and if the farmer holds them out for sale to others, they become "inventory." [U.C.C. §9-102, Comment 4a]

(d) "Equipment" [§58]

Goods are "equipment" if they *do not fit into any of the other three categories* of goods (*e.g.,* long-lasting goods used in a business, such as machinery used in a factory or a painting on an office wall). "Equipment," therefore, is the catchall category for goods that are used as collateral but are not classifiable as "consumer goods," "inventory," or "farm products." [U.C.C. §9-102, Comment 4a]

(e) Illustration of categories of goods [§59]

Under the above definitions, a piano sitting in a music store and used as collateral by the store is "inventory." However, if the piano is sold to an amateur pianist for home enjoyment and used by the amateur as collateral for a loan, it is "consumer goods." And if the piano is owned by a professional pianist and is so used, it is "equipment." [U.C.C. §9-102, Comment 4a]

b. Quasi-tangible collateral [§60]

Quasi-tangible assets are *legal rights usually represented by pieces of paper.* When used as collateral, such assets are classified as follows:

(1) "Instruments" [§61]

"Instruments" includes Article 3 *negotiable and nonnegotiable instruments* (*i.e.,* checks, promissory notes, drafts, and certificates of deposit). [U.C.C. §3-104(2), (3)]

(a) Distinguish—"chattel paper" [§62]

If the above instruments are coupled with an agreement creating a security interest in favor of a creditor (regardless of whether the agreement is contained in the same piece of paper), they are collectively called "chattel paper" (*see* below).

(2) "Documents" [§63]

"Documents" refers to *documents of title,* such as bills of lading and warehouse receipts. (A company's business documents—such as research reports or corporate papers—do *not* fall under this definition.) [U.C.C. §§9-102(a)(30), 1-201(15)]

(3) "Chattel paper" [§64]

"Chattel paper" refers to a *record* (*i.e.,* written or electronically stored information) that evidences both a *monetary obligation and a security interest in or a lease of* specific goods. The Code provides that a group of records evidencing those two essentials also constitutes chattel paper. [U.C.C. §9-102(a)(11)] Chattel paper that is stored in an electronic medium is further classified as "*electronic chattel paper,*" and chattel paper that is in writing is called "*tangible chattel paper.*" [U.C.C. §9-102(a)(31), (78)]

Example: Consumer buys a car from a car dealer and signs a contract promising to pay for the car and granting the car dealer a "*security interest*" in the car (thereby making the car collateral, so that it can be repossessed on default). The car dealer then sells the contract outright to a finance company or uses it as collateral for a loan. In either event, the contract constitutes "chattel paper" within Article 9. (*Note:* Because the contract is in writing, it also constitutes tangible chattel paper. If the contract instead had been electronically stored on a computer, it would have been electronic chattel paper.)

Example: Consumer *leases* a car from a car dealer. The lease is "chattel paper" when used by the car dealer as collateral for a loan, or when the car dealer sells the lease to another entity. *Note:* Since Article 9 does not apply to interests in real property (*see infra,* §97), a real estate lease used as collateral would *not* be covered by Article 9 and would not be "chattel paper." [U.C.C. §9-109(d)(11)]

Example: Consumer buys a car and signs *two* pieces of paper: a promissory note and a separate security agreement in favor of the car dealer. If the promissory note alone is sold to a finance company, it is an "instrument," but if the two papers are sold together, they constitute "chattel paper."

(a) Distinguish—"accounts" [§65]

Where a consumer buys goods (*e.g.,* groceries) on credit and signs nothing, the seller may use the consumer's *oral promise* of repayment as collateral for a loan. However, in such a case the collateral is called an "account," not chattel paper (*see infra,* §68).

(4) Investment property [§66]

Stocks and bonds, whether represented by a physical piece of paper (a *"certificated* security") or merely listed on the records of the issuing corporation (an *"uncertificated* security"), commodity contracts, and accounts in which such investments are held ("securities accounts" or "commodity accounts") are given special treatment in Article 9, and thus are all dealt with under the designation of *"investment property."* [U.C.C. §9-102(a)(49)]

c. Intangible collateral [§67]

Some types of collateral have *no physical form* (*i.e.,* they are intangible). There are five types of intangible collateral, which are classified as follows:

(1) "Accounts" [§68]

The term "accounts," commonly called "accounts receivable," refers to a *right of payment* for goods or services sold or leased that is not evidenced by an instrument or chattel paper. Certain similar rights to payment, such as rights to payment arising out of the use of a *credit card* or for *lottery winnings,* are also considered to be accounts. [U.C.C. §9-102(a)(2)]

Example: When a lawyer wants to borrow money, she may use as collateral the debts owed to her by her clients; these debts would be *accounts,* and this is true both as to currently owed obligations and those with *future clients* that have not yet come into being. These debts are therefore accounts whether or not the lawyer has performed the work necessary to earn them. Recall also that the *sale of accounts* (and not just their use as collateral) is also an Article 9 transaction (*see supra,* §45), so if the lawyer sells her clients' accounts to a bank, she is a "debtor" and the bank is a "secured party."

Compare: A *loan of money* is *not* an account. Thus if a bank loans money to its customers and then turns around and uses those debts as collateral when the bank itself borrows money, the debts would be classified as "general intangibles" (*see* below) and not accounts. Or, if the loan of money is coupled with the signing of a written promise to repay the money, it would be an "instrument" (*see supra,* §61).

(a) Health-care-insurance receivables [§69]

Health-care-insurance receivables are a *subcategory of accounts.* Thus when a hospital treats its patients and receives from them the right to get payment from their insurance companies, the hospital is the owner of an account. [U.C.C. §9-102(a)(2)]

(2) Letter of credit rights [§70]

A letter of credit is a payment device used to finance various transactions, and it is mostly regulated by Article 5 of the U.C.C. In a typical letter of credit transaction, a seller of goods does not trust a buyer to make payment but instead requires the buyer to get a letter of credit from a bank in favor of the seller, so that the bank makes the payment to the seller (the *"beneficiary"* of the letter of credit). The beneficiary's rights against the bank issuing the letter of credit, when used as collateral, are governed by Article 9. [U.C.C. §9-102(a)(51)]

(3) Deposit accounts [§71]

Deposit accounts are accounts maintained with a bank, such as checking, savings, or passbook accounts. Article 9 covers the use of deposit accounts as original collateral, but does not cover *consumer* deposit accounts (those used for personal, family, or household purposes), except to the extent they include proceeds (*see infra,* §103). [U.C.C. §9-102(a)(29), 9-109(d)(13)]

(4) Commercial tort claims [§72]

Tort claims that are filed by *organizations* (*e.g.,* partnerships and corporations) are commercial tort claims. Tort claims that are filed by *individuals* that arose out of the individuals' business and do not involve personal injury are also commercial tort claims. These tort claims can be used as collateral under Article 9 (assuming the law outside of Article 9 permits their assignment). [U.C.C. §9-102(a)(13)] Since the definition of "general intangible" (*see infra,* §73) specifically excludes commercial tort claims from its coverage, commercial tort claims are a new, separate category of Article 9 collateral.

Example: An employer's claim against a competitor for encouraging an employee to breach her employment contract and go to work for the competitor is a commercial tort claim that can be used as Article 9 collateral.

(5) "General intangibles" [§73]

"General intangibles" is vaguely defined to include any personal property *other than* that fitting in any of the above categories. The purpose of this catchall provision is to allow for commercial usage to make use of new forms of personal property as collateral. Some examples are goodwill, literary rights, and rights of performance. [U.C.C. §9-102(a)(42)]

Examples: Blueprints, bid packages, and research reports have been classified as general intangibles [**United States v. Antenna Systems, Inc.,** 251 F. Supp. 1013 (D.N.H. 1966)], as has the right to payment of a federal tax refund [*In re* **Certified Packaging, Inc.,** 8 U.C.C. Rep. 95 (D. Utah 1970)].

(a) **Note**

Although a *liquor license* is not "property" in the usual sense because it is not freely transferable (it is often described as a mere "privilege" and not a "right"), it is, nevertheless, very much an asset of a business. And many courts have held that it *is* "collateral," so that a security interest in a liquor license *can* be perfected under Article 9. [*In re* **Chris-Don, Inc.,** 308 B.R. 214 (Bankr. D.N.J. 2004)]

(b) **Software [§74]**

As explained *supra*, §53, software not embedded in goods qualifies as a general intangible, even if sold in a package in a computer store. [U.C.C. §9-102(a)(42)]

(c) **Payment intangibles [§75]**

Article 9 includes payment intangibles as a subcategory of general intangibles. A "payment intangible" is any general intangible under which the account debtor's principal obligation is the payment of money. Thus if you borrow money from your parents and give them an *oral* promise to repay, they would be the owners of a payment intangible. *But note:* If you sign a *written* promise to repay them, it is likely to be classified as an "instrument" since it now has physical form. [U.C.C. §9-102(a)(61)]

EXAM TIP · **gilbert**

Be sure to remember that types of *tangible collateral* are determined according to their *use* by the debtor, while types of *quasi-tangible and intangible collateral* are determined according to their *nature*. Therefore, a book can be "inventory" if it is on the shelves of a bookstore, a "consumer good" if it is bought from the bookstore by a person intending to use it for personal enjoyment, and "equipment" if it is bought from the bookstore by a person intending to use it as a reference book in her business. However, a promissory note will always be an "instrument," regardless of who owns it or how it is used.

SUMMARY OF TYPES OF COLLATERAL · gilbert

TANGIBLE	QUASI-TANGIBLE	INTANGIBLE
• Consumer goods • Inventory • Farm products • Equipment	• Instruments • Documents of title • Chattel paper • Investment property	• Accounts • Letter of credit rights • Deposit accounts • Commercial tort claims • General intangibles

3. Types of Transactions [§76]

Any *financing* transaction, regardless of its name or form, may be held subject to Article 9. If the purpose of the transaction was to *create a security interest* in collateral, Article 9 applies. [**Sierra Financial Corp. v. Brooks-Farrer Co.,** 15 Cal. App. 3d 698 (1971)—what appeared to be an outright *sale* of goods was held to be intended only as a security device and hence subject to Article 9 ("sale" was far below market price and "seller" had reserved the right to repurchase)]

a. Leases [§77]

A true lease is clearly *not* a secured transaction and is not subject to Article 9. However, leases are often structured so that the lessee may be entitled to purchase the "leased" goods at the end of the term. The question then arises whether the transaction is a true lease or, in reality, a financing arrangement designed to protect the seller by maintaining title in the seller as *security* for payments from the "lessee" (buyer). If the latter, the "lease" is subject to the filing requirements of Article 9, and the "lessor" had better take the steps required by Article 9 if it wishes to prevail over other creditors of the "lessee."

(1) True lease compared with security interest [§78]

Whether a transaction is a true lease or a sale on credit (*i.e.,* a secured transaction) disguised as a lease depends on the *facts of each case,* but section 1-201(37), defining "security interest," does provide a test to help answer the question: A transaction is a sale on credit rather than a lease if: (i) the lessee has *no right to terminate* the lease, *and* (ii) either the goods have *no economic value* at the end of the lease or the lessee can *purchase* the goods from the lessor for *little or nothing*.

(a) No right to terminate [§79]

If the lessee has the right to terminate the lease and return the goods, the transaction is a true lease. If there is *no right to terminate* the "lease," the transaction may be a sale on credit, since the right to terminate is not usually an option given to someone purchasing goods.

Example: Consumer leases a suite of furniture from Rent-To-Own Store, paying on weekly installments. The lease provides that at any time the consumer wishes, he may return the furniture and have no further liability. This is a true lease.

(b) Goods have no value when lease ends [§80]

If at the end of the lease term (either as originally set or as extended by renewals), the leased goods will have *no remaining economic value*, a disguised sale on credit may have occurred, and *not*

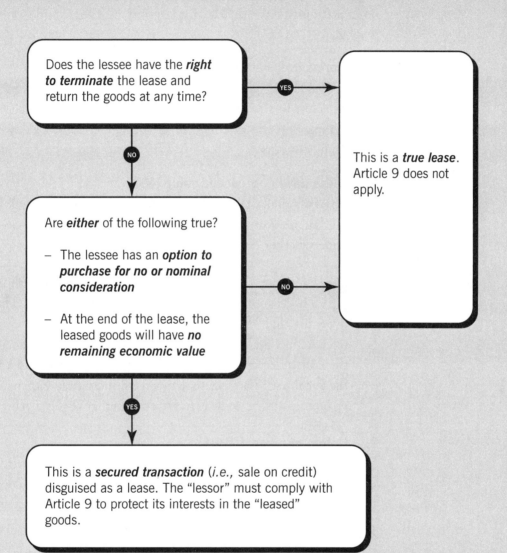

Does the lessee have the *right to terminate* the lease and return the goods at any time?

YES →

NO ↓

Are *either* of the following true?

- The lessee has an *option to purchase for no or nominal consideration*

- At the end of the lease, the leased goods will have *no remaining economic value*

NO →

This is a *true lease*. Article 9 does not apply.

YES ↓

This is a *secured transaction* (*i.e.,* sale on credit) disguised as a lease. The "lessor" must comply with Article 9 to protect its interests in the "leased" goods.

a true lease. This is sometimes called the "junk pile" test because at the end of the so-called lease, the goods are fit only for being discarded. [U.C.C. §1-201(37)(a) - (c)]

(c) Lessee can purchase goods for little or nothing [§81]

If the lessee has the *option to purchase* the property *for no or only nominal consideration*, the transaction may be a sale on credit. [U.C.C. §1-201(37)(d)]

(d) Other terms irrelevant [§82]

Section 1-201(37) lists a number of other terms of the lease that are *irrelevant* to the determination of whether a true lease or a secured transaction is intended, even though prior case law found these things important:

1) Lease payments exceed value [§83]

The fact that the payments made under the lease will exceed the fair market value of the goods does not in any way determine whether a true lease was intended.

---

e.g. Example: Consumer leases a suite of furniture from Rent-To-Own Store, paying on weekly installments. The lease provides that the furniture will be owned by the consumer once he has made rental payments that are *double* the amount the consumer would have had to pay if he had paid cash for the furniture. The fact that this is an incredibly expensive way to buy furniture in no way affects whether this is a true lease.

---

2) Option to renew [§84]

The fact that the lease gives the lessee the option to renew is also irrelevant, as long as the goods will still have some useful economic life at the end of the lease period.

3) Risk of loss [§85]

A term providing that the lessee has the risk of loss is also irrelevant to the true lease/secured transaction issue.

4) Taxes and other charges [§86]

Finally, it is also irrelevant that the lessee must pay taxes, insurance, or other service or maintenance fees.

(2) Protective filing [§87]

As with consignments (*see infra,* §91), a lessor who is unsure whether a transaction will be deemed by the courts to be a true lease or a disguised security interest may file a financing statement to *guarantee priority* in any event. Such a filing is not an admission that Article 9 applies to the transaction. [U.C.C. §9-505]

b. Consignments [§88]

In a typical consignment, the manufacturer or wholesaler of goods (the "consignor") turns them over to a retailer (the "consignee"), who acts as the selling agent of the goods at the retail level. The consignor *retains title* to the consigned goods, and if they are not sold by the consignee at retail, the consignor expects to get the goods back free from any claims of the consignee's creditors. As with leases, it is sometimes difficult to distinguish a "true" consignment from a disguised inventory financing arrangement. If the "consignee" has no option to return the goods if they are unsold but must pay for them in any event, this is not a true consignment—it is a secured transaction *called* a consignment, and the usual rules of Article 9 would apply. In that case the "consignee" is really a buyer of the goods, and the "consignor" is an Article 9 secured party.

(1) True consignments that are covered by Article 9 [§89]

Some *true consignments* are also covered by the rules of Article 9. A true consignor must comply with the requirements of Article 9 to protect its interests in the consigned goods if the consignment has the following attributes: (i) the goods, which *cannot be consumer goods* in the hands of the consignor, have a value of *at least $1,000* at the time of delivery to a consignee, (ii) the consignee is a *merchant* not generally known by its creditors to be substantially engaged in the selling of goods of others, and (iii) the consignee's professional name is different than that of the consignor. [U.C.C. §9-102(a)(20)]

---

e.g. Example: The heir to the family fortune decided to sell a valuable painting of an ancestor, so she turned it over to an art dealership to sell for her. Article 9 would not apply to this true consignment because the item being sold qualifies as consumer goods, and also because an art dealership would be generally known to be selling goods belonging to others.

---

e.g. Example: When City Newspaper replaced its major printing press, it took the old one to Printing Machines Unlimited, a seller of its own new and used printing presses, and asked that company to sell it for City Newspaper if possible, taking a commission if it was able to do so. This is a true consignment but Article 9 applies to it because (i) the printing press, which is equipment, is worth at least $1,000, (ii) Printing Machines Unlimited does not usually sell the goods of others, and (iii) the consignee (Printing Machines Unlimited) runs its business under a *different name* than the consignor (City Newspaper).

(a) Consignment treated as purchase money security interest in inventory [§90]

If Article 9 applies to the true consignment, the transaction is treated

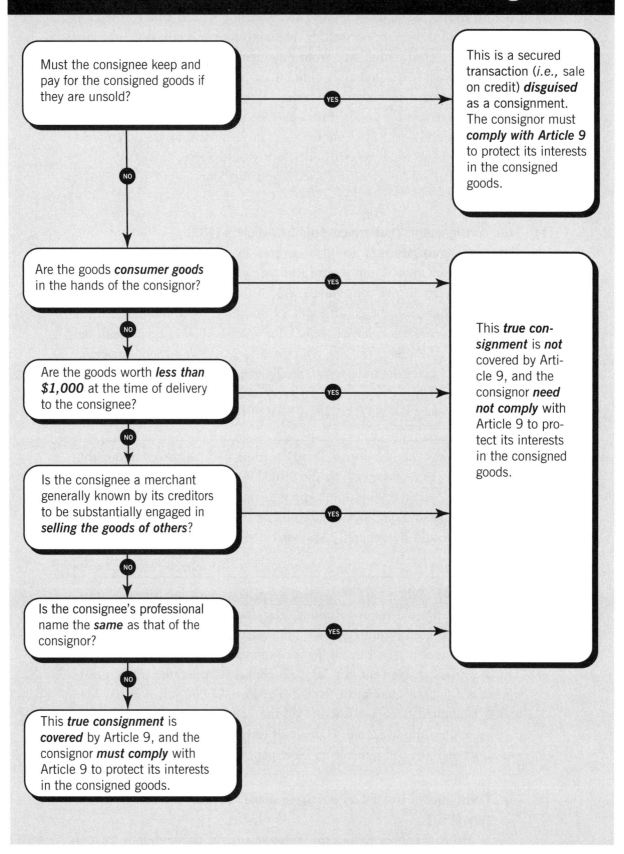

Must the consignee keep and pay for the consigned goods if they are unsold?

YES → This is a secured transaction (*i.e.,* sale on credit) *disguised* as a consignment. The consignor must *comply with Article 9* to protect its interests in the consigned goods.

NO ↓

Are the goods *consumer goods* in the hands of the consignor?

YES →

NO ↓

Are the goods worth *less than $1,000* at the time of delivery to the consignee?

YES →

This *true consignment* is *not* covered by Article 9, and the consignor *need not comply* with Article 9 to protect its interests in the consigned goods.

NO ↓

Is the consignee a merchant generally known by its creditors to be substantially engaged in *selling the goods of others*?

YES →

NO ↓

Is the consignee's professional name the *same* as that of the consignor?

YES →

NO ↓

This *true consignment* is *covered* by Article 9, and the consignor *must comply* with Article 9 to protect its interests in the consigned goods.

under the identical rules applicable to a secured party (here the consignor) claiming a purchase money security interest in goods that will go into the inventory of the debtor (here the consignee); *see infra*, §346.

(2) True consignments that are not covered by Article 9 [§91]

If a true consignment does *not* meet the definition of an Article 9 consignment, the consignor does not have to comply with the rules of Article 9 to protect its interest in the consigned goods. The consignment now falls under the *common law*, which usually allows the consignor to retrieve its goods from the consignee's inventory, even over the objections of the consignee's other creditors or a trustee in bankruptcy. [**Ludwigh v. American Woolen Co.,** 231 U.S. 522 (1913)]

(3) Protective filing [§92]

A consignor who is unsure whether Article 9 applies to the transaction or whether the transaction is a true consignment may make a protective filing of a financing statement, calling itself a "consignor" without this in any way being an admission that Article 9 does apply. The same thing may be done by a lessor who worries that his so-called lease is really a disguised secured transaction. [U.C.C. §9-505]

C. Transactions Excluded from Article 9

1. Introduction [§93]

Public policy and conflict with other bodies of law governing certain secured transactions give rise to a limited number of exceptions in the Article's otherwise broad coverage.

EXAM TIP   **gilbert**

Even if you find that one party has received an interest in another party's property, *do not automatically assume* the transaction is covered by Article 9. First, make sure the transaction does not fall within any of the exclusions from Article 9's coverage given below.

---

2. Federal Statutes [§94]

Security interests governed by any statute of the United States are exempt from the Code, but only to the extent that the statutes control the rights of the parties to the security agreement or the rights of third parties. [U.C.C. §9-109(c)(1)]

Example: The Federal Aviation Act [49 U.S.C. §1403] provides a method for recording title to airplanes and accords protection to titles thus recorded. This Act, therefore, *preempts* all state *filing* laws—although Article 9 must still be consulted on matters of priority, validity of title documents, good faith purchaser status, etc., as to which the federal statute is silent. [U.C.C. §9-109, Comment 8; **Philko Aviation, Inc. v. Shacket,** 462 U.S. 406 (1983)]

---

e.g. **Example:** The Ship Mortgage Act provides an exclusive method for recordation of interests in maritime vessels [46 U.S.C. §911], and the Assignment of Claims Act governs the assignment of payments due under U.S. government contracts [41 U.S.C. §15].

---

a. **Exception—federal loans [§95]**
The Supreme Court has held that federal loans are to be governed by the provisions of the U.C.C., which the Court adopted as a matter of federal common law. [**United States v. Kimbell Foods,** 440 U.S. 715 (1979)]

b. **Application of U.C.C. remedies [§96]**
In some instances, the federal statute merely determines ownership or priorities in the chattels in question but does not specify any *remedy* for enforcement or protection thereof. In such cases, courts apply the remedies available under the U.C.C.

3. **Landlord's Liens and Liens on Real Property Interests [§97]**
This exception simply emphasizes that Article 9 applies *only to personal property*; landlord's liens and other interests in real property are all excluded from the Article. [U.C.C. §9-109(d)(1), (11)]

4. **Mechanic's and Artisan's Liens [§98]**
Drafters of the Code felt that the rights of artisans and service people (holders of "statutory" liens) could adequately be governed by local statute or common law. [U.C.C. §9-109(d)(2)]

a. **Exception—agricultural liens covered [§99]**
Article 9 covers agricultural liens, even though these are *statutory liens,* and requires the lienor to take most of the steps required of Article 9 secured parties to protect the lien rights. An agricultural lien is a nonpossessory lien on farm products that is created by statute in favor of someone who furnishes a farmer with goods or services (lease payments for farm rental also qualify) and remains unpaid. [U.C.C. §9-102(a)(5)] The drafters brought such statutory liens under Article 9 so that the lienors would have to file in the usual Article 9 records and thus reveal their liens in the places that later creditors would search for interests in the debtor's farm products.

---

e.g. **Example:** Suppose that state law awards sellers who supply feed to a farm and who are not paid within 60 days a lien on the farmer's livestock. Such a seller has the benefit of an agricultural lien and must take the steps required of an Article 9 secured creditor taking an interest in similar collateral in order to protect the lien interest.

---

5. **Claims Arising Out of Judicial Proceedings [§100]**

Judgments, setoffs, rights, and tort claims generally do not serve as collateral in commercial transactions. Hence, they are excluded from the Code. *Note:* The Code does cover tort claims received by the debtor as *"proceeds"* on the sale or disposition of other collateral.

   a. **Exception—commercial tort claims and settled tort claims [§101]**

      Recall that commercial tort claims *are* covered by Article 9 as original collateral (*see supra,* §72). In addition, any tort claim, even a noncommercial claim, is covered by Article 9 once reduced to a *structured settlement*, since the collateral would then qualify as a "payment intangible." (*See supra,* §75.)

6. **Wage or Salary Claims [§102]**

The assignment of *current or future wages* represents a question of social importance rather than a purely commercial problem, and so it is left to local law. [U.C.C. §9-109(d)(3)]

7. **Insurance Policies and Consumer Deposit Accounts [§103]**

Sometimes insurance policies or consumer deposit accounts (*see supra,* §71) are put up as collateral, but they are not part of normal commercial financing and are therefore excluded from Article 9 (other than health-care-insurance receivables, *see supra,* §69). (Note, however, that these may be subject to Article 9 if received by the debtor as "proceeds" on the sale or disposition of other collateral; *see infra,* §375.) [U.C.C. §9-109(d)(8), (13)]

8. **Assignments Not for Financing Purposes ("One Shot Assignments") [§104]**

As previously mentioned, sales of accounts, chattel paper, payment intangibles, and promissory notes are normally subject to Article 9. [U.C.C. §9-109(a)(3); *supra,* §45] However, certain transfers of such intangibles have nothing to do with normal commercial financing and hence are specifically *excluded* from Article 9.

   a. **Assignment as part of sale of business [§105]**

      The sale of a business, along with its assets and liabilities, is not a normal financing transaction. Hence, if the owner of accounts, chattel paper, payment intangibles, or promissory notes transfers these assets as part of the sale of the business out of which those rights arose, no compliance with Article 9 is required. [U.C.C. §9-109(d)(4)]

   b. **Assignment for collection [§106]**

      Likewise, the assignment of an overdue account or note to a collection agency is not a financing transaction and is exempt from Article 9. [U.C.C. §9-109(d)(5)]

   c. **Assignment coupled with delegation of performance [§107]**

      Similarly, if the assignment of the right to payment under contract obligates the assignee to perform the work required for payment (*e.g.,* subcontracting work), this is not a financing transaction and is excluded from Article 9. [U.C.C. §9-109(d)(6)]

d. Assignment as payment of prior debts [§108]

Finally, no compliance with Article 9 is required if the assignment of a single account is made in *whole or partial satisfaction* of a preexisting indebtedness. Again, this is not a financing transaction. [U.C.C. §9-109(d)(7)]

9. Surety's Subrogation Rights [§109]

When a contractor fails to perform, so that the contractor's surety must therefore do so, the surety's equitable right of "subrogation"—which entitles the surety to the amounts still due the contractor—is *not* an Article 9 security interest, and the surety need not comply with Article 9 to prevail over the contractor's other creditors. [**United States Fidelity & Guaranty Co. v. First State Bank,** 494 P.2d 1149 (Kan. 1972)]

10. Subordination Agreements [§110]

An agreement whereby two creditors, both having security interests in the same collateral, decide to reverse which one is senior and which one is junior is enforceable, but it is *not* an Article 9 security interest. [U.C.C. §§1-209, 9-339]

TRANSACTIONS EXCLUDED FROM ARTICLE 9   gilbert

THE FOLLOWING GENERALLY ARE NOT COVERED BY ARTICLE 9:

- ☑ Security interests governed by United States statute
- ☑ Landlord's liens and liens on real property interests
- ☑ Local statutory or common law liens (except agricultural liens)
- ☑ Claims arising out of judicial proceedings (except commercial tort claims)
- ☑ Wage or salary claims
- ☑ Insurance policies
- ☑ Assignments not made for financing purposes
- ☑ Surety's subrogation rights
- ☑ Subordination agreements

---

11. Effect of Underlying Transaction Not Within Code [§111]

Even though the basic obligation that secures a security interest may be exempt from the U.C.C., subsequent transactions involving the security interest may fall within the coverage of Article 9. [U.C.C. §9-109(b)]

 Example: Buyer purchases a ranch from Seller, paying a portion in cash and giving a note and mortgage on the ranch for the remainder. This is a real property transaction and is excluded from the Code. [U.C.C. §9-109(d)(11); *see supra,* §96] However, suppose that Seller then takes Buyer's note and mortgage and pledges them to secure Seller's obligation to Third Party. Third Party's security interest in the note and mortgage *is governed by Article 9* because the collateral is a promissory note—the fact that the note is backed up by an interest in real property is irrelevant. Perfection of the security interest in the note automatically perfected a security interest in the realty (since, as the common law maxim has it, "security follows the debt"). [U.C.C. §§9-109(b) and Comment 7, 9-203(g), 9-308(d) and Comment 6]

12. Consumer Protection Statutes [§112]

The federal government and most states have enacted special statutes regulating security interests in consumer goods. These statutes provide important *additional* requirements in *consumer financing* arrangements to validate a security interest.

Example: Where a consumer credit transaction may result in the creation of a security interest in the debtor's principal residence, these statutes may require that the consumer be given certain notices and a three-day "cooling off" period in which to back out of the deal. [16 U.S.C. §1635]

Example: Similarly, consumer laws in most states require certain disclosures to be made in the security agreement, prohibit the creation of security interests in certain kinds of consumer collateral, and regulate the creditor's foreclosure rights on default. [Uniform Consumer Credit Code §§3.203, 3.103, 5.103; Cal. Civ. Code §§1803.2, 1804.3, 1812.2]

a. Consumers not always covered [§113]

Many sections of Article 9 specifically state that they do not extend to consumer transactions, leaving the resolution of the issues involved either to other statutes or to the common law.

Chapter Three: Creation of a Security Interest

CONTENTS

Chapter Approach

A.	Introduction	§114
B.	Attachment of a Security Interest—In General	§118
C.	Security Agreement	§122
D.	Value	§146
E.	Debtor's Rights in the Collateral	§147

Chapter Approach

In this chapter you are introduced to the first substantive area of the law of secured transactions—the basic steps necessary before the creditor's security interest *"attaches"* to the debtor's collateral.

Attachment is a condition precedent to the success of the creditor's attempt to reach any collateral protecting the credit extended by the creditor. Be careful to determine whether the mandatory rules for attachment of a security interest have been met:

1. Is there a *security agreement* that is complete (agreement accompanied by possession, control, or authenticated record)?

2. Did the secured party *give value* sufficient to support the agreement?

3. Does the debtor have *existing rights* in the collateral?

If you cannot answer yes to these three questions, there has been no attachment, and if a creditor makes a mistake here, the whole process thereafter is wasted.

A. Introduction

1. Basic Policies

a. Protection of lenders complying with Code [§114]
The Code contains a basic guarantee to lenders that if they follow its language and avoid the exceptions created therein, their security interests will be protected. Thus, the U.C.C. states: "Except as otherwise provided in the Uniform Commercial Code, a security agreement is effective according to its terms between the parties, against purchasers of the collateral, and against creditors." [U.C.C. §9-201]

(1) Effect
This greatly simplifies the problems in secured financing and is quite a departure from earlier systems of secured financing, where statutes or case law sometimes left "implied" or unstated exceptions to trip an unwary lender.

b. Prevention of systems outside Code [§115]
Lenders are also prevented from attempting to exploit gaps in the Code to

gilbert

A TYPICAL SECURED TRANSACTION SCENARIO

Creditor lends Debtor money to buy office furniture and has Debtor sign a security agreement describing the furniture to be purchased as the collateral.

↓

Debtor buys the furniture and the security interest *attaches*—the parties agreed to create a security interest as evidenced by the security agreement, Creditor gave value (the loan), and Debtor had an interest (ownership) in the collateral.

↓

Creditor *perfects* the security interest by filing a financing statement.

If Debtor defaults, Creditor can take the collateral and sell it, but probably not if third parties have rights in the same collateral.

If Debtor defaults, Creditor will have rights to the collateral against both the Debtor and most third parties.

create new types of security interests that need not be filed. U.C.C. section 9-310 provides that, with certain specific exceptions, a "financing statement must be filed to perfect *all* security interests and agricultural liens." Thus, the all-inclusive nature of the Code both protects the lender from unknown pitfalls and prevents the creation of a private system outside the framework of the Code.

2. Creation of a Security Interest—An Overview

a. Attachment and perfection [§116]

The process by which the debtor and creditor create a security interest in the debtor's collateral effective *between these two parties* is called *"attachment"* (*see* detailed discussion, below). The process by which this security interest is then made good against most of the *rest of the world* (*e.g.,* buyers, other creditors, the debtor's trustee in bankruptcy) is called *"perfection"* (*see infra,* §§154 *et seq.* for the steps required for "perfection").

b. Security agreement and financing statement [§117]

The two primary documents usually involved in an Article 9 financing transaction are the security agreement and the financing statement (each of which is discussed in detail, *infra*). Basically, the *security agreement is a contract between the debtor and creditor* that spells out the rights and duties of the parties regarding the collateral and is required for "attachment" of the security interest. The *financing statement is a document containing certain information* about the creditor's security interest and is typically (although not always) used to accomplish "perfection"; *i.e.,* the creditor perfects by *filing* the financing statement in the public records, where it is indexed under the debtor's name. Thus, the function of the financing statement is to give *notice* to others of the creditor's interest in the debtor's property.

B. Attachment of a Security Interest— In General

1. Definition [§118]

As indicated above, "attachment" is the label the U.C.C. uses to describe the *process* by which the security interest is *created* in the property of the debtor in favor of the secured party. The steps required for "perfection" of a security interest (*infra*) may be taken before or after the time the security interest attaches to the collateral, but the security interest is not perfected until it has attached—*i.e.,* it cannot be good against other parties ("perfection") until it is effective between the debtor and creditor ("attachment").

2. Requirements [§119]

There are three requirements for "attachment" of a security interest:

(i)   The parties must have an *agreement* that the security interest attach;

(ii) *Value* must be given by the secured party; and

(iii) The *debtor* must have *rights* in the collateral.

[U.C.C. §9-203] Each of these requirements is discussed in detail in the following sections (*and see* the chart *infra*).

a. Coexistence required [§120]

The security interest attaches as soon as these three requirements have been met, unless the parties have explicitly agreed to postpone the time of attachment. The three events may occur in *any order*, but they must *coexist* before the interest attaches. [U.C.C. §9-203(a)]

Example: Borrower borrowed $10,000 from Lender on May 1 and signed a security agreement giving Lender a security interest in Borrower's existing factory equipment. Lender also agreed to lend an additional $20,000 to Borrower against Borrower's existing inventory and an automobile Borrower was planning to buy. Borrower received this $20,000 loan June 1 and bought the automobile on July 1. The security interest in the factory equipment attached on May 1, when the three steps were completed. The security interest in the inventory did not attach until June 1, when Borrower received value from Lender. The security interest in the car did not attach until July 1, when Borrower acquired the automobile.

Example: On April 10, Borrower signed an agreement with Lender giving Lender a security interest in Borrower's stamp collection. On April 15, Lender filed a financing statement in the appropriate place. On April 18, Lender loaned Borrower the money. Attachment did not occur until April 18, when Lender gave *value*.

---

b. Agreement as to time of attachment [§121]

As mentioned above, the parties may specifically agree to postpone the time of attachment, due to such matters as accounting or taxes.

Example: On June 1, the debtor and creditor sign an agreement giving the creditor a security interest in collateral the debtor owned, with the creditor giving current "value" in the form of a binding commitment to make the loan (*see infra*, §146). However, the agreement provides that attachment will not take place until July 10. The agreement will be given effect.

REQUIREMENTS FOR ATTACHMENT

Security Agreement

- Agreement plus possession

  or

- Agreement plus control

  or

- Agreement plus authenticated record

and

Creditor Gives Value

- Consideration (*e.g.,* money) sufficient to support simple contract

  or

- Creditor's preexisting claim against debtor

  or

- Buyer's acceptance of delivery under a preexisting contract for purchase

  or

- Creditor's commitment to give future value

and

Debtor Has Rights in Collateral

- Debtor already owns or has possession of collateral

  or

- In a sale of goods, collateral has been identified by the seller as intended for the buyer

C. Security Agreement

1. **Necessity of a Record [§122]**

   In the past, the debtor usually had to sign a written security agreement for attachment to occur. As the world moves away from paper and into electronic media, Article 9 now requires that in most cases the debtor *"authenticate"* (*i.e.,* sign in writing *or* by electronic means) a *"record"* (*i.e.,* written or electronically stored information) of the security agreement in lieu of merely signing a written security agreement. The meaning of these terms is explored in more detail below, but first consider the situations in which *no authenticated record* is required for attachment and an *oral understanding* will suffice. Whether an authenticated record of a security agreement is required depends on whether the secured party has possession of the collateral or otherwise has control thereof.

   a. **Collateral in possession of secured party—oral agreement sufficient [§123]**

      If the secured party has *possession* of the collateral to which the security agreement attaches (a "pledge" transaction), an authenticated record of a security agreement is *not* required. *Note:* A security agreement is still necessary for attachment, but it may be *oral* since the collateral is pledged. [U.C.C. §9-203(b)(3)(B)]

      Example: Bummer leaves his wristwatch at the pawn shop in exchange for $10 and a pawn ticket. Even though Bummer did not sign a security agreement, the oral agreement is enough to give the pawn shop a security interest.

      ---

   b. **Collateral under "control" of secured party—oral agreement sufficient [§124]**

      For certain kinds of collateral (*i.e.,* investment property, letter of credit rights, deposit accounts, electronic chattel paper) the secured party need only obtain *"control"* over the property to prevail against other parties. How this is done is considered later (*see infra,* §§211-222), but when the secured party has control pursuant to any kind of agreement, no authenticated record of the transaction is required for attachment. [U.C.C. §9-203(b)(3)(D)]

   c. **Collateral not in secured party's possession or control—authenticated record of security agreement required [§125]**

      If the secured party is *not* in possession or control of the collateral, the security interest will be valid *only if* there is a security agreement *"authenticated" by the debtor* and *containing a description* of the collateral. [U.C.C. §9-203(b)(3)(A)]

When an exam question requires you to determine whether a security agreement is adequate for attachment, remember that one of the following **must accompany** the debtor's and creditor's **agreement** that a security interest in the debtor's collateral has been created:

(i)   The creditor's **possession** of the collateral;

(ii) The creditor's **control** of the collateral; or

(iii) A **record authenticated by the debtor** that describes the collateral.

If these requirements are not met, the security interest cannot attach.

(1) Effect of authenticated record requirement [§126]

The formal requirement of an authenticated record is not only a condition to the enforceability of a security interest against third parties, but it is also in the nature of a *Statute of Frauds* requirement; *i.e.,* a nonpossessory, noncontrol security interest without an authenticated record is *not enforceable* against the debtor and cannot be made so under any common law lien theory. [U.C.C. §9-203, Comment 3]

(2) "Authenticated" record of security agreement [§127]

The requirement of an authenticated record of a security agreement is broader than the requirement of a signed written security agreement found in prior versions of the Code. *"Authenticate"* is broadly defined to include signing a record, as well as executing or adopting a symbol or encrypting a record in whole or in part, with present *intent* to (i) *identify the authenticating party*; and (ii) *adopt or accept the record*. [U.C.C. §9-102(a)(7)] *"Record,"* in turn, means "information that is inscribed on a tangible medium or which is stored in an electronic or other medium and is retrievable in perceivable form." [U.C.C. §9-102(a)(69)] By this broad language, the drafters hoped to encompass all possible forms—written, electronic, or whatever—in which information might be contained and kept for future reference.

Note that the requirement of an authenticated record is often not that hard to meet because the terms "authenticated" and "record" are intended to be broad enough to cover many forms (e.g., a simple **signed writing** is an authenticated record). Nevertheless you must look for and point out in your answer:

(i) **A record**—information in a **tangible form** (e.g., on paper) or **electronically stored and retrievable** (e.g., in a computer file); and

(ii) **Authentication**—a **signature** or **other symbol or encryption intended to identify** the authenticating party **and accept** the record.

(3) Description of the collateral [§128]

The security agreement must always contain a description of the collateral involved. (Where the collateral is timber to be cut, it must also contain a description of the land on which the timber is located.) [U.C.C. §9-203(b)(3)(A)]

(a) Sufficiency of description [§129]

Following its policy of reducing formal requirements, the U.C.C. provides that the description is sufficient if it *reasonably identifies* what is described. [U.C.C. §9-108]

1) Test [§130]

The description must be such that it can be determined therefrom *what collateral the parties intended* the security interest to cover. Any method of identifying the collateral is allowed as long as it is not confusing. [U.C.C. §9-108(b)]

---

e.g. Example: A security agreement description of Debtor's collateral as "Debtor's John Deere tractor, serial number 009545698" is sufficient. A description of the collateral as "Debtor's tractor," if Debtor only has one tractor, is also sufficient. In addition, a broader description of the type of Debtor's collateral as "all of Debtor's farm equipment" suffices.

---

2) Exception—collateral that cannot be described by type alone [§131]

The following collateral cannot be described by type alone: (i) *commercial tort claims*, and (ii) *consumer goods, consumer securities accounts, and consumer commodity accounts.* Instead, such collateral must be described more specifically to be covered by the security agreement. [U.C.C. §9-108(e)]

---

e.g. Example: A description of Debtor's collateral as "all of Debtor's consumer goods" (a description of the collateral by type) is ineffective, but a description of the collateral as "Debtor's Toshiba television," if Debtor only owns one Toshiba television, is effective because it is more specific.

---

3) Supergeneric descriptions not allowed in security agreement [§132]

Because the security agreement must alert both the secured party and the debtor as to what property is specifically covered, supergeneric descriptions (*e.g.,* "*all* the debtor's property") are not sufficient to describe the collateral. Something more revealing is required (*e.g.,* "all of debtor's farm equipment"). [U.C.C. §9-108(c)]

a) Distinguish—description in financing statement [§133]

Note that in the *financing statement*, which must also describe the collateral (*see infra*, §261), a supergeneric description *is permitted*, because it would alert those looking at the financing statement to the necessity of further inquiry as to whether particular collateral is covered. [U.C.C. §9-504]

4) Effect of errors in description [§134]

An error in description is *not fatal* as long as there is some other proof that the parties intended the collateral in question to be covered by the security agreement.

e.g. **Example:** An error in copying the *serial or license numbers* of vehicles or equipment may be disregarded if the agreement also contains a correct description of the make, model, and year of manufacture. [U.C.C. §9-108, Comment 2]

SUFFICIENCY OF DESCRIPTION OF COLLATERAL IN SECURITY AGREEMENT — **gilbert**

TEST: CAN IT BE DETERMINED FROM THE DESCRIPTION WHAT COLLATERAL WAS INTENDED?

EXAMPLES:		SUFFICIENT?
Specific:	"Debtor's John Deere tractor serial number . . ."	Yes
General:	"Debtor's tractor"	Yes, if only one tractor
Type:	"All of Debtor's farm equipment"	Yes, but **cannot** be used for commercial tort claims, consumer goods, or consumer securities or commodity accounts
Supergeneric:	"All of Debtor's property"	No

(b) "After-acquired property" [§135]

A security interest may be created in "after-acquired property"—*i.e.,* collateral that the debtor does not now own, but that the debtor *may or will acquire in the future.* [U.C.C. §9-204(a); and *see infra,* §336] This means that as the debtor becomes the owner of new property in the future, the creditor's security interest will automatically attach to that property without the need to do anything further. Whether it is wise to allow the debtor to encumber future as well as existing property was a much debated issue when the Code was being drafted, but, with the exceptions mentioned below, the drafters decided to allow this much freedom of contract.

1) Exceptions—consumer goods [§136]

There are two major exceptions to this rule for consumer goods. Under the U.C.C., no security interest attaches to *consumer goods* given as additional security under an after-acquired property clause unless the debtor acquires rights in the consumer goods *within 10 days* after the secured party gives value. (This is to prevent overreaching creditors from tying up all the property of consumers.) [U.C.C. §9-204(b)(1)] The second exception is mandated by federal regulation and is called the "Credit Practices Rule." Under the Rule, both the Federal Trade Commission and the Federal Reserve Board prohibit the creation of nonpurchase money, nonpossessory security interests in *household goods*. [16 C.F.R. §444; 12 C.F.R. §227; for a discussion of what constitutes a purchase money security interest, *see infra,* §184] The policy here is to prevent overreaching creditors from seizing property having value only to the consumer.

Example: Mr. and Mrs. Debtor applied for a general loan from Finance Company. They signed a security agreement that claimed as collateral "all Debtors' personal sewing machines now owned or hereafter acquired until their deaths." The Debtors received a $1,000 loan from Finance Company on October 10. On October 31, they bought a sewing machine to use at home. Finance Company's security interest does *not* attach to the sewing machine. Under U.C.C. section 9-204, the sewing machine constitutes consumer goods purchased more than 10 days after value was given, and so no attachment occurs. In addition, under the federal regulations, an after-acquired interest cannot arise because the sewing machine is a household good, and the secured party does not have a purchase money security interest therein, and has not taken possession.

Compare: Farmer borrowed $10,000 from the Farmer's Friend Bank on October 10, signing a security agreement giving the bank a security interest in "all livestock now owned or hereinafter acquired." On October 31, Farmer bought 20 new cows. The bank's security interest attaches to the 20 cows since they are farm products, not consumer goods.

2) Exception—commercial tort claims [§137]

An after-acquired property clause in a security agreement will not reach commercial tort claims that were not *in existence* when the security agreement was authenticated. To be covered, later arising commercial tort claims would need a new attachment process. [U.C.C. §9-204(b)(2)]

3) Specificity required [§138]

Where the security agreement is intended to cover "after-acquired property," most courts hold that the agreement itself must *expressly* use that term or otherwise clearly refer to collateral to be acquired in the *future*. [*In re* **Atlantic Stud Welding Co.**, 503 F.2d 1133 (3d Cir. 1974)]

a) Distinguish—inventory [§139]

However, it is generally held that if the security agreement covers *"inventory,"* this term *implies* that it covers not only present inventory, but also inventory *to be acquired* in the future. *Rationale:* Inventory by its nature changes from day to day; thus, the parties must have intended the security interest to do likewise. [*In re* **Filtercorp, Inc.**, 163 F.3d 570 (9th Cir. 1998)]

b) Accounts and farm equipment similar [§140]

Similarly, if the collateral is accounts receivable or farm equipment, most courts hold that there is no need to use the words "now owned or after-acquired" since in the usual case the parties would contemplate that after-acquired collateral of this type would automatically be covered by the security agreement. However, the careful attorney will not leave this in doubt and will actually put "now owned or after-acquired" in both the security agreement and the financing statement. [*In re* **Nightway Transportation Co.**, 96 B.R. 854 (N.D. Ill. 1989)—accounts; **Kubota Tractor Corp. v. Citizens & Southern National Bank**, 403 S.E.2d 218 (Ga. 1991)—farm equipment]

EXAM TIP	gilbert

Even if the security agreement clearly is intended to cover "after-acquired property," remember that the security interest itself *attaches* only when the debtor *acquires* the property. However, once the debtor has an interest in the collateral, the security interest attaches *automatically* (no further agreement or formalities are required).

(c) "Floating liens" [§141]

A "floating lien" is one that attaches to a debtor's accounts, stock, inventory of goods, or other aggregation of items of collateral. However, the debtor has the right to transfer and dispose of *individual* items of collateral. Thus, the actual identity of the collateral may always be changing, but the inventory or aggregation as a whole continues to be subject to the lien; *i.e.,* the lien "floats" over the collateral, attaching to an item when it comes into the debtor's possession and terminating when the item is sold or the account is paid.

1) Code provisions [§142]

Although the term "floating lien" is not expressly used in the Code, it is authorized by the provisions of U.C.C. section 9-204(a), validating after-acquired property clauses (above), and U.C.C. section 9-205, validating arrangements under which the debtor has the right to transfer or dispose of the collateral.

2) Caution—bankruptcy proceedings [§143]

However, there is a problem with using a floating lien on inventory or accounts if the debtor goes bankrupt. The trustee in bankruptcy may try to attack the transaction as creating a *voidable preference* (*see infra,* §§490-492).

2. Other Terms of Agreement [§144]

In addition to the minimum requirements for validity (*i.e.,* authenticated record and description of the collateral) [U.C.C. §9-203], the security agreement (*i.e.,* the loan agreement between the parties) typically contains the details of the entire credit transaction, including the rights and duties of the parties.

a. Provisions for default [§145]

For example, although U.C.C. section 9-607 permits the creditor to repossess the collateral on "default," the term "default" is not defined in the Code. Therefore, a well-drafted security agreement will specify what circumstances constitute "default"—*e.g.,* nonpayment, the debtor's death, etc.—even though this is not required by the U.C.C.

D. Value

1. Value Must Be Given [§146]

The security interest cannot attach until the creditor has given "value." [U.C.C. §9-203(b)(1)] This is usually an advance of money or a delivery of goods, but may be anything satisfying the definition of "value" in U.C.C. section 1-201(44). Under this section, a person gives "value" for rights in collateral by acquiring the rights:

a. *In return for any consideration sufficient to support a simple contract*;

b. *As security for a preexisting claim* or in partial or total *satisfaction* thereof;

c. *By accepting delivery* under a preexisting contract for purchase; or

d. *In return for a commitment to give future value* (even though no money has yet been lent). *Note:* The commitment must be definite (as a matter of contract law) and not subject to the secured party's later change of mind on whether to make the advance. [*See* U.C.C. §9-102(a)(68)—defining when a promise to give an advance is made "pursuant to commitment"]

E. Debtor's Rights in the Collateral

1. Rights in Collateral [§147]

Before a security interest can attach, the debtor must have "rights in the collateral." This makes sense, since a debtor can hardly grant a security interest in property in which the debtor has no interest. [U.C.C. §9-203(b)(2)]

a. Definition [§148]

The term "rights in the collateral" is not defined by the Code, but it would seem to mean that the debtor must have some *ownership interest or right to obtain possession*. The term "rights" is defined to include *remedies*. [U.C.C. §1-201(36)]

b. Title to collateral irrelevant [§149]

Since the provisions of the Code on rights, obligations, and remedies of parties apply whether title to the collateral is in the secured party or the debtor, the concept of *title can be ignored* in considering whether the debtor has "rights in the collateral." [U.C.C. §9-202; **Border State Bank of Greenbush v. Bagley Livestock Exchange, Inc.**, 690 N.W.2d 326 (Minn. 2004)]

c. When "rights" acquired [§150]

The question as to whether and when "rights" have been acquired is left to determination by the courts on a case-by-case basis.

(1) "Identification" [§151]

In a sale of goods transaction, a buyer has rights in the goods as soon as they have been *"identified"* by the seller *as intended for the buyer*, even though the buyer has yet to receive possession. [U.C.C. §2-501; *and see* Sale & Lease of Goods Summary] Thus, if the other steps are met, a creditor's security interest in goods purchased by the debtor will attach upon the seller's "identification" of those goods. [*In re* **Pelletier**, 5 U.C.C. Rep. 327 (D. Me. 1968)]

Example: Bank loaned Farmer $20,000 to buy a tractor from Tractor Co., and Farmer signed a security agreement in favor of Bank. Farmer ordered the tractor on February 6. On February 10, Tractor Co. picked out a tractor from its warehouse and tagged it for eventual shipment to Farmer. The moment the tractor was picked out, "identification" occurred, Farmer obtained "rights in the collateral," and Bank's security interest "attached" to the tractor. (And this is true even though Farmer had not yet received or paid for the tractor.)

EXAM TIP   **gilbert**

When analyzing an exam question, be sure to note the time at which the debtor acquired rights in the collateral. This may affect the timing of attachment, and determining the *exact* moment of attachment may be important in establishing priorities among creditors—*e.g.*, if the debtor were to go bankrupt prior to delivery of identifed goods (*see infra*, §§490-492).

---

2. **Effect of Restriction on Debtor's Right to Transfer the Collateral [§152]**

Any provision in the security agreement that purports to prohibit transfer of the debtor's rights in the collateral is *void and unenforceable*, and the debtor's interest may be transferred notwithstanding. This includes both voluntary transfers and involuntary transfers (*e.g.*, by execution sale or other judicial process). [U.C.C. §9-401(b)]

   a. **Distinguish—acceleration or insecurity clauses [§153]**

   However, a provision in the security agreement giving the secured party the right to *accelerate payment* or *demand additional security* in the event of the debtor's transfer of the collateral may be valid and enforceable (*see infra*, §§513-514).

   b. **Other rights**

   Also, the debtor's transfer of the collateral in spite of this restriction does not necessarily preclude the secured party from finding and repossessing the collateral (*see infra*, §429), and, if the security agreement so provides, it may itself be a ground for default.

Chapter Four:
Perfection

CONTENTS

Chapter Approach

A.   Methods of Perfection   §154

B.   Time of Perfection   §224

C.   Place of Perfection—Multistate Transactions   §226

Chapter Approach

"Perfection" is the process that the parties must go through to make sure that the creditor's security interest in the collateral is good *against most of the rest of the world*. Particularly important is the creditor's freedom from the possibility that the debtor will go bankrupt and the debtor's trustee in bankruptcy will be able to find a way to attack and destroy the security interest.

You will learn in this chapter that there are a number of ways that a creditor can perfect the security interest. Be sure to examine the facts of your question to look for perfection by:

1. **Filing a Financing Statement**

    This is the *usual method of perfection*—the *filing* of a public notice (the "financing statement") in the appropriate office. This notice describes the encumbered collateral and gives the names and addresses of the parties. Since it is indexed under the debtor's name, later creditors who are contemplating a transaction with the same debtor can check the records and discover what property is already subject to the claims of creditors. Be sure that the financing statement has been filed in the *proper place*.

2. **Possession of Collateral**

    If the creditor takes *possession* of the collateral (*i.e.*, a pledge), the security interest is perfected.

3. **Control over Collateral**

    For some forms of collateral (*i.e.*, deposit accounts, letter of credit rights, investment property, and electronic chattel paper) the secured party perfects by going through the various steps required to give the creditor *control* over the collateral.

4. **Automatic Perfection**

    Some security interests can be perfected *without* filing, possession, or control. In such cases, perfection is accomplished by attachment alone (*e.g.*, purchase money security interest in consumer goods). Also, if an interest has been perfected, the protection may be lost if instruments, goods, or negotiable documents are released to the debtor to effect a sale or refinancing. In this situation, be sure to consider the rules regarding *temporary perfection*.

Also, when the facts of your question involve more than one state, consider the rules governing *choice of law* in secured lending problems. For example, if collateral is located in one jurisdiction but the debtor is located in another, in which jurisdiction should the steps for perfection be taken?

A. Methods of Perfection

1. Definition of Perfection [§154]

The U.C.C. does not include a definition of perfection. However, section 9-317 of the Code, in listing the classes of creditors over whom an *unperfected* security interest will not prevail, obliquely indicates that the process of perfection is a set of actions that, when complied with, give the secured party *priority over certain other classes of the debtor's creditors* in the exercise of the security interest.

2. Four Methods of Perfection [§155]

The Code provides four methods of perfecting a security interest: (i) the *filing* of a financing statement; (ii) *possession* of the collateral; (iii) *control* over the collateral; and (iv) the mere *attachment* of the security interest. The applicability of each method depends on the type of collateral; however, as a general rule, *filing is available for most types* of collateral.

COMPARISON OF ATTACHMENT VS. PERFECTION		gilbert
	ATTACHMENT	**PERFECTION**
PURPOSE	Establishes secured party's rights in the collateral as *against the debtor*.	Establishes secured party's rights in the collateral as *against third parties*.
REQUIREMENTS	(i) An *agreement* plus *possession, control, or an authenticated record*; (ii) *Value* given by the secured party; and (iii) Debtor has *rights in the collateral*.	(i) *Attachment*; and (ii) One of the following: • *Filing* (in the proper place) of *a financing statement* describing the collateral, • *Taking possession* of the collateral, • *Taking control* over the collateral, or • *Automatic* perfection.

3. Filing of a Financing Statement [§156]

A financing statement is a document that (i) notes the secured party's interest and (ii) generally describes the type of collateral included under the security agreement. The document is filed in the public office specified under each state's adoption of the Code. (The method is discussed in detail *infra*, §§258 *et seq*.)

a. **Note—filing sometimes exclusive method [§157]**

Filing is the most common method of perfecting a security interest. However, as to certain kinds of property—*accounts and general intangibles*—it is the *only* method by which an interest can be perfected. [U.C.C. §9-310]

4. Perfection by Possession [§158]

A *pledge* occurs when the creditor takes *physical possession* of the collateral (*e.g.,* creditor bank takes debtor's stamp collection and places it into its vault) and holds onto it during the term of the loan. The Code provides that the creditor's *possession* of the collateral results in perfection as soon as all the requirements for attachment have been met. [U.C.C. §9-313]

a. **Pros and cons [§159]**

If there is a single "best way" to perfect a security interest, it is for the creditor to take physical possession of the collateral. With one stroke, this solves any Statute of Frauds problems (*see supra,* §§123-126) and assures perfection. [U.C.C. §9-310(b)(6)]

(1) And note

Possession of the collateral also reduces the risk of third parties being misled: Since the debtor's assets are in "hock," they cannot be used to deceive potential lenders as to the debtor's solvency, and as a result, the secured party in possession of the collateral is generally entitled to priority in any contest with third parties (*see infra,* §325).

(2) But note

On the other hand, of course, physical possession carries with it problems of storage, care, and maintenance (*see infra,* §170).

EXAM TIP **gilbert**

Note that possession is a method of obtaining *both attachment and perfection.* Thus, if a secured party takes possession of the collateral, the security interest will be *simultaneously attached and perfected,* as long as the other requirements for attachment have been met (*i.e.,* secured party gave value and debtor has rights in collateral).

---

b. **Types of property covered [§160]**

Possession of the collateral by the secured party (without filing) perfects the security interest when the collateral consists of *goods, money, negotiable documents, certificated securities* (*see infra,* §214)*, instruments,* or *tangible chattel paper.* [U.C.C. §9-313(a) - (b)]

(1) Distinguish—property not covered [§161]

Property that does not fall within the above categories is not "pledgeable." This includes general intangibles such as a liquor license, country club membership, seat on a stock exchange, or debt.

c. **Means of taking "possession" [§162]**

"Possession" is not defined in the Code. At common law, it means unequivocal, absolute *physical control* over the property sufficient to put third parties on *notice* of the possessor's interest. However, the means of acquiring such control vary according to the type or location of the collateral involved. [**Transport Equipment Co. v. Guaranty State Bank,** 518 F.2d 377 (10th Cir. 1975)]

(1) Inventory [§163]

A common method for obtaining possession of the debtor's inventory is for the creditor to have the inventory placed in a warehouse (sometimes a *field warehouse, supra,* §24) and then take possession of the negotiable warehouse receipt (a document) issued by the warehouser. Since no one can get the warehoused goods without surrendering the warehouse receipt [U.C.C. §7-403(3)], possession of the document constitutes possession of the goods [U.C.C. §9-312(c)].

(2) Goods in possession of bailee [§164]

If goods are being held by a bailee, a secured party cannot directly take possession of them. The secured party can file a financing statement to perfect a security interest in the goods, but is not limited to this method of perfection. Instead, the secured party may work with the bailee to indirectly perfect a security interest by possession through the bailee using the methods described below:

(a) Goods covered by negotiable document of title [§165]

Documents of title are labeled as either "negotiable" or "nonnegotiable." Since a negotiable document of title (*e.g.,* a warehouse receipt or bill of lading) represents the goods being held by the bailee (*see supra,* §163), *possession of the document* perfects a security interest in both the *document and the goods* covered thereby. [U.C.C. §9-312(c) and Comment 7]

Example: Creditor loans Debtor $10,000, and Debtor gives Creditor *possession* of a negotiable warehouse receipt to secure the debt. Creditor's possession of the warehouse receipt perfects Creditor's security interest in both the warehouse receipt and the goods covered by the receipt.

(b) Goods covered by nonnegotiable document of title [§166]

A nonnegotiable document of title is nothing more than a contract by the bailee to deliver the goods to whomever the *bailor* later directs. Therefore, the secured party's possession of the nonnegotiable document does not result in perfection. However, the secured party can perfect a security interest in the *goods* by: (i) having the document *issued directly to the secured party*, or (ii) sending the bailee *notice* of the secured party's interest in the goods. [U.C.C. §9-312(d)]

Example: Farmer stored grain in an elevator and received in return a *nonnegotiable* warehouse receipt listing Farmer as the bailor. Farmer then borrowed money from Bank using the grain as collateral. If Bank gets the document reissued in Bank's name *or* notifies the grain elevator that Bank now has an interest in the goods, its security interest will be perfected.

(c) Bailment with no document of title [§167]

If the goods are in the hands of a bailee who has not issued any kind of a document of title covering the goods, the secured party can perfect *by getting the bailee to authenticate a record* (*see supra*, §127) acknowledging that the bailee holds the goods for the benefit of the secured party. [U.C.C. §9-313(c)] The bailee is *not required* to give such an acknowledgment, and if the bailee refuses to do so, the *only* recourse for the secured party would be to file a financing statement to perfect an interest in the goods. [U.C.C. §9-313(f)]

Example: Debtor's pet lion grew too large to keep at home, so she boarded it at the local zoo. Thereafter, Debtor used the lion as collateral for a loan from Bank. Bank's interest will attach and become perfected as soon as Bank and Debtor sign a security agreement, Bank loans the money, and the zoo authenticates a record acknowledging it holds the lion for Bank. [U.C.C. §9-313(c)]

---

d. Duration of perfection [§168]

When a security interest is perfected through possession, it becomes effective from the time *possession is taken* and continues only so long as possession continues. [U.C.C. §9-313(d)]

e. Rights and duties of secured party in possession [§169]

The U.C.C. confers certain rights and imposes certain duties on a secured party in possession of collateral:

(1) Duty of reasonable care [§170]

First, the secured party must use reasonable care in storing and preserving the collateral. In the case of instruments or chattel paper, this requires the secured party to take all steps necessary to preserve the rights of the debtor in the paper. [U.C.C. §9-207(a); **Grace v. Sterling Grace & Co.**, 30 App. Div. 2d 61 (1968)]

> **Example:** Bank took possession of certain debentures of XYZ Corporation as collateral for a loan to Debtor. These debentures were convertible into XYZ common stock. Bank received notice from XYZ that it was going to redeem the debentures—the redemption price being significantly lower than the value of the common stock into which the debentures were convertible. Bank failed to convert the debentures and allowed XYZ to redeem them. Bank was held liable to Debtor for the difference between the redemption price and the value of the XYZ common stock. [**Reed v. Central National Bank,** 421 F.2d 113 (10th Cir. 1970)]

(a) Notice to debtor [§171]

The creditor in possession may satisfy the duty of reasonable care by *notifying the debtor* of any act that must be taken with respect to the collateral and allowing the *debtor* to perform the act.

(b) No liability for market slump [§172]

A pledgee in possession of securities is not liable for a *decline in value* of the pledged securities—even if timely action could have prevented the decline after the nervous owner of the stock contacted the secured party and demanded an immediate sale. [**Layne v. Bank One, Ky., N.A.,** 395 F.3d 271 (6th Cir. 2005)]

(c) Waivers of liability void [§173]

An *exculpatory clause* (totally absolving the secured party from any liability) is unenforceable. Section 1-102(3) prohibits disclaimers of the due care obligation. (However, reasonable limitations on what is required by the secured party may be upheld.) [**Brodheim v. Chase Manhattan Bank,** 75 Misc. 2d 285 (1973)—parties may not disclaim liability, but may set standards by which to measure duties]

(2) Right to reimbursement for expenses [§174]

The secured party may charge the debtor for any reasonable expenses incurred during the secured party's custody of the collateral, including insurance costs. In addition, the secured party may hold the collateral as security for these expenses. [U.C.C. §9-207(b)(1)]

(3) Accounting for rents, issues, and profits [§175]

The secured party may keep any increase in profits on the collateral as additional security; however, any *money* received from the collateral must either be returned to the debtor or applied against the secured obligation. [U.C.C. §9-207(c)]

(4) Risk of loss [§176]

The risk of accidental loss or damage to the collateral is borne by the *debtor* to the extent that the *secured party's insurance is insufficient.* [U.C.C. §9-207(b)(2)]

(a) Secured party's duty to insure [§177]

However, the Code imposes *liability* for loss on the secured party for any *failure to meet the duty of reasonable care.* Note that it is arguably unreasonable for a secured party to take possession of collateral without any *insurance* on the collateral. [U.C.C. §9-207(a)]

(b) Use of insurance proceeds [§178]

Where insurance covers loss of the collateral, the insurance is used to pay the debt. The insurance company *cannot* pay the creditor and then (through the doctrine of subrogation) turn around and sue the original debtor. [*See* G. Gilmore, *Security Interests in Personal Property* §42.7 (1965)]

(5) Right to repledge [§179]

The secured party may *repledge* the collateral to a third party if this action does not impair the ability of the debtor to redeem. [U.C.C. §9-207(c)(3), and Comment 5]

Example: When Consumer borrowed money from Big Bank, the bank made him pledge his valuable stamp collection as collateral, keeping it in the bank vault. If *Big Bank* needs to borrow money, it may use Consumer's stamp collection as collateral, as long as the terms of the deal between Big Bank and its lender in no way affect the ability of Consumer to pay off the original debt and retrieve the stamp collection.

(6) Right to use collateral [§180]

The secured party may operate or use the collateral *only* for the following reasons: (i) for purposes of *preserving* the collateral or its value (*e.g.,* cows have to be milked, or they will dry up); (ii) pursuant to *court order;* or (iii) except for consumer goods (for which this is not allowed), *as agreed to by the debtor.* [U.C.C. §9-207(b)(4)]

EXAM TIP   **gilbert**

If an exam question indicates that a secured party has taken possession of the debtor's collateral, you should discuss issues concerning attachment and perfection, but you should *also make sure* that the secured party has *not breached the duties* required of a secured party in possession (*e.g.,* reasonable care in storing and preservation of collateral).

---

5. Perfection with Neither Possession Nor Filing—"Automatic" Perfection [§181]

The Code carves out a set of transactions that may be perfected simply by the *attachment* of a security interest; *i.e.,* upon attachment, perfection occurs *automatically,* and no further steps are necessary. The logic behind the U.C.C. drafters' decision to allow perfection upon attachment in these cases is based on commercial convenience and the availability of other methods for protecting creditors.

a. Purchase money security interest in consumer goods [§182]

A security interest in *consumer goods* that arises in connection with the purchase of the goods is perfected automatically upon attachment; *i.e.,* no filing is required. [U.C.C. §9-309(1)]

(1) Rationale for automatic perfection [§183]

Retail merchants typically advance credit in the form of retail installment contracts (*e.g.,* store credit cards). The financial burden that filing would place on them would outweigh any interest in protecting other creditors of the consumer who might look to the collateral in payment of their claims. Furthermore, since consumer goods are rarely used twice as collateral, there are usually no later creditors who would benefit from a filing.

(2) "Purchase money" transactions [§184]

A purchase money security interest ("PMSI") arises when the secured party advances money or credit *to enable the debtor to purchase* the collateral. [U.C.C. §9-103]

e.g. **Example:** Buyer buys a dishwasher on credit from Seller, who reserves "title" to the dishwasher in himself until Buyer pays for it (a "conditional sale"; *see supra,* §16). Since this extension of credit enables Buyer to buy the goods, Seller's interest qualifies as a purchase money security interest [U.C.C. §9-103(b)], which is perfected automatically on attachment [U.C.C. §9-309(1)].

cf. **Compare:** Borrower needs money to finance her child's tonsillectomy and borrows it from Consumer Finance Co. ("CFC"), giving CFC a security interest in her valuable stamp collection. In this case, CFC must file or take possession for perfection since its money was not used to *buy the stamp collection* and hence its interest is not of the "purchase money" variety.

(a) Who holds PMSI [§185]

A purchase money secured party may be either the *seller* who has advanced credit for all or part of the price or *any other person* (*e.g.,* finance company, lender) who gives value or incurs an obligation to enable the debtor to acquire the collateral or rights in it, but *only* if the value is *actually used* in the transaction by the debtor. [U.C.C. §9-103(a)(2)]

e.g. Example: In the first example above, if a *bank,* rather than Seller, had loaned Buyer the money to buy the dishwasher, the bank's lien therein would also qualify as a "purchase money security interest" *if* Buyer actually used the borrowed money to buy the dishwasher. If Buyer told the bank that Buyer planned to use the money to buy the dishwasher (and signed a security agreement giving the bank an interest in the dishwasher), but *actually* used the money to pay a tax bill and bought the dishwasher with money taken from a savings account, the bank's interest would not be of the "purchase money" type, and the bank would have to file a financing statement to perfect its interest. [U.C.C. §9-103(a)(2)]

(b) Note—security agreement required [§186]

Even though the creditor is not required to *file* notice of his interest in a purchase money transaction involving consumer goods, the creditor must still have an *authenticated security agreement* with the debtor to obtain a valid security interest in the first place. [*See* **Food Service Equipment Co. v. First National Bank,** 174 S.E.2d 216 (Ga. 1970); U.C.C. §9-203] *Note:* Possession by the creditor generally is not a viable alternative to an authenticated security agreement in a PMSI situation because the buyer will generally need to use the goods purchased.

EXAM TIP   **gilbert**

When answering an exam question, be sure to check whether each creditor has a PMSI in the debtor's collateral. In addition to achieving automatic perfection of a security interest in *consumer goods*, a creditor with a PMSI in *any type of goods* has special priority (*i.e., super-priority*) over most other creditors if the creditor meets certain other requirements (*see infra,* §§330-347).

---

(3) "Consumer goods" [§187]

As indicated *supra,* §55, the Code defines "consumer goods" as goods "used or bought primarily for personal, family or household purposes." [U.C.C. §9-102(a)(23)]

(a) Primary use test [§188]

Whether a particular purchase falls under the definition depends on the purchaser's *primary* use. Thus, a sofa sold for use in a dentist's reception room would not constitute consumer goods because of the business use; however, the purchase of the same sofa for the dentist's living room in his family home would fall under the definition.

(b) Creditor may trust consumer [§189]

However, actual use of the goods may not be determinative if it differs from what the consumer told the creditor at the time of *attachment.*

In other words, if the consumer says the goods are for personal use and is lying (really planning a business use), the creditor is still protected without filing if the creditor believed the debtor. [**Balon v. Cadillac Automobile Co.**, 303 A.2d 194 (N.H. 1973); **Commercial Credit Equipment Co. v. Carter**, 516 P.2d 767 (Wash. 1973)]

(c) Exception—motor vehicles [§190]

In all states, certificates of title are issued evidencing the ownership of certain motor vehicles (*e.g.*, cars, trucks, mobile homes). Security interests in such vehicles *must* be perfected by notation of the interest *on the face of the certificate;* neither automatic perfection nor the filing of a financing statement would work for such motor vehicles, even if they are classified as "consumer goods." *Note*: This exception does *not* apply to vehicles that are part of a dealership's inventory. A security interest in such vehicles can be perfected using the ordinary perfection rules (*e.g.*, by filing a financing statement). [U.C.C. §§9-309(1), 9-311(a), (d)]

1) When certificate of title effective [§191]

Under prior law there was much disagreement about *when* a certificate of title became effective—on submission of an application to the issuing authority or only when the certificate is finally issued by that authority. The answer was important for reasons of priority over later parties acquiring rights in the automobile (buyers, the trustee in bankruptcy, etc.). Article 9 provides that the submission of a *valid application and payment* of the fee to the right office makes the certificate of title effective, and would date the secured party's perfection from then. The security interest continues in the collateral as long as this certificate is still valid. [U.C.C. §9-303(b)]

2) Validity of a foreign certificate [§192]

Must the state or country issuing the certificate of title have some *connection* with the transaction? Suppose that the debtor lives in California, buys a car in California, keeps the car in California, and borrows money from a California bank to finance the car's purchase, but somehow gets a certificate of title for this car that is issued by the state of Maryland. If the California bank makes sure its lien interest is noted on the Maryland title (the only title for the car in existence), is the bank perfected even though the state of Maryland has nothing to do with this transaction? Courts had disagreed, but Article 9 allows the title to be valid even if issued by a foreign jurisdiction having no connection with the transaction. The policy reason is that this will cause no real harm; any later parties acquiring an interest in the vehicle will want to see the certificate of title, so anything written on the Maryland title will come to their attention. [U.C.C. §9-303(a)]

(d) Exception—fixtures [§193]

Consumer goods that are to become fixtures (*e.g.,* a furnace) require special steps for perfection (*see infra,* §§348-350).

(4) Combining PMSIs with other security interests [§194]

Under prior law, there was a great deal of controversy about whether PMSI status was lost if the debt was *refinanced* or *consolidated* with other loans. The issue is particularly important in bankruptcy, in which debtors can protect their exemption rights from non-PMSIs, but not PMSIs [*see* Bankruptcy Code §522(f)]. Suppose, for example, that a creditor with a PMSI in a debtor's factory equipment allows the debtor to refinance the debt when payment proves difficult, and at the same time loans the debtor more money, taking a security interest in additional non-PMSI collateral as well as keeping the existing PMSI in the factory equipment. Has the creditor now lost PMSI status as to the original factory equipment? Some courts said "yes," applying the so-called *transformation rule*—any change in the PMSI debt *transformed* it into a non-PMSI transaction. However, other courts *allowed* the creditor to retain its PMSI status as to the original collateral if it could prove how much of the original debt remained unpaid, under the so-called *dual status* rule. For *nonconsumer* transactions, Article 9 adopts the dual status rule, allowing the parties to specify how payments are to be allocated to preserve the PMSI status of the original debt, and providing default rules allocating payments if the parties fail to so specify. [U.C.C. §9-103(e) - (g)]

---

e.g. **Example:** Bank loaned Debtor money to buy a business computer, taking a PMSI in the computer. When Debtor needed to borrow more money, Bank refinanced the loan, giving Debtor more money, keeping its PMSI in the computer, and also taking a security interest in Debtor's accounts receivable. The security agreement provided that payments would first be allocated to the non-PMSI portion of the debt, so that Bank kept its PMSI status as to the computer as long as possible. The Code approves of this arrangement.

(a) Default rules as to payments [§195]

If the parties fail to specify in the security agreement how payments are to be applied to the debt, the debtor/obligor may do so when making payment (*e.g.,*"Use the payment to pay off the computer debt first"). [U.C.C. §9-103(e)(2)] If the debtor gives no instructions, the payments are applied first to *unsecured* debts (*i.e.,* ones for which there is no collateral) and then to pay off secured debts in the *order in which they were incurred.* [U.C.C. §9-103(e)(3)]

(b) No Code rule for consumer debts [§196]

Consumer groups preferred the transformation rule described above, since it allowed the consumers to preserve more property from creditors in bankruptcy, so they persuaded the drafters to omit *all* consumer transactions from the Code's dual status rule, leaving the issue to be decided by the bankruptcy courts without any Article 9 guidance. [U.C.C. §9-103(h) and Comment 8]

b. Assignment of beneficial interest in decedent's estate [§197]

Like purchase money security interests, perfection of a security interest created by an assignment of a beneficial interest in a decedent's estate is automatic; *i.e.,* no filing is required. [U.C.C. §9-309(13)]

Example: Debtor borrows $1,000 from Lender, and to secure payment, he assigns to Lender his beneficial interest in his deceased uncle's estate. Lender need not file to perfect his security interest.

---

(1) Rationale

Such an assignment is not normally a commercial transaction, and hence the Code drafters decided to exclude it from the filing requirements of Article 9.

c. Assignment of certain accounts and payment intangibles [§198]

Another exemption to the filing requirement (*i.e.,* another automatic perfection transaction) covers assignments of accounts or payment intangibles that—either alone or combined with other assignments to the same assignee—do *not* constitute a *significant portion* of the assignor's outstanding accounts or payment intangibles. [U.C.C. §9-309(2)]

(1) What constitutes "significant" portion [§199]

For the purposes of determining a "significant portion," the Code focuses on all transfers made to the *particular assignee,* including other earlier assignments made in conjunction with the assignment that is supposedly exempt. Thus, an assignor cannot avoid the Code perfection requirements by serial assignment.

(a) Minority view—percentage of assigned accounts or payment intangibles measured [§200]

Some courts measure a "significant portion" *mathematically*—comparing the unfiled assignment amount to the assignor's total accounts or payment intangibles—and hold the assignee unsecured if the assignment is a large percentage of the total. [*See, e.g.,* **Consolidated Film Industries v. United States,** 547 F.2d 533 (10th Cir.

1977)—assignment of assignor's *only* account receivable held "significant" so that assignee who did not file was deemed unperfected]

(b) Majority view—regularity of assignments measured [§201]

Most courts, however, take the position that whatever the percentage, the true test is whether the assignment is *"casual or isolated"* or part of a regular commercial financing pattern. [U.C.C. §9-309, Comment 4]

1) Rationale

An assignee who does not regularly engage in assignments may not realize filing is required; furthermore, as a practical matter, it may be difficult for an assignee to discover the total amount of the assignor's accounts or payment intangibles. [*See, e.g.,* **Architectural Woods, Inc. v. Washington,** 562 P.2d 248 (Wash. 1977)—assignee not in the regular business of taking assignments of accounts held perfected and hence not required to file]

(2) Distinguish—assignment of perfected security interest [§202]

If the creditor perfects by filing a financing statement in the proper place and then assigns or sells the debtor's obligation to another creditor, the second creditor may wish to change the records to reflect that the name of the creditor has changed. This may be accomplished by the filing of an *assignment statement,* but such a filing is *permissive* and not mandatory, so that even without it, the second creditor's security interest remains perfected. [U.C.C. §9-514]

(a) Constitutes sale of an account [§203]

Recall, however, that assignments of accounts are treated as security interests (*see supra,* §45). Thus, even though the second creditor's security interest remains perfected as to the **original debtor,** the second creditor must file a financing statement to be perfected as to the *first creditor's creditors*. If the second creditor fails to do this, it risks losing the account to other creditors of the first creditor. [U.C.C. §9-310, Comment 4]

---

e.g. **Example:** Debtor borrowed money from Lender A and gave Lender A a security interest in her accounts receivable, which Lender A perfected by filing a financing statement in the appropriate place. Lender A then assigned this debt to Lender B, so that the debtor would have to make the payments directly to Lender B. There is no legal duty to change the name of the secured parties on the financing statement, and whether or not this is done, Lender B will be protected against those trying to seize the accounts receivable from the original debtor. However, the transaction between Lender A and Lender B is itself a secured transaction (the sale of an account), and for Lender B to have priority over the creditors of Lender A, Lender B will have to file a financing statement showing that Lender A has granted it a security interest in these accounts.

d. Sale of promissory notes and payment intangibles [§204]

While the outright sale of both promissory notes and payment intangibles are Article 9 transactions (even where these items are not in any way being used as collateral—*see supra*, §45), the buyer of such property is *automatically perfected* on attachment and need take no other steps to perfect its security interest. [U.C.C. §9-309(3) - (4)]

e. Supporting obligations [§205]

Rights against sureties and issuers of letters of credit are called "supporting obligations" in the Code, and, as long as the creditor is perfected in the *underlying obligation*, the supporting obligations are automatically perfected without the creditor having to take any special steps to preserve these secondary rights. [U.C.C. §§9-102(a)(77), 9-308(d) and Comment 5]

Example: Buyer agreed to buy goods on credit from Seller (thus creating an "account") and to get both a surety who would guaranty the payment and a bank's letter of credit in favor of Seller. If Seller borrows money and uses the account as collateral, and Seller's lender perfects as to the account, the lender is automatically perfected as to rights against both the surety and the issuer of the letter of credit.

f. Temporary "automatic" perfection [§206]

The Code provides for *temporary* perfection of a security interest in certain situations. [U.C.C. §9-312]

(1) New value given [§207]

A secured party as to *negotiable documents, certificated securities, or instruments* who advances *new value* obtains a *20-day* perfection period from the moment of attachment, even if the secured party does not file and the collateral remains with the debtor. [U.C.C. §9-312(e)]

(a) Rationale

There are often commercial reasons why the debtor must remain in possession of such collateral, and there would be no point in forcing the secured party, who is willing to extend new value, to first file or take possession of the collateral or else lose perfection. The briefness of the period of perfection assures that the secured party will be watchful.

(2) Other twenty-day extensions [§208]

There are two other situations (besides the giving of new value) in which the Code specifies that a security interest already in existence in certain collateral shall remain perfected (without additional filing) for a 20-day "grace" period:

(a) Delivery of goods or negotiable documents [§209]

If a secured party makes available to the debtor *either* negotiable documents or goods in the hands of a bailee that were not covered by a negotiable document, for the purpose of ultimate sale or exchange, or for loading, shipping, storing, or like purposes, the Code grants a 20-day extension of perfection. [U.C.C. §9-312(f)]

(b) Delivery of instruments or certificated securities [§210]

A secured party is granted a similar extension when delivering instruments or certificated securities to the debtor for the purpose of sale, exchange, collection, renewal, or registration of transfer of the instruments or certificated securities. [U.C.C. §9-312(g)]

> **EXAM TIP** **gilbert**
>
> Remember that if a security interest is *temporarily* perfected under one of the above rules, the perfection *only lasts for 20 days*. If the creditor does not perfect by *some other means* within the 20 days, the creditor becomes *unperfected* and loses any priority it has over competing creditors.

6. Control over Investment Property [§211]

For investment property (stocks, bonds, commodity contracts, and rights in securities held with a broker), there are two methods of perfection: *filing* a financing statement and getting "*control*" over the investment property.

a. Priority [§212]

It is important to appreciate the following rules: If one creditor perfects by gaining control and another by filing, the *creditor with control* prevails over the creditor who perfected merely by filing. [U.C.C. §9-328(1)] If two creditors have control, the *first* creditor to gain control has priority. [U.C.C. §9-328]

b. Methods of obtaining control [§213]

A creditor has *control*, and is therefore perfected, by doing one of the following things:

(1) Certificated securities [§214]

If stocks or bonds are represented by physical certificates (*i.e.*, they are *certificated securities*), the creditor gains control by taking *delivery* of the certificates with any necessary *indorsements*. [U.C.C. §8-106(a) - (b)]

(2) Uncertificated securities [§215]

Some corporations issuing stocks or bonds do not issue physical pieces of paper, but instead simply record the names of the owners of these securities at the corporate office or with its transfer agent. Such securities are said to be *"uncertificated."* [U.C.C. §8-102(a)(18)] In this case, a creditor gains control, and thus is perfected, either by becoming the *registered owner* in the records of the issuer or by having the issuer agree to *comply with instructions by the creditor* without further consent by the registered owner (the debtor). [U.C.C. §§8-106(c), 8-301(b)]

(3) Securities or commodity accounts or rights to particular investments in such accounts [§216]

If the stocks or bonds are deposited in an account with a broker or a clearing corporation (both are called *"securities intermediaries"*), or commodity contracts are similarly held, a security interest can be taken in the entire account or portions thereof (a *"security entitlement"*) by gaining control over the account. This is done by *changing the name* of the account to that of the creditor, or by obtaining the agreement of the broker/clearing corporation that it will *act according to the instructions of the creditor* without any further consent of the debtor. [U.C.C. §8-108(d)]

---

e.g. **Example:** Investor bought 100 shares of Monopoly Telephone Co. stock through her broker and allowed the broker to register the stock in the broker's name so that the stock could be easily sold when Investor so decided. Investor needed to borrow money and use this stock as collateral, so she applied to Bank for a loan. Bank can perfect its security interest in the stock in a number of ways: (i) have the stock moved to an account of which Bank is the record owner, (ii) have the broker transfer the stock to Bank so that Bank becomes the registered owner, or (iii) have Investor procure the agreement of the broker that it will act according to the instructions of Bank without having to get the consent of Investor. Any of these methods would establish *control* and lead to perfection. Bank could also file a financing statement covering the stock, but it would then risk losing priority to another creditor who perfected by gaining control.

---

(4) Securities intermediary as creditor [§217]

If the securities intermediary (*i.e.*, the broker or clearing corporation) itself becomes the creditor, the securities intermediary will have control because the securities will be in its possession. In this situation, the securities intermediary gets *super-priority* over all other creditors, even those having prior control. [U.C.C. §9-328(3)]

> **Example:** Suppose, in the last example, that Bank gained control by having Investor instruct her broker to follow the instructions of Bank, but in the meantime to also follow her instructions (such dual ownership is permitted). If Investor then borrows money from her own broker, granting the broker a security interest in the Monopoly Telephone stock, both the broker and Bank have perfected security interests, but the broker has priority over Bank.

7. Control over Deposit Accounts [§218]

Filing is *not* an available method to perfect a security interest in a bank account—getting "control" over the account is the *only way to perfect* an interest in it. [U.C.C. §9-312(b)(1)]

a. Three methods of control of deposit account [§219]

There are three different ways to get control over a deposit account. First, the *bank in which the deposit account is maintained* automatically has control over the deposit account when it makes a loan to a customer using that deposit account as collateral. If *creditors other than the bank in which the account is maintained* want control, they must use one of *two other methods*: *changing* the account name to the name of the creditor (which is the safest method of getting control), or, if this is not done, having the bank agree in an authenticated record (*see supra*, §127) that the bank will *follow the instructions of the creditor* without further consent of the debtor. [U.C.C. §9-104(a)]

> **Example:** Company borrows money from the bank where it has its checking account and signs a security agreement using that account as collateral. The bank has control over the account and is perfected without having to do anything more.

> **Example:** When Business Corporation borrowed money from its own president, it gave the president a security interest in the bank account Business Corporation had at Octopus National Bank. The president got Business Corporation to agree to change the name on the account to the president's name. The president has control of the account.

> **Example:** Same facts as in the example above, except all three parties (Business Corporation, the president, and the bank) agreed in writing that if the president so informed the bank, it would transfer all monies in the account over to the account the president had at another bank. The president has control over the collateral, and this is true even though the account is still carried in the name of Business Corporation and the corporation could itself take all the money out of the account at any time. [U.C.C. §9-104(b)]

8. **Control over Letter of Credit Rights [§220]**

Filing is **not** an available method to perfect a security interest in rights against the issuer of a letter of credit—getting "control" over the letter of credit rights is the **only way to perfect** a direct interest in such collateral. [U.C.C. §9-312(b)(2)] A creditor gets such control by having the issuer of the letter of credit **consent to an assignment to the creditor** of the proceeds of the letter of credit. [U.C.C. §9-107]

---

e.g. **Example:** To pay for its order of 1,000 sweaters from Seller, Buyer had Big Bank issue a letter of credit to Seller (the "beneficiary" of the letter of credit), guaranteeing that Big Bank itself would pay for the sweaters if Seller sent Big Bank the relevant paperwork showing that the sweaters had been shipped to Buyer (the "applicant" of the letter of credit). If Seller wants to borrow money using the letter of credit rights as collateral, Seller's creditor will get control only if Big Bank agrees to this assignment.

---

a. **Issuer not obligated to give consent [§221]**

The issuer of the letter of credit is **not** obligated to consent to the assignment, and if the issuer refuses to give consent, the seller's creditor will not have achieved control and will be **unperfected**. [U.C.C. §5-114(c)] In this case, the creditor could still achieve perfection by perfecting its security interest in the **account** that the buyer owes to the creditor, and this would automatically perfect a security interest in the letter of credit supporting this account (*see supra*, §205). The drawback to perfecting in this manner is that the seller might still collect under the letter of credit, get the money, and spend it before the creditor could collect it from the seller. The seller's creditor would have been better off talking the issuer of the letter of credit into agreeing to the assignment of the proceeds of the letter of credit, in which case the issuer would have paid the money directly to the creditor.

9. **Control over Electronic Chattel Paper [§222]**

A security interest in electronic chattel paper (*i.e.*, chattel paper that has no physical form—*see supra*, §64) may be perfected by **filing or taking control**. Section 9-105 provides for such control if the creditor can figure out a way to have a **single authoritative copy** of the electronic chattel paper marked so that the creditor is the assignee of record, and the copy is maintained by the creditor in such a way that it can be changed only with the agreement of the creditor. Whether the technology yet exists to do this is debatable. [U.C.C. §9-105 and its Comments]

10. **Rights and Duties of Secured Party in Control [§223]**

While a secured party has control of collateral, it has the same duty to account for rents, issues, and profits of collateral and the same right to repledge the collateral as a secured party in possession of collateral (*see supra*, §§175, 179).

SUMMARY OF METHODS OF PERFECTION	**gilbert**
FILING—	Effective for *all types* of collateral *except deposit accounts and letter of credit rights*.
POSSESSION—	Effective for goods, money, documents, certificated securities, instruments, and tangible chattel paper.
AUTOMATIC—	Effective for PMSIs in *consumer goods*, assignments of an insignificant portion of the assignor's accounts or payment intangibles, assignments of beneficial interests in decedents' estates, the sale of promissory notes and payment intangibles, and all supporting obligations. There are also *temporary periods of automatic perfection:* 20 days from the moment of attachment when a secured party gives new value and the collateral is a negotiable document, certificated security, or instrument; and 20 days where a secured party makes available an instrument, negotiable document, or goods in possession of a bailee (not represented by a negotiable document) on a temporary basis (*e.g.,* for the debtor to sell).
CONTROL—	Effective for investment property, deposit accounts, letter of credit rights, and electronic chattel paper.

B. Time of Perfection

1. Completion of Filing or Other Requirements [§224]

A security interest becomes perfected when (i) it has *attached and* (ii) *all the required steps* for the method of perfection being used by the secured party have taken place. A secured party may take the steps necessary for perfection (such as filing or acquiring possession of the collateral) *in advance* of the attachment of the security interest, but perfection does not take place until the interest has attached. [U.C.C. §9-308(a); *and see supra,* §§119-120]

2. Effect of Secondary Perfections [§225]

A security interest may be perfected more than once. If this occurs, the later perfection by another means is deemed to *relate back* to the date of the original perfection, *provided* that there has been no intervening unperfected period. [U.C.C. §9-308(c)]

Example: On June 1, Debtor pledges his crop of corn, placing the entire harvest in a silo in Secured Party's name in return for an advance of $1,000. (Secured Party's interest is therefore perfected by possession under section 9-310(b)(6).) On July 1, Debtor needs to regain possession of the corn, so Secured

Party files a financing statement covering the transaction and then allows Debtor to have possession. The perfection is still deemed to have taken place on June 1, since there was no intervening period of nonperfection.

Example: Suppose instead that Secured Party released the corn to Debtor on July 1, without filing a financing statement, so that Debtor could sell the corn at a market. Secured Party no longer enjoys perfection by possession, but has a 20-day temporary perfection period commencing on July 1, since the secured party has released the collateral to allow Debtor to sell. [U.C.C. §9-312(f); *supra*, §209]

Compare: But suppose Secured Party released the corn for a purpose that does not fall within section 9-312(f) or failed to file within the 20-day period. In such a case, Secured Party's perfected interest will no longer date from June 1, the original date of perfection, since there was a lapse in the continuity of perfection, and intervening liens or purchasers could prevail. [U.C.C. §9-308(c)]

EXAM TIP   **gilbert**

Determining the *time of perfection* often is very important when determining which creditor has *priority* over the debtor's collateral. For example, in a contest between two perfected secured parties, the first secured party to file a financing statement or perfect generally prevails. Thus, the exact moment of filing or perfection is crucial in the determination of which party will have priority. (See Chapter VI for a full discussion of the rules of priority.)

C. Place of Perfection—Multistate Transactions

1. Introduction [§226]

The question of which state's law governs perfection arises when collateral is moved from one state to another and in multistate transactions. This question is particularly important when perfection has been accomplished by filing. If a filing is not made in the proper state, a party will not be perfected. Therefore, the Code provides special rules to determine which state's law governs. [U.C.C. §9-301]

2. General Rule—Debtor's Location Governs Perfection [§227]

The law of the jurisdiction in which the *debtor is located* generally governs perfection. This is a significant change from prior law, which generally involved more complicated tests, typically choosing the law of the jurisdiction where the collateral was physically located. [U.C.C. §9-301(1)]

a. **Where is debtor located? [§228]**

Usually it is obvious where a debtor is located, but there are thorny cases, and therefore section 9-307 contains definite rules establishing the debtor's location for purposes of Article 9.

(1) **Corporations and other "registered organizations" [§229]**

Regardless of where it is physically headquartered, a corporation is located in the state of its *incorporation*. This means that Delaware, which has more corporations than people, will have the lion's share of the nation's corporate filings, and the state will collect a hefty amount in filing fees through the years. [U.C.C. §9-307(e)]

(2) **Organizations other than corporations [§230]**

Noncorporate organizations (*e.g.*, partnerships, trusts, and societies) are located at their *place of business* if they have only one place of business, and at their *chief executive office* if they have more than one place of business. [U.C.C. §9-307(b)(2) - (3)]

(a) **Definition—place of business [§231]**

For purposes of determining a debtor's location, the debtor's "place of business" is the place where a debtor *conducts its affairs*. [U.C.C. §9-307(a)]

(3) **Individuals [§232]**

Individuals are located at their *primary residence*. [U.C.C. §9-307(b)(1)]

(4) **Federal government as debtor [§233]**

When the United States borrows money, it is deemed to be located in the *District of Columbia*. [U.C.C. §9-307(h)]

(5) **Foreign debtors [§234]**

If the debtor is located in a foreign country, that country's law governs perfection if it has laws similar to Article 9 permitting the recording of nonpossessory security interests to obtain priority over the rights of a lien creditor with respect to the collateral. If the country does *not* have such laws, the debtor is located in the District of Columbia. [U.C.C. §9-307(c)]

3. **Exceptions**

a. **Possessory security interests and security interests in fixtures and timber to be cut [§235]**

If the secured party perfects by taking *possession* of the collateral (*see supra*, §158), or if the collateral is a fixture (*see infra*, §§348-350) or timber to be cut, the location of the *collateral* determines issues relating to perfection. [U.C.C. §9-301(2) - (3)]

b. Minerals [§236]

Security interests in oil, gas, and other as-extracted collateral are governed by the law of the jurisdiction of the *wellhead or minehead*. [U.C.C. §9-301(4)]

c. Goods covered by certificate of title [§237]

Recall that a security interest in goods covered by a certificate of title is perfected by placing a notation of the security interest on the certificate. Thus, the law of the *state issuing the certificate* governs perfection. [U.C.C. §9-303]

d. Deposit accounts [§238]

The law of the *depositary bank's jurisdiction* governs perfection of a security interest in a deposit account. The bank's jurisdiction is usually provided in *agreements* or other communications between the debtor and the bank. If no jurisdiction has been designated by the parties, the law of the state in which the bank has its *chief executive office* governs perfection. [U.C.C. §9-304]

e. Investment property perfected by control [§239]

If a security interest in investment property is perfected by control, rather than by filing or automatic perfection, the following rules apply: If the collateral is a *certificated security,* the law of the state where the *certificated security* is located governs perfection. If the collateral is an *uncertificated security, a securities account, or a commodity account,* the law of the *issuer's, securities intermediary's, or commodity intermediary's jurisdiction* governs perfection. As is the case with deposit accounts, such parties' jurisdictions are usually provided in *agreements* or other communications between the debtor and either the issuer, securities intermediary, or commodity intermediary. If no jurisdiction has been designated, the law where the *issuer was incorporated*, or the law where the *securities intermediary's or commodity intermediary's chief executive office* is located, governs perfection. [U.C.C. §§8-110, 9-305]

f. Letter of credit rights [§240]

If a security interest in letter of credit rights is *not perfected as a supporting obligation* (*see supra,* §205), and the letter of credit was *issued within the United States,* the law of the *issuer's jurisdiction* governs perfection. Again, the issuer's jurisdiction is usually provided in *agreements* or other communications between the issuer and the debtor. If no jurisdiction has been designated by the parties, the law of the jurisdiction in which the *debtor is located* governs perfection. [U.C.C. §§5-116, 9-306]

g. Agricultural liens [§241]

The perfection of an agricultural lien is governed by the law of the state in which the *farm product covered by the lien* is located. [U.C.C. §9-302]

4. Location of Collateral Governs Issues Other than Perfection [§242]

Although the *debtor's* location generally dictates the law governing perfection, the jurisdiction where the *collateral* is located nonetheless governs the *effect of perfection and issues of priority*. [U.C.C. §9-301(3)]

Example: Debtor is located in State A, but has a valuable art collection located in State B. If Debtor uses the art collection (consumer goods) as collateral for a loan, the secured party making the loan should file a financing statement in State A, where Debtor is located. Suppose that State A provides that when consumer goods are sold at a foreclosure sale, the sale must be a public auction; State B allows both auctions and private foreclosure sales for consumer goods. If the secured party declares a default for nonpayment of the debt and seizes the collateral in State B where it is located, the secured party could use either the public auction or a private sale to dispose of the art collection, since State B's law controls the *effect* of perfection (as opposed to the method of perfection). If the two states had different rules about which of several creditors had priority in the same collateral, the state of the collateral's location would be used to resolve this priority issue as well.

---

5. **Change of Debtor's Location [§243]**

If the perfection of a security interest is governed by the law of the state in which the *debtor is located*, and the debtor changes its location (*see supra*, §§228-234 for rules as to where the debtor is located), a reperfection is required in the new location within *four months* after the change (even if the secured party does not know of the change). [U.C.C. §9-316(a)(2)]

Example: Sara borrows money from Best Bank and gives Best Bank a security interest in all of her equipment. Sara is an individual residing in the state of Illinois, so Best Bank perfects by filing a financing statement in Illinois. Sara then moves to Tennessee. Best Bank has *four months* to reperfect by filing in Tennessee or by taking possession of the equipment.

---

a. **Similar rule applies to deposit accounts, letter of credit rights, and most investment property [§244]**

Recall that the perfection of security interests in deposit accounts, letter of credit rights, uncertificated securities, securities accounts, and commodity accounts is governed by the law of the jurisdiction of the bank, issuer of the letter of credit, issuer of the uncertificated security, securities intermediary, or commodity intermediary. If the jurisdiction of any of these parties *changes*, the secured party must perfect within *four months* of the change (even if the secured party does not know of the change). [U.C.C. 9-316(f)]

b. **New perfection "relates back" [§245]**

As long as the secured party reperfects the security interest in the new state within the four-month period (by a new filing or taking possession), the interest is deemed perfected from the date of the original perfection—*i.e.*, there is a "relation back" as against any subsequent interest holder. [U.C.C. §§9-308(e), 9-316(b)]

c. Effect of failure to reperfect [§246]

On the other hand, if the secured party fails to reperfect within four months of removal, the interest becomes unperfected as against *any* "purchaser" of the collateral after removal (and under section 1-201, "purchaser" includes secured parties). In this case, there is *no* "relation back," so that even if the secured party later perfects in the new state, the interest will be subordinate to intervening secured creditors, etc. [U.C.C. §9-316(b)]

Example: Big Bank perfected a security interest in the inventory of Retailer, whose only store was located in Utah. On January 1, Retailer moved the store and its inventory to Texas. On February 1, Retailer used the same inventory as collateral for a new loan from Texas Bank, which promptly filed a financing statement in the appropriate Texas filing office. If Big Bank files a financing statement in Texas before the end of April, it will prevail over Texas Bank. If not, Texas Bank has priority in the inventory, even if Big Bank were to perfect in, say, August, after the four-month grace period had expired.

(1) Note—judicial lien creditor not protected during grace period [§247]

The Code's definitions of "purchaser" and "purchase" [U.C.C. §1-201(32), (33)] *require a voluntary transaction*. A judicial lien is not voluntary, so a judicial lien creditor whose lien attaches to the collateral during the four-month grace period is junior to the original security interest, even if the original creditor never reperfects in the new jurisdiction.

(2) Judicial lien acquired after grace period expires has priority [§248]

If the collateral is moved to a new jurisdiction and four months elapse but the original creditor does not reperfect, the security interest becomes unperfected at the end of the grace period. A judicial lien first attaching *after* the four-month period, and before the original creditor reperfects, would have priority over the original creditor's security interest. As discussed *infra*, §320, *unperfected security interests are junior to judicial lien creditors*.

Example: Big Bank perfected a security interest in the inventory of Retailer, whose only store was located in Utah. On January 1, Retailer moved the store and its inventory to Texas. On February 1, Retailer's employee negligently ran over a pedestrian with the company truck. The pedestrian sued and recovered a judgment against Retailer on April 1, and promptly had the sheriff seize the inventory to satisfy the judgment. Big Bank will have priority in this inventory over the pedestrian's judicial lien since the latter first attached during the four- month grace period, and this is true even if Big Bank never reperfects its security interest in Texas. However, if the pedestrian's judicial lien attached *after* the four-month grace period, and before Big Bank reperfected, the judicial lien would have priority in the inventory.

d. Effect of lapsing perfection [§249]

As discussed *infra,* §287, a filed financing statement is effective only for five years and then it lapses unless renewed. If the debtor's location changes and the financing statement lapses in the first state *before* four months have passed since the move, there is *no four-month "grace" period*; rather, the time for reperfecting in the second state ends when the financing statement lapses in the first state. [U.C.C. §9-316(a)(1)]

Example: Big Bank filed a financing statement in Utah on March 1, 2005, to perfect a security interest in Retailer's inventory. This financing statement will lapse (cease to be effective) at the end of five years (March 1, 2010). If on February 1, 2010, Retailer moves the business to Texas, Big Bank will have only until March 1, 2010, to refile in Texas, or its security interest will become unperfected.

---

e. Exception to four-month rule—automatic perfection [§250]

If the collateral is of the type requiring no steps other than attachment for automatic perfection (*e.g.,* a purchase money security interest in consumer goods; *supra,* §182), the four-month rule does *not apply*. Thus, on removal of the collateral to a new state, no steps need be taken to continue the original perfection.

Example: Debtor purchased a dog in Arkansas on credit, giving Seller a purchase money security interest. One year later, Debtor and the dog moved to North Carolina. No filing was required in Arkansas since Seller's perfection occurred automatically on attachment. [U.C.C. §9-309(1)] Therefore, perfection continues without filing in North Carolina. [*In re* **Marshall,** 10 U.C.C. Rep. 1290 (N.D. Ohio 1969)]

---

f. Change in identity of debtor [§251]

Revised Article 9 has a number of rules about what happens if the debtor makes a substantial change in its identity—*e.g.,* merges with another company, reorganizes into a new entity in or outside of bankruptcy, or sells the collateral to a buyer who assumes the debt. The Code calls this new entity a *"new debtor."* When such a new debtor arises, the original perfection against the old debtor continues only for *one year* if the new debtor is located in a different state than the original debtor. [U.C.C. §9-316(a)(3)]

Example: Business Corporation gave a security interest to Bank in return for a loan, using its inventory located in stores across the United States as collateral. Bank filed a financing statement in Delaware, where Business Corporation was incorporated. Shortly thereafter Business Corporation merged with Monopoly, Inc., a New York corporation, and the new corporation they formed was incorporated under the laws of the state of Maryland. Bank has one year from the merger to file a new financing statement in Maryland.

---

6. Movement of Collateral Covered by Possessory Security Interest [§252]

Recall that if a security interest is perfected by possession, perfection is governed by the law of the *state in which the collateral is located* (*see supra*, §235). If such collateral is moved from one state to another, the security interest will remain perfected *without any further action* as long as the security interest is also perfected by possession under the laws of the *new* state. [U.C.C. 9-316(c)]

EXAM TIP   **gilbert**

If an exam question states that a debtor or collateral moves from one state to another, you should consider whether the move threatens a creditor's security interest in the collateral (*i.e.,* if a new state's law governs perfection due to the move, the secured party may become **unperfected** unless it takes steps to reperfect in the new state). However, it is important to remember that the move **might not affect perfection at all**. For example, if the **debtor's location** determines the governing law, movement of the **collateral** to a new state has no effect on perfection. Therefore, you should **first** decide what factor influences which state's law governs perfection. If that factor has changed, only **then** should you apply the interstate transfer rules.

---

7. Protective Filings Wise [§253]

When in doubt as to where to file or whether filing is required, the smart attorney will file a financing statement in *every place* that is arguably relevant to the transaction. The old adage is "filing is cheap—lawsuits are expensive."

8. Interstate Transfer of Motor Vehicles

a. General rule—no action needed [§254]

If a motor vehicle is covered by a certificate of title and the secured party's interest is properly noted on the certificate, interstate movement of the vehicle generally has *no effect* on the security interest, even if the vehicle is re-registered in the new jurisdiction. Perfection of the interest generally is governed exclusively by the law of the state that issued the certificate, and the secured creditor remains perfected without doing anything. [U.C.C. §§9-303(c), 9-316(d)]

Example: Debtor purchased a car in Virginia and Finance Company's security interest was noted on the certificate of title. Later, Debtor moved to the District of Columbia. Finance company's security interest will remain perfected as long as no new certificate is issued by the District of Columbia (*see* below).

(1) New certificate obtained—four-month grace period [§255]

If a vehicle is already covered by a certificate of title on which a creditor's lien is noted, and the debtor moves the vehicle to a new jurisdiction and somehow obtains a new certificate of title not showing the creditor's lien (which in theory should not happen—the new jurisdiction typically will not issue a new certificate until the old one is surrendered, and liens are transferred to the new certificate), the creditor's security interest remains perfected for only *four months* after the issuance of the new certificate. After the four-month period, the creditor, unless it reperfects within that time, will lose to later buyers or Article 9 secured parties (*i.e.*, "purchasers for value"). [U.C.C. §9-316(e)]

---

e.g. Example: Bank loaned Debtor money to buy a new car and made sure its lien interest was noted on the certificate of title. Debtor moved to a new state a year later and on March 1 of that year managed to get a new certificate of title issued that showed no liens (a "clean" certificate). Even if Debtor sells the car to a used car dealership in the new state, Bank can repossess the car from the dealership as long as it takes action within four months of March 1. After that period, Bank will become unperfected and lose to an innocent buyer of the collateral. (For the rules of priority versus buyers of the collateral, *see infra*, §§419-435).

(a) Judicial lien creditors not protected [§256]

The four-month grace period only protects later buyers and Article 9 secured parties—it does not protect judicial lien creditors or the debtor's trustee in bankruptcy. If the new clean certificate is issued, four months go by, and then a judicial lien creditor tries to seize the car, the judicial lien will be junior to the original creditor for as long as the original certificate of title is in effect. [U.C.C. §9-316, Comment 5, Example 8]

(b) Innocent buyers and secured parties—no four-month grace period [§257]

There is no four-month grace period for reperfection if the vehicle is either sold to a later innocent party or used as collateral in favor of a later creditor who does not know of the earlier security interest. The original creditor *loses* to these later parties, even during the four months after the new certificate is issued (unless that new certificate warns later parties that there may be security interests not shown on the new certificate). *Note:* A used car dealership does not qualify as an innocent buyer; being in the business of buying cars, it should be better able to police these matters. [U.C.C. §9-337]

Chapter Five:
Filing

CONTENTS

Chapter Approach

A.	The Financing Statement	§258
B.	Where to File	§281
C.	Mechanics of Filing	§284
D.	Request for Statement of Account or List of Collateral	§299

Chapter Approach

This chapter looks into the *formalities* of the financing statement, which are important because failure to create a valid financing statement means that the creditor is unperfected (unless perfection was achieved by possession, by control, or automatically). If the debtor goes bankrupt while the creditor is unperfected, or if other creditors perfect a security interest in the collateral, the creditor with the unperfected security interest will not be able to reach the collateral if the debtor defaults on the debt.

The chapter also discusses the *mechanics* of filing: where to file, how often to file, and what documents can be filed. It is important for you to analyze the facts of your question to determine whether these technical requirements have been met.

A. The Financing Statement

1. **Notice Filing [§258]**
   The parties may, if they choose, file a copy of their *security agreement* as a financing statement, thus giving complete notice of the debt and collateral to all who read the record. However, the Code also authorizes the filing of a brief *financing statement*—a system favored by most debtors and creditors. The financing statement may give little specific information about the details of the underlying transaction, but it does put other creditors "on notice" that a security agreement of *some* kind is in effect.

   a. **Form of financing statement [§259]**
      A sample form of a financing statement is set forth in U.C.C. section 9-521, and blank forms (commonly referred to as "U.C.C. 1s") are available at the office of the secretary of state and at other filing offices.

   b. **Indexed under debtor's name [§260]**
      The financing statement is indexed in the records under the debtor's name. The idea here is that later creditors, contemplating a loan to the debtor, can then search the records under the debtor's name and see what property of the debtor is already encumbered in favor of other creditors.

2. **Required Contents of Financing Statement [§261]**
   The following is the information required to be included in the financing statement under the Code [U.C.C. §§9-502, 9-516]:

   (i)   The *name and address of the debtor;*

(ii) The *name and address of the secured party;* and

(iii) A *description of the collateral* covered by the financing statement. *Note:* If the collateral is *real property-related,* the real property to which the collateral is related also must be described (*see infra,* §278).

a. Rejection of financing statement [§262]

Under prior law, filing officers sometimes took on the role of judge and made legal decisions about whether the proffered financing statement was sufficient. The 1999 revision gives the filing office only very limited grounds for rejecting a financing statement. [U.C.C. §9-516] If the filing office *wrongfully rejects* a financing statement, the secured party is nonetheless protected, except against a purchaser of the collateral who gives value in reasonable reliance on the absence of the record from the files. [U.C.C. §9-516(d)] However, in such a situation, the smart thing for the secured party to do would be to correct the alleged problem and actually put an appropriate financing statement on file.

b. Open drawer concept [§263]

The original financing statement will be given a filing number, and all later filed items relating to this transaction (continuation statements, assignments, termination statements, etc.—all part of the "record") must refer to this file number. [U.C.C. §9-516(b)] Everything later filed is then kept in the same file, thus creating what is sometimes called an "*open drawer,*" and later searchers asking to see what is on file will be shown *everything* that is contained therein (and not just the original financing statement, which is typically all that filing offices used to provide). [U.C.C. §9-519(f)] Requests for the items in the filed record must be honored by the filing office within two business days. [U.C.C. §9-523(e)]

c. Retention of filed items [§264]

Even if the transaction ends and a termination statement is filed (*see infra,* §292), the filing office is required to keep on record all that has been filed for *one year.* [U.C.C. §9-519(g)] This is useful if there are conflicts about what the filing used to say, as long as the matter is brought in the year after the financing statement ceased to be effective.

d. Copies [§265]

It may prove important to establish exactly what was filed and when, so the secured party may request a copy of the filed items, and the filing office must provide the copy either in writing or electronically. Requesting such a copy is a wise move every time the secured party files anything. [U.C.C. §9-523]

e. Debtor's authorization required [§266]

Prior law required that the debtor sign the financing statement (this was an extra cautionary step to warn the debtor about what was going on), but the

Code now only requires that all such filings be *"authorized by an authenticated record."* [U.C.C. §§9-509(a); 9-502, Comment 3] The debtor's authentication of the original *security agreement* (*see supra*, §126) is *automatically* an authorization for the secured party to file a financing statement without the necessity of any further steps. [U.C.C. §9-509(b)] The idea here is to encourage and facilitate electronic filings and thereby speed things up.

3. Sufficiency of the Financing Statement

a. Financing statement without seriously misleading errors generally effective [§267]

The stated policy of the Code is that a financing statement *substantially complying* with the requirements of section 9-502 is effective even though it contains *minor errors* that are *not seriously misleading*. The courts are bluntly told to avoid the supertechnical reading of statutory requirements sometimes practiced in the past. [U.C.C. §9-506(a), *and see* Comment 2]

---

e.g. Example: Nightflyer Trust and Finance takes a security interest in Debtor's equipment. However, the financing statement lists the secured party as "Nightflyer Finance Company." This financing statement will still be effective, despite the error in the secured party's name, because financing statements are indexed under the debtor's name, and thus an error as to the secured party's name is likely to be labeled as minor and not seriously misleading. [U.C.C. §9-506, Comment 2]

---

(1) Errors in debtor's name—search logic test [§268]

Courts had all sorts of tests under prior law as to whether an error in the *debtor's* name was seriously misleading, but Article 9 uses a simple test. It asks whether a later search under the debtor's correct name, using the filing office's *standard search logic*, would find the initial financing statement. "Search logic" is a computer term relating to the method in which computer programs search for files (*e.g.*, capitalization does not affect the search, the word "Inc." is irrelevant to the search, etc.). [U.C.C. §9-506(c); **Pankratz Implement Co. v. Citizens National Bank**, 102 P.3d 1165 (Kan. 2004)]

b. Name and address of secured party [§269]

The requirement that the address of the secured party be listed on the financing statement is intended to give anyone interested notice of where to go for more information. Hence, creditors may jeopardize their secured status by providing incomplete or inadequate names and addresses. On the other hand, a complete street address is not always required. The Code merely requires an address that is *"reasonable under the circumstances."* [U.C.C. §9-516, Comment 5] *Note:* If a filing office *accepts* a financing statement containing an inadequate address, or no address at all, the financing statement nonetheless will be *effective*.

Example: Coca-Cola sold a Coke machine on credit to a gas station. The financing statement gave the address of the secured party as "Coca-Cola Bottling Co., East Hartford, Conn." The court held the address sufficient because there was only one Coca-Cola Bottling Co. in the entire Hartford phone book, so a creditor would not have been misled by the incomplete address. [*In re* **Bengtson**, 3 U.C.C. Rep. 283 (D. Conn. 1965)]

Compare: Creditor lived on a rural route outside the small town of Harvard, Illinois. The financing statement gave the creditor's address only as "Harvard." This was held insufficient since another creditor trying to get more information would have a "difficult task" locating the creditor. [**Burlington National Bank v. Strauss**, 184 N.W.2d 122 (Wis. 1971)]

(1) Representative's name allowed [§270]

Sometimes creditors do not want their names in the public record, so they may loan money through an agent or straw organization. This is *allowed*, and properly perfects a security interest in the real creditor whose name is not used. This is true even if no indication is given of agency status. *Rationale:* Using a different name hurts no one, since the debtor typically knows who the real creditor is, and later creditors searching the files are warned of the fact that the named collateral is already encumbered in favor of someone. [U.C.C. §9-503(d)]

c. Name and address of debtor [§271]

The name and mailing address of the debtor must be included in the financing statement to give notice of the existing interest to the other creditors of the debtor—especially future creditors considering extending credit. Since the financing statement is indexed under the name of the debtor, it is particularly important that this information be correct. *Note:* Just as in the case of an inadequate or missing secured party's address, a financing statement with an inadequate or missing debtor's *address is effective if accepted* by the filing office.

(1) Trade names [§272]

Individuals doing business under trade names must be identified by their *real names,* not their company names. Trade names are too uncertain (and may be unknown to a person searching the record) to serve as the basis for a filing system. [U.C.C. §9-503(c)]

Example: Lender took a security interest in the inventory of "Carolyn's Fashions," a dress store owned by Mary Carolyn Hill. The financing statement listed "Carolyn's Fashions by Mary Carolyn Hill." When the store went bankrupt, the Lender's security interest was held *invalid* because the financing statement had been filed under the debtor's trade name instead of her real name. [*In re* **Hill**, 363 F. Supp. 1205 (N.D. Miss. 1973)]

(2) Partnerships [§273]

If a partnership is the debtor, the financing statement *is* sufficient if it states the *partnership name*; it need not name the individual partners. [U.C.C. §9-503(a)(4)]

(3) "Seriously misleading" rule [§274]

If the debtor so changes her name (or a corporation so changes its identity or structure, *e.g.*, by merger) that a filed financing statement becomes *"seriously misleading,"* the filing ceases to be effective as to any *new* collateral acquired by the debtor after *four months*, unless a new statement or amendment is filed before then. [U.C.C. §§9-507(c), 9-508(b)]

Example: Bank loaned Business Corporation money, taking a security interest in the company's equipment "now owned or after-acquired," and filed a financing statement to this effect. A year later Business Corporation changed its name to Consumer Corporation. Bank's security interest is perfected as to all the debtor's equipment at the time of the name change and all new equipment acquired by the debtor in the four months after the name change, but Bank's floating lien will not attach to any equipment first acquired by the debtor *more* than four months after the name change (unless Bank amends the financing statement to reflect the debtor's new name within that period).

EXAM TIP   **gilbert**

Remember that although the question of whether an error in a financing statement is seriously misleading is often a fact-based inquiry, there are *much stricter rules for errors in the debtor's name* than for other errors in the financing statement. An error in the debtor's name that prevents a filing office's computer search logic from finding the financing statement (which is indexed under the debtor's name) is seriously misleading. Therefore, if *debtor* Kevin Smith's name is misspelled as "Kevin Zmith," the error will be considered seriously misleading because a computer searching under the debtor's last name will not be able to locate the financing statement. However, if *creditor* Kevin Smith's name is misspelled in the same fashion, the error probably will *not* be considered seriously misleading, especially if the creditor's correct address is listed on the financing statement, allowing the creditor to be located.

d. Description of collateral [§275]

The financing statement must contain a description of the collateral. The description of the property must be sufficient to allow a party to identify it by *reasonable further inquiry*. *Less specificity* of description is required in the financing statement than in the security agreement because the financing statement's purpose is to provide mere *notice* to others to check further, whereas the security agreement's description is the more specific contractual understanding of the two parties. For the financing statement, the description need not be complete, nor completely accurate, as long as the collateral is reasonably identified; a trade description or statement of the *type* of collateral will usually suffice. [U.C.C. §§9-108, 9-504]

Example: Seller sold a tractor to Buyer under a conditional sales contract. The financing statement described the collateral by model type and serial number, but did not state what type of appliance or object it was. The description was held sufficient, on the basis that the collateral was obviously some type of vehicle sold by Seller, and inquiry of the parties would have definitely determined what it was. [*In re* **Richards**, 455 F.2d 281 (6th Cir. 1972)]

---

(1) Supergeneric description allowed [§276]

If the debtor is willing to give the secured party a security interest in *all* of the debtor's collateral, the financing statement may simply state this. Language describing the collateral as "all the debtor's assets" or "all the debtor's personal property" would suffice. [U.C.C. §9-504(2)] Note that such "supergeneric" descriptions are *never* allowed in the *security agreement* (*see supra*, §131). *Rationale*: The security interest creates the understanding between the parties and must be specific, but the financing statement merely serves to put later creditors on notice that the debtor has encumbered its property, so the later creditors are not harmed when told the debtor has encumbered *all* of its assets.

(2) After-acquired property [§277]

The security agreement may cover not only existing collateral but also collateral to be acquired in the future—*i.e.*, "after-acquired property" (*supra*, §134). This does *not have to be mentioned in the financing statement*, as long as the *types* of collateral subject to the after-acquired property provision are sufficiently described. [**Bank of Utica v. Smith Richfield Springs, Inc.**, 58 Misc. 2d 113 (1968)—security agreement covered auto dealer's present inventory and after-acquired cars as well; financing statement specified merely "motor vehicles," but this was sufficient description to alert other creditors that secured party's interest might extend both to present and after-acquired stock of cars]

(3) Fixtures, timber to be cut, and minerals [§278]

Where the collateral is goods that are or will be affixed to realty (excluding crops), the financing statement must expressly state this fact, must describe the realty, must provide the name of the record owner of the realty if the debtor is not the record owner, and must further recite that the financing statement is to be recorded in the real estate records. [U.C.C. §9-502(b)] (*See* further discussion of fixture filings, *infra*, §§348 *et seq.*)

AUTHENTICATED SECURITY AGREEMENT VS. FINANCING STATEMENT	**gilbert**	
	AUTHENTICATED SECURITY AGREEMENT	FINANCING STATEMENT
REQUIREMENTS	• Language creating a security interest in the debtor's collateral; • A description of the collateral; and • Authentication (*e.g.,* signature) by the debtor.	• The debtor's and creditor's names and addresses; and • A description of the collateral.
IS AFTER-ACQUIRED PROPERTY CLAUSE NEEDED?	Yes (except for inventory and accounts)	No
WHEN DOES REALTY ATTACHED TO COLLATERAL NEED TO BE DESCRIBED?	If the collateral is timber to be cut	If the collateral is fixtures, timber to be cut, or minerals
IS SUPERGENERIC DESCRIPTION OF COLLATERAL ALLOWED?	No	Yes

4. Amendments [§279]

Amendments to the original financing statements that merely change names, amounts, or descriptions are considered part of the original financing statement and therefore have *no effect* on perfection or priority of the security interest. However, if an amendment *adds collateral,* it is deemed effective (as to the added collateral) only from the filing date of the amendment. [U.C.C. §9-512]

a. Distinguish—"floating lien" [§280]

Note the important distinction between a floating lien (*supra,* §140) and an amendment adding collateral:

(1) "Floating lien"

The specific items of inventory covered by a "floating lien" are *covered from the date of filing,* regardless of when they come into the inventory.

Example: Retailer gives Bank a security interest in its "inventory, now existing or after-acquired," and Bank files a financing statement in the proper place. This creates a lien (security interest) in favor of Bank that "floats" over the inventory as it changes components—*i.e.,* Bank does *not* have to file amendments to the financing statement each time the specific items in the inventory change.

(2) Amendment adding collateral

On the other hand, an amendment enlarging the collateral to include a new item covers the *new* item only from the *date of amendment.* (This underscores the advantage of an "after-acquired property" clause in the original security agreement; *supra,* §134.)

> **Example:** Thus, in the above example, if Retailer had given Bank a security interest in its "office furniture," and then later, in return for a new loan, gave Bank a new security interest in its truck, the financing statement would have to be amended to cover the truck, and perfection as to the security interest in the truck would date only from the filing of the amended financing statement.

B. Where to File

1. General Rules [§281]

Article 9 has a simple set of rules about where the financing statement should be filed. The default rule is that it should be filed in *one central state office* (the office of the *secretary of state* in most states). The only exception is for financing statements covering *collateral related to realty* (*i.e.*, minerals, timber to be cut, and fixtures, but not crops), which must be filed in the relevant office where a *real estate mortgage* would be filed (typically the *county recorder's office* in the county where the realty is located). [U.C.C. §9-501]

> **EXAM TIP** gilbert
>
> Remember that financing statements for non-realty-related collateral must be filed centrally with the secretary of state in the *state whose laws govern perfection* (usually the state in which the debtor is located; *see supra,* §227). Therefore, if the debtor moves from one state to another, the creditor must file another financing statement with the secretary of state for the *new state* within four months, or the creditor's security interest will become unperfected.

2. Federal Filing Acts [§282]

Local filing is not required for certain types of security interests covered by federal statutes. [U.C.C. §9-311(a)(1)] For example, railroad equipment filing is with the National Surface Transportation Board, and aircraft, aircraft parts, and engines require filing with the Administrator of Civil Aeronautics. Ship mortgages are required by the Ship Mortgage Act of 1920 to be filed with the office of the collector of customs of the ship's port of documentation. For interstate trucks and buses, Congress has provided that compliance with the filing and perfection laws of any state perfects the security interest in all jurisdictions. [49 U.S.C. §313]

3. Transmitting Utility [§283]

A transmitting utility is defined in the Code to mean a utility (*e.g.*, the phone company, gas company, or railroad) whose primary business involves the movement of goods or communications from one place to another. [U.C.C. §9-102(a)(80)] Such entities tend to have many power lines or tracks across many counties (or the entire country). These assets typically qualify as *fixtures* (*see infra*, §§348-350), but the Code drafters wanted to avoid the time and expense of having to file in every county in the state in which the utility sticks a power line or runs a track, so transmitting utilities using their fixtures as collateral need file only a *single* financing statement in the usual *central filing office* of the state (*see supra*, §281). [U.C.C. §9-501(b)]

C. Mechanics of Filing

1. When Effective [§284]

Filing under the Code is deemed effective on the presentation of a financing statement for filing and tender of the filing fee or acceptance of the statement by the filing officer. What the filing officer does with the statement does not matter, as long as the secured party *presents* a conforming statement and *pays* the filing fee. [U.C.C. §9-516(a)]

a. Indexing [§285]

The filing officer must mark each statement with a unique file number and the date and hour of filing, and must allow public inspection of the statement. The officer is required to index the statements according to the name of the *debtor*. [U.C.C. §9-519]

b. Errors in filing or indexing [§286]

However, the creditor's job is over on delivery of the financing statement and proper filing fee at the proper filing office. The security interest is protected even if the filing officer somehow fails to file the financing statement or files it under the wrong name. [U.C.C. §9-517; *In re* **Masters**, 273 B.R. 773 (Bankr. E.D. Ark. 2002)—erroneous termination of financing statement by filing clerk did not destroy perfection]

(1) Note

In this situation, a creditor has a perfected security interest even though no other creditor could discover it! It is simply a question of protecting the earlier of two innocent parties.

2. Duration of Filing [§287]

The financing statement is effective for a period of *five years* from the date of filing. [U.C.C. §9-515(a)]

a. Effect of lapse [§288]

Unless a continuation statement is filed in the six months before the expiration of the five-year period, the security interest becomes **unperfected.** The effect is that purchasers and junior security interest holders whose interests have attached before the lapse **gain priority** over the lapsed security interest. [U.C.C. §9-515(c)]

Example: A and B both make advances against the same collateral. A files on March 1, 2008, and B files on September 1, 2009. Unless A files a continuation statement before March 1, 2013, his filing lapses, his security interest becomes unperfected, and B will have priority until September 1, 2014. Any purchaser whose interest attaches on or after March 1, 2013, and before A refiles will also have priority over A.

---

(1) Judicial liens unaffected by lapse [§289]

Judicial lien creditors are not similarly protected. A lapsed financing statement still grants priority over a judicial lien that arose during the period when the financing statement was effective. This is because section 9-515(c), giving priority to some parties on lapse of the original statement, only protects "**purchasers**," a term defined to include **only voluntary transactions.** [U.C.C. §1-201(32), (33)] Since a judicial lien is not voluntary, it does not gain priority on lapse of the financing statement.

b. Public finance and manufactured home transactions [§290]

In a **public finance transaction,** a governmental entity issues debt securities (*e.g.,* municipal bonds) that have a maturity of 20 years or greater. [U.C.C. §9-102(a)(67)] A **manufactured home transaction** is one creating a PMSI (*see supra,* §184) in which the primary collateral is a manufactured home (*i.e.,* permanently installed personal property, such as a mobile home or home assembled from a kit). [U.C.C. §9-102(a)(53), (54)] For these transactions, which typically have a very long life span, the initial financing statement is effective for a period of **30 years,** rather than five years. [U.C.C. §9-515(b)]

3. Continuation Statements [§291]

The secured party can extend the effectiveness of a financing statement about to expire by filing a **continuation statement.** Such a statement may be filed within **six months** before the expiration of the financing statement. The continuation statement must identify the original statement by file number, and must either indicate that it is a continuation statement or that it is filed to continue the effectiveness of the identified financing statement. [U.C.C. §9-102(a)(27)] This adds **another five years** to the effectiveness of the financing statement; succeeding continuation statements can be filed to add additional five-year periods. [U.C.C. §9-515(d)]

4. Termination Statement and Release of Collateral [§292]

Whenever there is no outstanding secured obligation and no commitment to make advances, incur obligations, or otherwise give value, the secured party *must, on authenticated demand* by the debtor, within 20 days send the debtor a termination statement providing that the secured party no longer claims a security interest under the financing statement, identified by file number. [U.C.C. §9-102(a)(79)] The debtor can then file this termination statement. If the secured party does not send such a termination statement within 20 days after a proper demand is made, the debtor may recover for any damages suffered plus a statutory $500 penalty. [U.C.C. §9-625(b), (e)(4)]

a. Necessity of demand [§293]

As to *consumer goods* financing, an affirmative duty is placed on the secured party to file a termination statement within one month following full payment *regardless of demand* by the debtor (consumer). In all other cases, however, the secured party is *not* under a duty to file until the debtor makes written demand therefore. [U.C.C. §9-513(b)]

b. Who can demand [§294]

Only the debtor can force the secured party to give such a statement; another potential creditor cannot, although such a creditor can condition a new loan to the debtor on having the old outstanding security interest canceled.

c. Releases [§295]

A secured party can also *release collateral* described in the financing statement from the security interest by filing an amendment to the financing statement. The amendment must contain a description of the collateral being released, the name of the debtor, the name of the secured party, and the file number of the financing statement. [U.C.C. §9-512]

d. Bogus filings [§296]

Anarchist groups (sometimes called various kinds of "militia") in recent years have been causing a lot of trouble by filing financing statements in the public records even though there has been no secured transaction, meaning to cloud up the title of the property of their perceived enemies. First of all, it should be clear that the filing of a financing statement by someone who has no right to file it is *ineffective*. [U.C.C. §9-510(a)] A bogus filing therefore has no legal effect except to make difficult the life of the alleged debtor, who must get the financing statement removed from the files. The Code provides a number of avenues of relief: (i) the debtor may file a *termination statement* (*see supra*, §292) [U.C.C. §9-509, Comment 3]; (ii) the debtor may file a *correction statement* explaining the facts [U.C.C. §9-518]; or (iii) the debtor may sue the offender (a suit for *conversion* under common law). Section 9-625 also gives the debtor a statutory right to recover *actual damages* plus *punitive damages of $500*. [**United States v. Orrego**, 54 U.C.C. Rep. Serv. 2d 145 (N.Y. 2004)]

5. Assignment [§297]

A secured party may assign all or part of his rights under a financing statement by filing an amendment to the financing statement. The amendment must state the name of the assignor, the name and address of the assignee, and the file number of the financing statement to which the amendment relates. [U.C.C. §9-514]

a. Procedure permissive [§298]

Note that the section 9-514 procedure is only a *permissive* method whereby a secured party can have an assignment noted "of record" (so that inquiries regarding the transaction will be addressed to the assignee). A secured party who assigns ("sells") the security interest of another creditor *need not file* to preserve the perfected status of the assignee. [U.C.C. §9-514, Comment 2]

SUMMARY OF TYPES OF FILED RECORDS			**gilbert**
TYPE	**DEFINITION**	**WHEN FILED**	**DURATION**
FINANCING STATEMENT	Document noting a creditor's security interest in the debtor's collateral and describing the types of collateral covered by the security interest	Any time (even before the security interest has attached)	Five years
CONTINUATION STATEMENT	Document continuing the effectiveness of the financing statement (successive continuation statements can be filed)	Within six months before the expiration of the prior financing statement or continuation statement	Five years
AMENDMENT	Document making a change to a financing statement or continuation statement	Any time	Same duration as financing statement or continuation statement being amended
TERMINATION STATEMENT	Document stating that the creditor no longer claims a security interest under the filed financing statement	Any time	Unlimited

D. Request for Statement of Account or List of Collateral

1. **Request by Debtor [§299]**

   The debtor has the power to force the secured party to provide information under the Code. [U.C.C. §9-210] The debtor may send the secured party a statement indicating the aggregate amount of the unpaid debt as of a specified date, and may request that the secured party approve or correct the statement and return it to the debtor. The debtor may also request an *accounting* of the amount still due. If the security agreement or some other record kept by the secured party identifies the collateral, the debtor may request that the secured party approve or correct a list of the collateral.

   a. **Response by secured party [§300]**

      The secured party has 14 days in which to comply by sending (in an authenticated record) an accounting, a correction, or an approval. If the secured party claims a security interest in all of a particular type of collateral owned by the debtor (*e.g.*, all inventory), the secured party may state that in the reply and does not have to approve or correct an *itemized* list of such collateral.

   b. **Failure to reply [§301]**

      If the secured party fails to comply without a reasonable excuse, the secured party is *liable for any loss* caused to the debtor and a penalty of $500. [U.C.C. §9-625(b), (f)] If the debtor included a good faith statement of the total obligation or a list of collateral, or both, in the statement, and the secured party failed to comply without a reasonable excuse, the secured party is barred from claiming a security interest in anything not shown in the statement against any person who has been misled by the failure to comply. This penalty provides a secured party with a strong incentive to reply in order to avoid losing part of the collateral. [U.C.C. §9-625(g)]

2. **Protection of Secured Party [§302]**

   The secured party is protected against burdensome requests by U.C.C. section 9-210(f), which limits a debtor to *one* such statement every six months without charge. A debtor has a right to receive statements more often, but the secured party may charge up to $25 for each additional one.

3. **Third Party Problems [§303]**

   A secured party is often unwilling to disclose to third parties detailed information about the secured party's security interest, either because it is costly or because the interests of the inquirer conflict with those of the secured party. Third parties *cannot* compel the secured party to provide such information; they are limited to the information on file—and usually, only the *types* of collateral are described in financing statements.

   a. **Third party recourse [§304]**

      As a result, a third party (*e.g.*, a prospective lender) must prevail upon the *debtor* to get a statement of the secured party's claim.

(1) Note

Of course, this is of no help where the third party is a present creditor trying to learn the extent of another creditor's security interest in order to levy upon the goods for a prior debt.

(2) And note

Even for a prospective lender aided by the debtor, the statement relates only to obligations and collateral existing at the time of the statement and does not protect against future advances or after-acquired property.

b. Estoppel [§305]

Although there is no duty to reply to a third party's inquiry, the secured party may be *estopped* to deny *misstatements* regarding the secured party's relationship with the debtor, if the misstatements cause detriment to a third party who advances credit based on this information. [**United States v. Gleaners & Farmers Cooperative Elevator Co.**, 314 F. Supp. 1148 (N.D. Ind. 1970)—where government told prospective buyer it did not have lien on farmer's crops, it was held estopped to claim one later]

Chapter Six: Priorities

CONTENTS

Chapter Approach

A.	Competing Interests in Collateral—the Claimants	§306
B.	Priority—Unperfected Creditors	§317
C.	Priority Among Perfected Creditors—General Rule	§324
D.	Priority Among Perfected Creditors—Special Rules for Purchase Money Security Interests	§330
E.	Priority Among Perfected Creditors—Special Rules for Certain Types of Collateral	§348
F.	Priority Among Perfected Creditors—Perfection by Control	§400
G.	Priority Among Perfected Creditors—As Affected by Terms of Security Agreement	§404
H.	Priority Among Perfected Creditors and Other Claimants	§419

Chapter Approach

If more than one person claims the right to certain property, which of them prevails over the others? This is the issue of priority, and the Code contains a wealth of rules on point. The competitors in the fight to claim the property include not only the original lender and debtor, but also people such as other secured parties, judicial lienors, buyers of the collateral, taxing authorities, and the debtor's trustee in bankruptcy.

To establish the priorities, ask:

1. Is the secured party's interest *unperfected*? If so, that party may be entitled to little priority (only over certain subsequent parties).

2. Is the secured party's interest *perfected*? If so, then that party may be entitled to priority over unperfected creditors and perfected creditors under the *"first-to-file-or-perfect"* rule, *purchase money security interest* rules, the *control* rules, and *special rules* applicable to fixtures, accessions, and commingled goods.

Remember that more than one creditor may claim the *proceeds* of the sale or disposition of the collateral. The priority rules regulate this dispute as well.

Finally, recall that there are certain kinds of parties against whom even a perfected security interest affords *no protection*—*e.g.,* a bona fide purchaser from a dealer in goods, a holder in due course of a negotiable instrument, and certain statutory lien holders.

A. Competing Interests in Collateral—the Claimants

1. Introduction [§306]
Sometimes there are several competing interests in the same piece of collateral. In such a case, the question arises as to which of these interests is entitled to priority. Of course, the simplest answer would be to rank each according to the time it arose. However, the Code has rejected this approach in favor of protecting certain classes of interest holders over others (*e.g.,* creditors who have gone through the requisite formalities to perfect their interests take priority over unperfected creditors). Therefore, before considering specific rules of priority, it is necessary to keep in mind who the possible claimants to a piece of collateral are.

2. Obligor and Debtor [§307]
The person who *owes payment or other performance* of the secured obligation is

the "obligor." The *owner* of the collateral is the "*debtor.*" Often, the obligor and debtor are the same person. (*See supra,* §48.)

3. Unsecured ("General") Creditor [§308]

A creditor who has no security interest in the collateral but has a *personal* claim against the debtor (*e.g.,* a doctor to whom bills are owed) is called an unsecured creditor. Note that this type of creditor may acquire an interest in the debtor's collateral if the debtor *agrees* to grant the creditor a security interest or if the creditor *sues* the debtor, recovers judgment, and uses the judicial process to *levy* on the collateral (thereby creating a judicial "lien" on it; *see* below).

4. Judicial "Lien Creditor" [§309]

A creditor who was formerly unsecured ("general"), but who has acquired a lien on the debtor's property by judicial process (attachment, levy, etc.) is a judicial "lien creditor." Under the U.C.C., the term "lien creditor" *also includes* the trustee appointed in the debtor's bankruptcy, the assignee appointed to represent the debtor's creditors in a state liquidation procedure (called an "assignment for the benefit of creditors"), and a receiver appointed by a court of equity to take over and control the debtor's property. [U.C.C. §9-102(a)(52)]

a. Time of lien [§310]

In most states, a lien creditor's interest arises at the time of "levy," meaning the moment a judicial officer (typically the sheriff) physically *seizes* the property. In a minority of states, the moment of "levy" relates back to the moment the court clerk issued the writ of execution.

(1) Insolvency proceedings [§311]

For a trustee in bankruptcy, a judicial lien is automatically created on all the bankrupt debtor's nonexempt property at the moment the *bankruptcy petition is filed* (*infra,* §489); in an assignment for the benefit of creditors, the judicial lien on all the debtor's nonexempt property arises on *assignment*; and for a receiver in equity, the lien arises at the time of *appointment* of the receiver. [U.C.C. §9-102(a)(52)]

EXAM TIP gilbert

Exam questions will often contain a debtor who cannot pay debts, thus triggering the priority rules of Article 9. If the debtor goes a step further and declares **bankruptcy**, you will need to include the rights of the bankruptcy trustee in your answer. It is important to remember that for Article 9 purposes, *a trustee in bankruptcy is equivalent to a judicial lien creditor* who has placed a lien on all the debtor's property.

---

5. Secured Creditor [§312]

If the debtor has agreed to give a security interest in specific collateral to a creditor, and that creditor has taken the steps necessary for the security interest to "attach" (become valid between the two parties), the creditor is "secured." [U.C.C. §9-203; *see supra,* §§117-150]

6. **Perfected and Secured Creditor [§313]**

A secured creditor who has also taken the steps necessary to protect the security interest from other claimants is both *secured and perfected* (*see supra,* §443).

7. **Statutory Lien Creditor [§314]**

A creditor whose lien interest arises *automatically* by statute or common law is called a statutory lien creditor. "Statutory" liens are granted to taxing authorities (*e.g.,* the federal tax lien, discussed *infra,* §443), landlords, mechanics, artisans, lawyers, innkeepers, and certain other people who have performed services for the debtor.

   a. **When lien arises [§315]**

   The lien attaches to the debtor's property at the time specified in the statute creating the lien (typically on the lien holder's *possession* of the collateral).

8. **Buyers of the Property [§316]**

If the debtor (owner) sells the collateral, the buyer may then face the claims of the debtor's various creditors having interests in the property. As a general rule, the law tends to favor a good faith buyer over such creditors—although, as will be seen, the buyer does not always win.

B. Priority—Unperfected Creditors

1. **Unperfected Creditor vs. Other Unperfected Creditor—First-to-Attach Rule [§317]**

Where there are two conflicting attached security interests in the same collateral, neither of which has been perfected, the *order of attachment determines* priority in the collateral. [U.C.C. §9-322(a)(3)]

   a. **Note**

   As a practical matter, this type of dispute is never litigated because it is simply easier for a creditor to perfect prior to suit and thus prevail as a perfected creditor (*see* below). This means that when the collateral is repossessed and sold, the perfected creditor will first be paid in full, and only then, if there is any surplus money, will the unperfected creditor be paid. Thus, if the sale's proceeds are insufficient to pay the full amount the debtor owes the unperfected creditor, the unperfected creditor's only recourse is to sue the debtor personally for the "deficiency" (the amount still owing).

2. **Unperfected Creditor vs. Perfected Creditor [§318]**

An unperfected creditor is *junior* (or "subordinate") to a creditor who has *perfected* a security interest in the collateral first. [U.C.C. §9-322(a)(2)]

   a. **Knowledge and time of attachment irrelevant [§319]**

   The above rule (perfected over unperfected) applies no matter which security interest attached first, and regardless of whether the perfected creditor had *knowledge* at all times of the unperfected creditor's interest.

Example: Debtor gives a security interest in collateral to Creditor A and another security interest in the same collateral to Creditor B. Both creditors know of each other. If *neither* perfects, they have priority in the collateral according to the order in which their interests attached (*supra,* §317). However, if one creditor perfects, that creditor has the senior interest, no matter whose security interest attached first.

3. **Unperfected Creditor vs. Judicial Lien Creditor [§320]**

   An unperfected creditor is also junior to a judicial lien creditor. [U.C.C. §9-317(a)(2)]

4. **Unperfected Creditor vs. Statutory Lien Holder [§321]**

   Holders of statutory liens (*e.g.,* auto mechanics, landlords, taxing authorities) are *senior* to unperfected security interests unless the statutes creating their liens state otherwise (and typically they do not). [U.C.C. §9-333]

5. **Unperfected Creditor vs. Buyer [§322]**

   Purchasers of the collateral from the debtor who *pay value and receive delivery* take *free* of unperfected security interests in the collateral as long as they have *no knowledge* of the unperfected interest. [U.C.C. §9-317(b)] *Note:* If the collateral is an account, electronic chattel paper, or investment property other than a certified security, there is *no delivery requirement* because there is nothing tangible to deliver. [U.C.C. §9-317(d)]

   a. **Purchase of inventory [§323]**

      Moreover, if the collateral is *inventory* and the buyer purchases in the *ordinary course of business* (*i.e.,* a "normal" retail sale), the buyer takes free of *all* security interests in the inventory (perfected or not), even if the buyer *knows* of the security interest. [U.C.C. §9-320(a), *and see* Comment 3; *see infra,* §420, for detailed discussion on buyers of inventory]

EXAM TIP   **gilbert**

The above priority rules highlight the importance of achieving a perfected security interest. If the facts in an exam question indicate that a creditor *has not properly perfected* its security interest in collateral (*e.g.,* if the creditor filed a financing statement in an improper place), the creditor will *lose* to perfected secured creditors, judicial lien creditors, most statutory lien holders, and most buyers.

C. Priority Among Perfected Creditors— General Rule

1. **Introduction [§324]**

   As mentioned above, perfected security interests are senior to unperfected security interests in the same collateral. But when two *perfected* security interests exist in the same collateral, who prevails?

2. General Rule—First to File or Perfect [§325]

Priority goes to whichever secured party is the first either to *file or perfect* the security interest (whichever is earlier), provided there is no period thereafter when there is neither filing nor perfection. [U.C.C. §9-322(a)(1)]

a. Effect

This gives the party who *files first* top priority—even though a later creditor *perfected* first (*e.g.,* by taking possession after the first creditor's filing). Alternatively, an interest perfected by a method *other than filing* is entitled to priority over a filed interest only if the nonfiling creditor in fact perfected *before* the other creditor's filing.

Example: Debtor sought to borrow $10,000 from Bank using her valuable art collection as collateral. The parties signed a security agreement and financing statement as to this, and Bank filed the financing statement in the appropriate place, but did not immediately loan the money nor make a commitment to do so. Two days later, Debtor borrowed $8,000 from Loan Company, also using the art collection as collateral, which Loan Company then took into its possession as it loaned her the money (a perfection by pledge). The day after that, Bank loaned Debtor the $10,000. In this situation Bank has filed its financing statement *first* but perfected its security interest *second* (since perfection cannot occur before attachment, and attachment cannot occur until the creditor gives value—*see supra,* §224). Nonetheless, Bank has priority over Loan Company because Bank filed first, and section 9-322(a)(1) gives priority to the *first to file or perfect*, whichever came first between the two. This rule permits reliance on the filing system; Bank got on file first, and its filing should have alerted later creditors, like Loan Company, that it would therefore claim top priority in the collateral.

3. Knowledge and Time of Attachment Not Determinative [§326]

One creditor's knowledge of the other's unperfected security interest is irrelevant. Furthermore, the time when the competing security interest first *attached* is also immaterial. [**St. Paul Mercury Insurance Co. v. Merchants & Marine Bank**, 882 So. 2d 766 (Miss. 2004)]

Example: First Finance files a financing statement on June 1 but does not actually advance any funds to Dana Debtor until July 1 (hence, its security interest in the collateral does not attach or become perfected until July 1; *see supra,* §119). Quick Loan advances value on the same collateral on June 15 (hence, its security interest attaches on that date), but does not file (perfect) until July 10. First Finance is entitled to priority. Even though Quick Loan's security interest attached first (June 15), it was not the first to "file *or* perfect." *Rationale:* The fact that First Finance's security interest did not arise until after the filing does not affect its priority, because the subsequent creditor (Quick Loan) was given *constructive notice* by the filing that First Finance might have an interest in the collateral; thus, Quick Loan has no cause to complain.

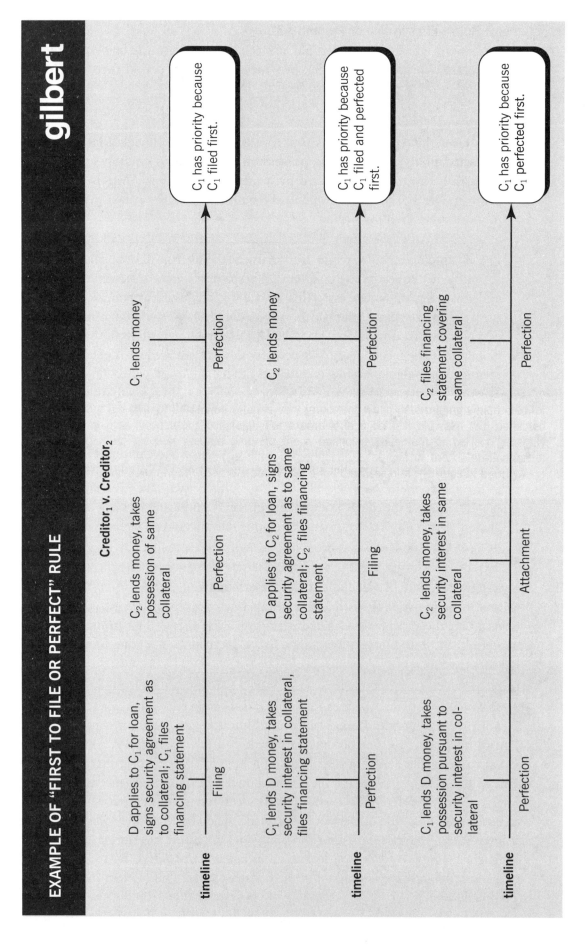

EXAMPLE OF "FIRST TO FILE OR PERFECT" RULE

Creditor₁ v. Creditor₂

timeline

D applies to C_1 for loan, signs security agreement as to collateral; C_1 files financing statement	C_2 lends money, takes possession of same collateral	C_1 lends money
Filing	Perfection	Perfection

C_1 has priority because C_1 filed first.

---

timeline

C_1 lends D money, takes security interest in collateral, files financing statement	D applies to C_2 for loan, signs security agreement as to same collateral; C_2 files financing statement	C_2 lends money
Perfection	Filing	Perfection

C_1 has priority because C_1 filed and perfected first.

---

timeline

C_1 lends D money, takes possession pursuant to security interest in collateral	C_2 lends money, takes security interest in same collateral	C_2 files financing statement covering same collateral
Perfection	Attachment	Perfection

C_1 has priority because C_1 perfected first.

Example: The result in the example above would be the same even if First Finance had perfected by some means other than filing before Quick Loan filed or perfected. For instance, suppose Quick Loan had advanced funds to Dana Debtor on May 15, but had neither filed nor otherwise perfected its security interest at that time. First Finance comes along on June 1 and advances funds to Dana, taking possession of the collateral (and thus perfecting its interest). If Quick Loan finally gets around to filing a financing statement on June 15, First Finance prevails. Even though Quick Loan's interest had attached first (May 15), First Finance was the first to "file *or* perfect."

4. New Debtors [§327]

If two different debtors merge into one "new debtor," how do we adjust the rights of creditors of the original debtors?

Example: Company A gave a perfected security interest in its inventory to Bank A. The next year, Company B did the same thing in favor of Bank B. One year later, the two companies merged, combining their inventories and buying new inventory under the name of the new company formed by the merger. What are the rights of the two banks, and which has priority over the other?

a. Original collateral still covered [§328]

When collateral is transferred to the new entity, this entity is called a *"new debtor"* in revised Article 9, but since there are *two* original debtors, this creates what the Code calls a *"double debtor"* problem. [U.C.C. §9-102(a)(56); Comments to §9-325] The basic rule is that perfected security interests in the *original* collateral *remain attached* to the property now in the hands of the new debtor without the need for a new security interest or financing statement. [U.C.C. §§9-203(d) - (e), 9-508(a)] Therefore, the usual priority rules described in this chapter apply. However, note that the creditor must be able to identify its collateral or trace it—which may be difficult if the collateral is inventory.

Example: In the last example, the merged inventory still will be encumbered in favor of the original creditors to the extent it can be identified as still unsold. The *proceeds* of the sale of this inventory will also belong to the original creditors.

(1) Note

Recall that if the new debtor has a substantially different name from the original debtor, the original creditor can also claim that its floating lien attaches to after-acquired inventory for four months following the seriously misleading name change. If a new financing statement is not filed, collateral acquired more than four months after the name change will not be covered by the original financing statement (see *supra*, §274).

b. New collateral acquired by the new debtor [§329]

Normally the merger will be accompanied by an agreement between all parties involved (debtors and creditors) as to what assets will be collateral for what debts. Assuming that the new debtor has agreed to be bound by the original financing statements, the new debtor's *order of assumption* of the old debtor's security agreements will control the priority between the old creditors as to newly acquired collateral. [U.C.C. §9-326(b)]

D. Priority Among Perfected Creditors— Special Rules for Purchase Money Security Interests

1. Introduction [§330]

As indicated previously, the "general rule" of priority (first to file or perfect) is subject to modification where certain types of security interests are involved. In these cases, the Code grants special priority to holders of such interests regardless of whether they would prevail under the general "first-to-file-or-perfect" rule. The first type of security interest having such "super-priority" is the purchase money security interest ("PMSI"). (*See supra*, §184, for a discussion on how PMSIs are created.)

2. Non-Inventory, Non-Livestock PMSIs [§331]

Recall that a creditor who advances value to a debtor enabling the debtor to acquire an interest in collateral has a PMSI. A creditor with a PMSI stands in a different position than other creditors. Since the advance is directly related to the collateral, it is right that such a creditor be given additional protection in that collateral over other creditors of the debtor. The Code accomplishes this by declaring that a *PMSI* (in collateral other than inventory or livestock) *takes priority* over conflicting security interests in the same collateral and its identifiable proceeds (*i.e.*, things received upon the sale or disposition of collateral, such as money; *see infra*, §373) if the interest is perfected when the debtor takes possession of the collateral *or within 20 days* thereafter. [U.C.C. §9-324(a)]

a. Rationale for PMSI priority [§332]

Other creditors of the debtor cannot complain. They are in no worse position than if the debtor had not entered into the purchase money agreement. They may, in fact, be in a better position to the extent the PMSI is less than the value of the collateral, because otherwise the debtor would not have purchased the collateral. There is an additional pragmatic reason for giving priority to a PMSI: The debtor would have no way to finance new purchases if the debtor could not assure the party advancing such funds of priority in the property purchased. The existence of purchase money super-priority prevents debtors from being captives of their existing creditors. (This is particularly true in the case of an after-acquired property agreement, discussed *infra,* §§336-341.)

b. Effect on general rule of priority [§333]
This super-priority cuts across the "first-to-file-or-perfect" rule both from the standpoint of time and from the standpoint of method of perfection.

Example: Big Bank advances purchase money to Debtor to acquire collateral on December 1, and Debtor takes possession of the collateral on that date. On December 5, Small Bank advances Debtor value in return for a security interest in the same collateral. Small Bank perfects on December 5. Big Bank perfects its PMSI on December 10, within the 20-day period after possession. Big Bank will take priority over Small Bank, regardless of the fact that Small Bank perfected its interest before Big Bank. [U.C.C. §9-324(a)] *Note:* This result is the same regardless of the *manner* in which the parties perfected. Thus, even if Small Bank perfected by taking possession of the collateral on December 5, Big Bank wins if it perfects by filing no later than December 20.

c. Knowledge of prior interest immaterial [§334]
The purchase money secured party who perfects within 20 days prevails against all conflicting security interests—even interests that were *filed* at the time of sale and of which the purchase money secured party actually *knew*. [**Noble Co. v. Mack Financial Corp.**, 264 A.2d 325 (R.I. 1970)]

d. Limitation to "purchase money" [§335]
The priority of the PMSI is limited to the *extent of the "purchase money"* (cash or credit) *used* in acquisition of the collateral.

Example: Freddie's Finance advances $1,000 to Debtor to purchase collateral worth $5,000 on August 1. On August 5, Bank advances $3,000 in a nonpurchase money transaction and perfects a security interest in the same collateral by filing on that date. On August 10, Freddie's Finance files a financing statement perfecting its security interest, but it also advances another $1,000, taking a security interest in the same collateral and includes this second $1,000 in the financing statement that it files on August 10. Thus, Freddie's Finance has a security interest totaling $2,000, and Bank has interests totaling $3,000. If it is clear that the first $1,000 that Freddie's Finance advanced is purchase money, Freddie's Finance will have priority even though it filed after Bank. However, this is the extent of Freddie's Finance's priority due to purchase money. In weighing Freddie's Finance's claim for the second $1,000 against Bank's claim, Bank will prevail since the case is governed by the usual rules—here, the "first-to-file-or-perfect" rule.

3. PMSIs in Inventory [§336]

A lender who advances money to a retailer and takes a security interest in the retailer's inventory expects to get top priority as to the debtor's *after-acquired* inventory as well as the existing inventory. If creditors selling inventory to the retailer on credit could get PMSIs that prevailed over the first lender's "after-acquired property" interest in the inventory, the first lender's security interest would in time be virtually nonexistent. For this reason, the usual rule of super-priority for PMSIs is modified somewhat when the collateral is "inventory" (defined *supra*, §56).

a. Requirements for priority [§337]

A creditor wishing to claim a PMSI in goods that will become inventory in the hands of the debtor is accorded super-priority over other creditors *only if* the following two requirements are first met:

(1) Perfection requirement [§338]

The PMSI must already be perfected *at the time the debtor receives possession* of the collateral. There is *no 20-day grace period* (as there is for PMSIs in non-inventory, non-livestock collateral). [U.C.C. §9-324(b)(1)]

(2) Notice requirement [§339]

In addition, the purchase money secured party must give an authenticated notification to any other security interest holder who has *previously filed a financing statement* covering inventory of the *same type of goods* as those that will be covered in the PMSI (but *not* to persons financing the debtor's accounts). The notice must be given *prior* to the date on which the debtor takes possession of the collateral. [U.C.C. §9-324(b)(2)]

(a) Contents of notice [§340]

The notice must state that the person filing has or expects to acquire a PMSI in the debtor's inventory, and it must *describe* the inventory. [U.C.C. §9-324(b)(4)]

(b) Duration of notice [§341]

Once properly given, the notice lasts for *five years* (same as the financing statement), and it will preserve the priority of the purchase money creditor for all later similar transactions. If at the end of the five years, the purchase money financing is still continuing, a new notice must be sent to and received by the conflicting interest holder. [U.C.C. §9-324(b)(3)]

Example: Retailer owned and ran a bookstore. She borrowed $20,000 from Bank, which took and filed a security interest in her inventory "now and after-acquired." While selling the original inventory to customers, Retailer bought a new shipment of books from Book Distributors, Inc. ("BDI") on credit, giving BDI a PMSI in the books it sold her. Before delivering the books, BDI filed a financing statement in the proper place and sent written notice of its interest to Bank. Since notice is deemed to give Bank the facts necessary to protect itself (*e.g.*, by cutting off further credit to Retailer and/or repossessing the unencumbered inventory), BDI takes priority over Bank in the new shipment of books.

b. Effect of rule [§342]

By requiring the purchase money secured creditor to perfect and give notice, the Code protects creditors with existing interests in the debtor's inventory. At the same time, the Code preserves the debtor's flexibility in making financing arrangements by giving the purchase money inventory creditor the same super-priority as other non-inventory purchase money creditors if the above requirements are met.

c. Proceeds covered [§343]

PMSI super-priority also extends to certain proceeds of inventory collateral. A creditor with PMSI super-priority in inventory also has super-priority in identifiable cash proceeds (*i.e.*, the amount given to the debtor/seller by a retail buyer of the collateral) that are received on or before delivery of the inventory to the buyer, chattel paper proceeds, and instrument proceeds.

Example: Bank lends Debtor money and properly perfects a security interest in Debtor's inventory on March 1. On July 1, Seller sells Debtor new inventory and perfects and gives notice to Bank before Debtor receives the inventory. Thus, Seller has PMSI super-priority in Debtor's inventory. Debtor later sells on credit some of the inventory it purchased from Seller to Buyer. Buyer signs a promise to pay for the inventory (an instrument). Seller now also has PMSI super-priority in the instrument as a proceed of the inventory. If Buyer pays cash at the time of the sale, Seller also has priority as to these monies.

d. How floating lien creditor protects itself [§344]

Of course, under these rules, a floating lien creditor (*see supra*, §141) becomes junior to a portion of the inventory every time the purchase money creditor uses the rules to gain priority. How can the floating lienor protect its security interest in the inventory? First of all, it may not care. The debtor's business may be sound enough that the floating lien creditor is comfortable with having the rest of the inventory protect its loan. If the floating lienor becomes alarmed by its increasingly junior priority position, it can probably declare a default (*see infra*, §510), and repossess the unencumbered portion of the inventory.

e. Livestock purchase money priority [§345]

A creditor claiming a PMSI in **livestock** of the debtor can prevail over a prior

PMSI SUPER-PRIORITY—EXAMPLES

Creditor₁ v. Creditor₂

timeline

C_1 lends D money, takes a security interest in D's equipment (present and after-acquired), files a financing statement
— Perfection

C_2 sells D a piece of equipment (the collateral) on credit, retaining a security interest (PMSI)

C_2 files a financing statement within 20 days after the sale
— Perfection

D defaults on payments to C_1 and C_2
— Default

> C_2 has priority in the equipment it sold to D because C_2's PMSI was perfected within the statutory period, but C_1 has priority as to D's other equipment.

timeline

C_1 lends D money, takes a security interest in D's inventory (present and after-acquired), files a financing statement
— Perfection

C_2 notifies C_1 that it is selling D more inventory (the collateral), files a financing statement, sells D the inventory on credit, and retains a security interest (PMSI)
— Perfection

D defaults on payments to C_1 and C_2
— Default

> C_2 has priority in the inventory because C_2 gave C_1 notice and properly filed its security interest.

timeline

C_1 lends D money, takes a security interest in D's consumer goods (present and after-acquired), files a financing statement
— Perfection

Two days later, C_2 sells D a television (the collateral) on credit and retains a security interest (PMSI)
— Automatic Perfection

D defaults on payments to C_1 and C_2
— Default

> C_2 has priority in the new television over C_1 because C_2's PMSI was automatically perfected upon attachment.

gilbert

floating lien on that livestock by taking the same steps as those required for taking a PMSI in inventory (*see supra*, §§336-341). This PMSI super-priority also extends to indentifiable proceeds and unmanufactured products (*e.g.*, wool) of the livestock. [U.C.C. §9-324(d)]

HOW TO GAIN PMSI SUPER-PRIORITY		**gilbert**
TYPE OF GOODS	**METHOD OF OBTAINING PMSI SUPER-PRIORITY**	**PROCEEDS COVERED**
CONSUMER GOODS	Automatic upon attachment	All identifiable proceeds
EQUIPMENT	Perfection before or within 20 days after debtor receives equipment	All identifiable proceeds
FARM PRODUCTS (EXCLUDING LIVESTOCK)	Perfection before or within 20 days after debtor receives farm products	All identifiable proceeds
INVENTORY	Perfection and authenticated notice given to other filed secured parties before debtor receives inventory	Cash proceeds received on or before delivery of inventory to buyer, chattel paper proceeds, and instrument proceeds
LIVESTOCK	Perfection and authenticated notice given to other filed secured parties before debtor receives livestock	All identifiable proceeds and unmanufactured products

f. **Article 9 consignments treated as PMSIs in inventory [§346]**

A similar problem exists where goods end up in a debtor's inventory on consignment from a supplier, and at the same time some prior inventory financer claims an interest in the consignee's (debtor's) inventory under an after-acquired property clause. If the consignment is covered by Article 9 (*i.e.*, the consigned goods, which are not consumer goods in the hands of the consignor, have a value of at least $1,000 at the time of delivery to the consignee, the consignee is a merchant not known by its creditors to be substantially engaged in the selling of goods of others, and the consignee's professional name is different from that of the consignor), it is treated as a *PMSI in inventory*. Therefore, if the consignor takes the steps required to gain super-priority in inventory, it will have priority in the consigned goods over all other inventory financers. [U.C.C. §§9-103(d), 9-324 and Comment 7] (For a detailed discussion of consignments, *see supra*, §88.)

4. Two PMSI Creditors with Interest in the Same Collateral [§347]

If the debtor buys goods on credit (thus creating a PMSI in favor of the seller), the buyer may also borrow money to make the payments (particularly the down payment), thus creating a PMSI in favor of the lender. If both PMSI creditors qualify for PMSI super-priority in the goods, which one has priority in the goods sold over the other? Article 9 answers this question by giving top priority to the *seller* over the lender, concluding that the seller's interest in goods it used to own should outweigh that of a lender of money used to buy the goods. [U.C.C. §9-324(g) and Comment 13]

Example: To buy a new $10,000 sign for its company headquarters, Business Company borrowed the $5,000 down payment from Lending Company, giving it a PMSI in the sign for this amount, which Lending Company promptly perfected by filing. Business Company paid the $5,000 to Sign Seller, Inc., which then sold the sign to Business Company, agreeing to finance the remaining $5,000 and taking a PMSI in the sign it sold. Sign Seller, Inc. perfected its PMSI by filing in the proper place one day after Lending Company filed. Since both Lending Company and Sign Seller, Inc. have PMSI super-priority in the sign (*see supra*, §331), the Code gives top priority in the collateral to the seller (Sign Seller, Inc.) over the lender (Lending Company), and this is true regardless of which party perfected first.

E. Priority Among Perfected Creditors— Special Rules for Certain Types of Collateral

---

1. Fixtures [§348]

The only circumstance in which Article 9 has major involvement in real property financing arises when the collateral is goods that are currently or are about to become "fixtures"—*i.e.,* personal property attached to real property.

a. "Fixtures" defined [§349]

The U.C.C. does not actually define a "fixture." Ordinary building materials that are incorporated into an improvement on land (*e.g.,* bricks, lumber, cement, and the like) are specifically *excluded*, but all other goods become "fixtures" as provided by *local (non-U.C.C.) law*. [U.C.C. §§9-102(a)(41), 9-334(a)]

(1) Under property law [§350]

In most states, the notion of what is a "fixture" is intuitive—a *permanent attachment of the goods to real property*. (*See* detailed discussion in Property Summary.)

(a) *Mobile homes* placed on leased land have been involved in a number of cases. Normally, the lessee (debtor) has the right to remove the mobile home, and consequently it is *not* regarded as permanently affixed to the land.

(b) *Prefabricated buildings* brought onto the land by the owner thereof may be classified as "fixtures" if the owner *intended* a permanent attachment to the land.

(c) *"Readily removable" factory or office machines* would *hardly ever* be classified as fixtures. However, if they are, a special rule provides that a security interest therein can be perfected by any method permitted under Article 9; *i.e.*, the special fixture filing rules below do *not* apply. This is also true for readily removable *replacements* of domestic appliances that are *consumer goods* (*e.g.*, a window unit air conditioner). [U.C.C. §9-334(e)(2)]

b. Priority rules

(1) PMSIs—fixture filing required [§351]

Most security interests in particular fixtures are PMSIs (*see supra*, §§184-185). Such interests prevail as against most existing and future interests in the real estate *provided* that the purchase money security interest is *perfected* by a *"fixture filing"* at the time the goods are *affixed* to the realty or within 20 days thereafter. In addition, the "debtor" must be the *owner* of the real estate or someone in possession thereof (*e.g.*, a lessee).

(a) "Fixture filing" defined [§352]

A "fixture filing" is a perfection of the fixture financer's security interest in the goods that is accomplished by *filing a financing statement* in the place where *real property records* are filed. [U.C.C. §§9-102(a)(40), 9-501(a)(1)(B)] In addition to the usual requirements for a financing statement (*see supra*, §261), a fixture filing financing statement *must recite* that it is to be filed in the real estate records, must describe the goods, and must contain a description of the related real estate. [U.C.C. §9-502(b)]

1) Description of realty [§353]

In most states, the real estate description need only be sufficiently detailed to give *"constructive" notice* of the security interest to those examining the real estate records. However, some states (*e.g.*, Utah) require the financing statement to contain a technical legal description of the real property.

2) Identity of record owner [§354]

If the fixture debtor is not the record owner of the realty, but is only in possession, the financing statement also must identify the record owner so that it can be indexed under the record owner's name as well (as are most real property recordings). [U.C.C. §9-502(b)(4)]

(b) Limitation—construction mortgages [§355]

A lender who finances the construction of a building takes top priority as to *all items* that become part of the building during construction. Thus, when a construction mortgage has been *recorded* against the property, even a perfected PMSI in goods becoming fixtures during construction will be *junior* to the construction mortgage. [U.C.C. §9-334(h) and Comment 11] The rationale for this is since the construction mortgagee advanced the money for the whole project, the construction mortgagee should have superior rights to all items that are installed during construction unless the mortgagee agrees to subordinate its interest (*see* below).

1) Effect of subordination agreements [§356]

Even where the U.C.C. grants priority to a construction mortgage (or any other prior recorded interest in the real property), the fixture financer will prevail if the real property creditor, in an authenticated record, *agrees to subordinate* its interest to the security interest in the fixture or *disclaims an interest* in the goods as fixtures. [U.C.C. §9-334(f)]

(c) Right of fixture removal on default

See infra, §§626-627.

(2) Status of non-PMSIs

(a) Non-PMSI vs. prior recorded interests in realty [§357]

A non-PMSI in fixtures (or a PMSI perfected *more* than 20 days after the goods become a fixture) *loses* to *prior recorded* interests in the realty even if the fixture financer perfects by a fixture filing. (Conversely, *unrecorded* prior interests in the realty are subordinate to the fixture financer's perfected security interest.) [U.C.C. §9-334(c)]

(b) Non-PMSI vs. subsequent interests in realty [§358]

But the non-purchase money fixture financer can prevail over *subsequent* parties (*i.e.*, later real property mortgagees and buyers) by making a fixture filing before the subsequent parties obtain rights in the realty. [U.C.C. §9-334(e)(1)]

1) Subsequent lien creditors [§359]

If the subsequent claimant to the property is a judicial lien creditor (*supra*, §309), the fixture financer can achieve priority by perfecting the security interest using *any* method (not necessarily fixture filing) before the judicial lien attaches to the realty. [U.C.C. §9-334(e)(3)] [*In re* **Allen**, 35 U.C.C. Rep. Serv. 2d 1029 (Bankr. S.D. Ill. 1998)] The avowed purpose of this special rule is to preserve the fixture security interest against invalidation by a trustee in bankruptcy, who is a hypothetical judicial lien creditor under the Bankruptcy Code (*see infra*, §489). [U.C.C. §9-334, Comment 9]

EXAM TIP   **gilbert**

To summarize, in a contest between a secured creditor who has made a fixture filing and a party with an interest in the real estate to which the fixture is attached (*e.g.*, a mortgagee), the *first party to file or record* wins. However, if the security interest in the fixture is a *PMSI filed within 20 days* after the goods were affixed to the realty, the *PMSI holder* has priority, *unless* the real estate interest is a *construction mortgage* and the fixture was affixed during construction (in which case the construction mortgagee would have priority).

---

2. Accessions [§360]

Goods that are attached to *other goods* (*e.g.*, a telephone installed in a car) are called "accessions." [U.C.C. §9-102(a)(1)] Since real property is not involved, security interests in accessions fall within the scope of the Code and are governed without undue complexity.

a. Perfection continues in accession [§361]

There are no special rules for perfecting a security interest in an accession; the usual methods suffice. If the security interest in the accession is perfected when the accession is installed in other goods, its perfection continues in the accession. [U.C.C. §9-335(b)]

b. Priority determined by other rules [§362]

With the exception noted below, the Code has no special rules for priorities in accessions, leaving the usual rules for obtaining priority in place. [U.C.C. §9-335(c) and Comment 6]

(1) Exception—goods installed in motor vehicles [§363]

If a vehicle is covered by a certificate of title on which the security interest must be noted in order to achieve perfection (which is true in all states for automobiles; *see supra*, §190), the secured party who is *listed on the certificate of title* has priority in all accessions added to the vehicle, no matter whether the accessions are prior or subsequent to the certificate of title perfection. [U.C.C. §9-335(d) and Comment 7]

3. Commingled Goods [§364]

Goods that are physically united with other goods so that their identity is lost in a product or mass are said to be "commingled." Suppose a party takes a security interest in baled cotton that the debtor later spins into thread and then weaves into cloth. The collateral has changed form but is still identifiable, and security interests need not be affected. But suppose that the cotton is spun into a blend of cotton and rayon. Now, the collateral not only has changed form but also is no longer entirely identifiable. It is commingled. [U.C.C. §9-336(a)]

a. Interest extends to ultimate product [§365]

The Code handles this problem by providing that a perfected security interest in goods that have become part of a product or mass *extends to the product or mass* if they have been manufactured, assembled, or commingled so that they are *no longer identifiable*. [U.C.C. §9-336(b) - (d)]

b. Competing interests in ultimate product [§366]

It is possible, of course, that more than one perfected secured party may have an interest in a mass of commingled goods (*e.g.,* several types of raw material, each covered by a perfected security interest, are commingled into one product). The Code *ranks the interests of such conflicting parties equally*—declaring that each has an interest in the mass or total product in proportion to the value of the collateral at the time of commingling. [U.C.C. §9-336(f)(2)]

Example: Boll perfects a security interest in $1,000 of raw cotton and Weevil perfects an interest in $2,000 of raw wool. Debtor textile producer then spins the raw materials into 50 bolts of glen-plaid, the total cost of which is $6,000. In determining the extent of Boll's and Weevil's interests in the total product, the Code would give Boll an interest to the extent of 1/6 (or $1,000 out of $6,000) and Weevil an interest of 1/3 (or $2,000 out of $6,000).

(1) Time of attachment and perfection irrelevant [§367]

Note that it makes no difference when the original interests in the commingled goods attached and were perfected; they are still treated equally.

(2) Unperfected security interests junior [§368]

Of course perfected security interests have priority over unperfected ones, and this is true of commingled goods as well. [U.C.C. §9-336(f)(1) and Comment 5]

4. Proceeds

a. Introduction [§369]

As will be explained below, "proceeds" includes anything received by the debtor on the sale or any other kind of disposition of the collateral, whether or not the disposition was authorized by the creditor.

(1) Background [§370]

Prior to the Code, if the debtor was allowed to use or to dispose of the collateral or to retain the *proceeds* from the sale thereof, the courts treated the security interest as a fraudulent transfer, which could be set aside by a trustee in bankruptcy. [**Benedict v. Ratner**, *supra*, §32]

(a) Code provisions [§371]

This rule frustrated the needs of modern commercial financing, and hence was overturned by U.C.C. section 9-205, which specifically provides that a security interest is not invalid or fraudulent against creditors by reason of such permission granted to the debtor. This allows the parties to agree that the debtor may use or dispose of all the collateral and use or dispose of the proceeds obtained thereby, without having the secured party police the matter.

(b) Security interest in proceeds [§372]

The problem discussed in this section is to what extent the secured party's interest attaches to proceeds.

(2) "Proceeds" defined [§373]

"Proceeds" includes *whatever is received* on the sale, lease, exchange, or other disposition of collateral or of proceeds (from some previous disposition of collateral).

Example: First Bank has a perfected security interest in the inventory of an automobile dealership, Crazy Al's Cars. If Crazy Al's sells one of the new cars in the inventory to a buyer who gives Crazy Al's in return a used car as a trade-in, a cash down payment, and a promissory note accompanied by a security agreement for the balance (*i.e.*, chattel paper), First Bank's security interest now attaches to the used car, the cash, and the chattel paper, all of which are *proceeds* of the interest in the inventory.

(a) "Second generation" proceeds [§374]

If, in the example above, Crazy Al's later resells the used car for $2,500, the $2,500 is also proceeds from sale of the new car. Such proceeds of proceeds are sometimes called "second generation proceeds."

(b) Insurance and tort claims proceeds as "proceeds" [§375]

While most insurance and tort claims are not covered by Article 9 (*see supra*, §§100, 103), when these items are *proceeds*, Article 9 does apply to them. However, in the case of an insurance claim, before the secured party can reach the insurance payoff, the insurance policy must have listed either the debtor or the secured party as the *beneficiary* of the policy. [U.C.C. §9-102(a)(64)(E)]

(3) Express reference to "proceeds" not required [§376]

No express reference to "proceeds" is required in the security agreement *or* in the financing statement. The secured party's rights with respect to proceeds are deemed to arise by operation of law, in accordance with the parties' *presumed intent*, unless otherwise agreed. [*See* U.C.C. §9-315(a)]

(4) Secured party's option between proceeds or collateral [§377]

It should be emphasized that in many cases the secured party is not limited to asserting an interest in the "proceeds." If the security interest continues in the original collateral notwithstanding transfer thereof to a third person (*see infra,* §419), the secured party may claim both the proceeds *and* the original collateral—although the secured party is entitled to but *one satisfaction* of the debt. [U.C.C. §9-315(a)]

(a) But note

Of course, in those cases in which the transfer cuts off the security interest, the secured party would be limited to asserting an interest against the "proceeds" (*e.g.,* purchase by buyer in ordinary course from dealer in goods; purchase of negotiable instrument by holder in due course; *see infra,* §§420, 435).

b. Rules regarding attachment and perfection of security interest in proceeds [§378]

As long as the secured party's interest in the original collateral was perfected, that interest often will continue *automatically* for as long as the original perfection is effective in any *identifiable proceeds* received by the debtor from the sale, exchange, or other disposition of the original collateral; *i.e.,* no new filing is necessary. [U.C.C. §9-315(a)(2)(c)] The date of priority in the proceeds will be the same as that for the *original* collateral.

(1) Security agreement violated [§379]

The fact that the "proceeds" were obtained in violation of the security agreement is *immaterial.* For example, Debtor receives payments on accounts receivable already assigned to Lender, but instead of turning the money over to Lender, Debtor puts it in a bank account. Lender's interest in the collateral (accounts receivable) continues in the bank deposits. [**Commercial Discount Corp. v. Milwaukee Western Bank,** 214 N.W.2d 33 (Wis. 1974)]

(2) Same filing office—no new perfection required [§380]

Ask yourself, "If the proceeds had been the original collateral, where would the creditor have filed the financing statement?" If the financing statement is already on file in that office, the creditor need do *nothing more* to continue its perfection, even if the filed financing statement is misleading when applied to the proceeds. [U.C.C. §9-315(d)(1)] This is sometimes called the "same office" rule.

e.g. **Example:** Secured Party perfected a security interest in Debtor's "office machines," and filed a financing statement in the proper place so describing the collateral. Debtor then traded a computer for new drapes for his office window. Secured Party need do nothing to continue its perfection in the drapes (which are proceeds of the computer), even though the description in the financing statement does not appear to cover drapes. Since both the computer and the drapes are *equipment*, a financing statement covering either would be filed in the same central filing office.

EXAM TIP **gilbert**

Because filing occurs *centrally* (usually with the secretary of state) for all types of collateral except fixtures, minerals, and timber to be cut, the filing office for the proceeds and the original collateral generally will be the *same*. Thus, when a security interest in this type of collateral is perfected by filing and a security interest in proceeds of the collateral could also be perfected by filing, the secured party generally does not need to take any further steps to continue perfection in the proceeds.

(a) Proceeds of cash proceeds—20-day rule [§381]

The above rule does not apply if *cash proceeds* (*i.e.*, money, checks, bank accounts; *see* §9-102(a)(9)) intervene in the creation of the new proceeds (which are "second generation proceeds," *see supra*, §374). In that case the secured party is given *temporary perfection* in the second generation proceeds for only *20 days* and must file a new financing statement describing the *second generation proceeds* in the appropriate office within that period or lose its perfection. [U.C.C. §§9-315(d)(1)(C), 9-315(e) and Comment 5]

e.g. **Example:** If in the example above Debtor had instead sold the computer to someone else, thus generating *cash proceeds*, and then used the cash to buy drapes, Secured Party would be perfected only for 20 days following the purchase of the drapes and would have to correct the filed financing statement to describe the drapes within that period or lose its perfection in the drapes.

---

(3) Cash proceeds—tracing rules applied [§382]

Perfection of a security interest in the original collateral continues in cash proceeds of the collateral as long as the cash proceeds are still *identifiable*. [U.C.C. §9-315(d)(2)] This is sometimes called the "cash proceeds" rule. Whether cash proceeds are identifiable is left to the *common law* rules of tracing money. [U.C.C. §9-315(b)(2)] One major common law rule that favors creditors is called the *"lowest intermediate balance"* rule (adopted by Comment 3 to U.C.C. section 9-315), which traces money into bank accounts by presuming that withdrawals from that account are of money in which *no one claims an interest.*

---

e.g. **Example:** Debtor had a bank account in which the balance was $2,000. Debtor then deposited $3,000 cash proceeds in that account and subsequently withdrew $1,000. Since the lowest intermediate balance rule presumes that the debtor withdrew money that no one claimed (the original $2,000), the cash proceeds are still in the bank account and may be traced there by the secured party claiming the $3,000 cash proceeds.

(a) **Proceeds creditor junior to bank's right of setoff [§383]**
In a reversal of the common law rules, Article 9 gives the bank in which the account is carried a *superior setoff right* to anything in that account, including identifiable cash proceeds. [U.C.C. §9-340]

---

e.g. **Example:** If in the prior example the bank where the proceeds were deposited had a right of setoff against its customer (the debtor) because the customer owed the bank $4,000 for an overdue bank loan, the bank's common law right of setoff against this account would be superior to the rights of all other parties in the account, including the creditor's right to identifiable cash proceeds deposited therein.

---

(4) **All other instances—creditor must perfect within 20 days [§384]**
If a creditor has a perfected security interest in the original collateral and neither the "same office" rule nor the "cash proceeds" rule applies to proceeds of the collateral, the creditor must obtain a perfected security interest in the proceeds within *20 days* after the debtor receives the proceeds to retain its perfected security interest.

---

e.g. **Example:** Creditor lends Debtor money and takes a security interest in Debtor's "investment property." Creditor perfects by taking control of the investment property. Debtor then sells a commodity account in exchange for a security agreement and promissory note (*i.e.,* chattel paper). Creditor must perfect a security interest in the chattel paper within 20 days.

---

c. **Rules of priority [§385]**
The usual priority rules (*e.g.,* the*"first-to-file-or-perfect"* rule) govern most priority disputes in proceeds. Special statutory variations from this norm are considered in this section.

(1) **Accounts as "proceeds" of inventory [§386]**
Wherever a security interest exists in the debtor's inventory and another

security interest exists in the debtor's accounts receivable, a conflict will exist if the debtor sells the inventory on credit, since the "proceeds" of inventory will be an account receivable.

(a) Illustration [§387]

Bank One files and perfects a security interest in Debtor's inventory on June 1. Debtor sells a portion of his inventory in the ordinary course of business to Purchaser (such sale cutting off the security interest in the goods) on open account payable within 30 days. Debtor's accounts are subject to a security interest held by Bank Two, which had filed a financing statement with regard thereto on May 1. Who has priority in Purchaser's account? In this case, the accounts receivable financer (Bank Two) prevails because it was the "first to file or perfect" *as to the accounts* (the general priority rule of section 9-322(a)(1)).

1) *Even though Bank One may claim the accounts were "proceeds"* of the inventory in which it had a perfected interest, it is not entitled to priority as to the accounts *unless it filed first*.

2) *Where, as here, the accounts receivable financer (Bank Two) filed first*, it is entitled to priority. This is true even though, in fact, the inventory financer (Bank One) was the first to extend credit (because the date of *attachment* of the secured interest is *immaterial*; *see supra,* §326). It is also true regardless of the purchase money or nonpurchase money nature of the inventory financer's security interest.

(b) Distinguish—chattel paper, instrument, and cash proceeds of PMSIs in inventory [§388]

The result may be different where the inventory was sold for *chattel paper, an instrument, or cash* and the inventory financer had a *PMSI* in the debtor's inventory. This is because section 9-324(b) provides that the super-priority given a PMSI in new inventory (*see supra,* §336) *continues in the chattel paper, instrument, and cash proceeds* of the sale of such collateral.

Example: On January 1, Alpha files and perfects a security interest in the inventory of Debtor's hat shop. In addition, Debtor's accounts receivable are subject to a perfected security interest in favor of Beta, who files a financing statement on March 1. On August 1, Debtor orders a shipment of felt hats on credit from Chi and signs a security agreement giving Chi a PMSI in the hats. Chi files a financing statement on August 2 and before delivering the hats to Debtor, Chi gives written notice to Alpha of its new financing arrangement with Debtor. When the hats are delivered, Debtor sells some for cash and some on credit. Since Chi complied with the early perfection and written notice requirements of section 9-324(b), Chi's interest in the felt hats prevails over Alpha's existing interest in the general inventory. Also, since Chi's super-priority *continues* as to *cash proceeds* resulting from the sale of its collateral, Chi prevails over Beta as to the cash traceable from sale of the felt hats. However, priority in the *noncash* proceeds (the accounts receivable from the hats sold on credit) depends on the general "first-to-file-or-perfect" rule. Thus, Alpha would have top priority as to the accounts receivable, with Beta and Chi taking second and third priority, respectively (*i.e.,* their order of filing).

(2) Chattel paper as proceeds [§389]

The common method of selling large items such as automobiles and appliances is for the dealer to take a cash down payment for part of the price and chattel paper for the balance. Whoever is financing the dealer's inventory will want its security interest to carry over to the chattel paper since the product is no longer in the inventory as collateral, and the financer's claim to the product sold is cut off by the good faith consumer-buyer. [U.C.C. §9-320(a); *infra,* §420] Some dealers prefer to sell the chattel paper to a second financer, which creates conflicting claims between the inventory financer and the chattel paper financer since a *sale* of chattel paper is also covered by Article 9 (*supra,* §45).

(a) Where interest in chattel paper claimed as "proceeds" of inventory [§390]

If the purchaser of chattel paper gives *new value* for it and *takes possession* in the ordinary course of business, the purchaser has a priority over another security interest in the chattel paper that is claimed merely as *proceeds of inventory* subject to a security interest. This is true even though the purchaser of the chattel paper *knows* that the paper being bought is subject to the security interest. [U.C.C. §9-330(a)]

Example: Dealer borrowed money from Bank to finance the purchase of a stock of new cars and gave Bank a security interest in the new cars, which Bank perfected. Dealer then sold a car to Buyer for cash and chattel paper. Dealer then sold the chattel paper to Discount. Bank has no security interest in the car because Buyer purchased in the ordinary course of business. [U.C.C. §9-320(a)] Bank's security interest in the chattel paper is subordinate to Discount's, because Discount took the chattel paper in the ordinary course of business and gave new value.

 Example: Financer had a security interest in Dealer's inventory. Dealer was short of cash and sold the chattel paper on

12 recently sold cars to an out-of-town Bank with which Dealer had never done business. Dealer had always carried his own chattel paper previously, so the sale was not in the ordinary course of his business. However, the Bank would still have had priority against Financer, because the Bank took in the ordinary course of *its* business.

EXAM TIP   **gilbert**

Remember that a creditor with PMSI super-priority *in inventory* can also claim super-priority in chattel paper proceeds of that inventory. However, because a purchaser of chattel paper who takes possession and gives value prevails over *all* creditors who claim a security interest in the chattel paper merely as proceeds of inventory, the chattel paper purchaser will *prevail* over the PMSI creditor.

(b) **Where chattel paper subject to security interest other than as inventory "proceeds" [§391]**

If the chattel paper is subject to a security interest perfected other than as the proceeds of inventory, a stricter rule is applied. To take priority in this case, the purchaser of chattel paper must not only give new value and take possession in the ordinary course of business, but must also take *without knowledge* that the purchase violated the rights of the secured party. [U.C.C. §9-330(b)]

Example: Ace advances Dealer funds against Dealer's conditional sales contracts, which are assigned to Ace to secure repayment. However, the contracts themselves are left in Dealer's possession. Dealer then dishonestly obtains new financing from Bob and transfers possession of the contracts to Bob. Bob prevails against Ace as long as Bob paid value and took in the ordinary course of business without knowledge of a violation of Ace's rights.

---

1) **Notice [§392]**

A secured party claiming an interest in chattel paper other than as a mere claim to proceeds can get protection and still allow the debtor to retain possession of the paper by stamping or marking the paper with a *notice* of the assignment (*e.g.*, "This account has been assigned to XYZ"). This would put any prospective buyer on notice of the prior interest in the paper. [U.C.C. §9-330(f)]

(c) **Effect [§393]**

The effect of these two sections is to leave open the possibility that a dealer can simultaneously use two sources of collateral financing for the inventory and the chattel paper created by the sale of the inventory. An inventory financer wanting to be protected against the claims of purchasers of the chattel paper must have a claim based on more than the mere "proceeds" of the inventory. One way to do this would be to take a broader security interest in *both* inventory and chattel paper. The secured party could then either take possession of the chattel paper *or* merely mark it with notice of the security interest and be fully protected.

d. Returned goods

(1) Background [§394]

Under the rule of **Benedict v. Ratner** (*supra,* §370), whether a secured party could claim any interest in goods that had been sold by the debtor but then had been returned to the debtor for any reason might depend on whether the debtor was required to *segregate* the returned goods. If the secured party failed to require the debtor to do this, the entire security agreement was sometimes held invalid as against the debtor's trustee in bankruptcy.

(2) Rule [§395]

Under the Code, the original security interest in the goods continues (reattaches) in returned goods. This is true regardless of the reason for their return as long as they go back into the inventory. [U.C.C. §9-330(c) and Comments 9 - 10] If the original security interest was perfected by a filing that is still effective, nothing further is required to continue the perfection. Otherwise, however, the secured party must take *possession* of the returned goods or must *file* in order to perfect.

(a) Repossessed goods [§396]

If the debtor *repossesses* goods that it sold (as automobile dealerships will do if a buyer of a car does not pay for it), the rights of the various creditors of the debtor do not attach to the repossessed item *until it becomes the property of the debtor again* (which will happen only if there is a foreclosure sale and the debtor buys the property at the foreclosure sale, or if the debtor and the buyer agree that the debtor will accept the repossessed car in satisfaction of the outstanding balance—a so-called strict foreclosure; *see infra,* §550). [U.C.C. §9-330, Comment 10a(2)]

(3) Rights of third parties [§397]

If the sale of the goods has created chattel paper or an account receivable, a purchaser of the chattel paper or account has a security interest in the returned goods—which is good against the debtor (retailer) who sold the chattel paper or account. [U.C.C §9-330(c)]

(a) Perfection required [§398]

However, the security interest in returned goods must be *perfected* for protection against creditors of the transferor, as well as purchasers of the returned or repossessed goods. Perfection of the original security interest in the chattel paper or account does *not* carry over automatically to the returned goods, as it does where the secured party originally financed the inventory (above). Rather, the chattel paper or account financer must take steps within 20 days to get perfection as to the returned goods by filing or by taking possession of them. [U.C.C. §9-315(d)]

Example: Dealer sells an automobile to Buyer and transfers the chattel paper to Bank (which had not previously financed the car as inventory). Thereafter, Buyer rightfully rescinds the sale for breach of warranty, and Dealer takes the car back. Bank has a security interest in the car good against Dealer. However, Bank must file a financing statement or possess the car to be perfected against later creditors of Dealer. *Note:* Of course, Bank cannot perfect its security interest against another buyer in the ordinary course of business, so Dealer could still resell the car and an innocent purchaser would prevail against Bank. [U.C.C. §9-320(a); *see infra*, §420]

---

(4) Inventory financer vs. chattel paper purchaser [§399]

If a dealer has financing arrangements with two separate parties—a secured party financing inventory and a purchaser of the chattel paper created by sale of the inventory—both may claim a security interest in the returned goods: the inventory financer since the goods go back into the inventory, and the purchaser of the chattel paper claiming the returned goods as proceeds of the chattel paper. The conflicting claims are resolved under the rules of section 9-330 (*supra,* §390); *i.e.,* the security interest of the purchaser of *chattel paper* has priority over that of the inventory financer if the purchaser of the chattel paper gave value for the paper and took it in the ordinary course of business. [U.C.C. §9-330(c)]

F. Priority Among Perfected Creditors— Perfection by Control

1. Introduction [§400]

For investment property, deposit accounts, and letter of credit rights, the secured party can achieve perfection by obtaining *control* over the collateral (*see supra*, §§211-222). The rules for priority in investment property have already been discussed (*see supra*, §212). The following rules deal with priority between creditors having control over deposit accounts and letter of credit rights.

2. Priority in Deposit Accounts [§401]

If a creditor has control over a deposit account (the only method of directly perfecting a security interest in a deposit account, *see supra*, §219), it prevails over all other claimants to the account who do not have control (*e.g.*, those claiming a perfected security interest in the deposit account as *proceeds* of other collateral). If more than one secured party has control, the secured parties rank in priority according to *time of obtaining control*.

a. Exception—account in secured party's name [§402]

The depository bank has a *superior right of setoff* for debts owed to it by the depositor, and prevails over the secured party having control of the account, *unless* the secured party obtained control by having the account put in its own name, in which case it prevails over the bank's right of setoff. [U.C.C. §9-327(3) - (4)]

---

e.g. **Example:** American Bank, Customer (the debtor), and Creditor agree that American Bank will follow the instructions of Creditor (as well as those of Customer) as to the disposition of the contents of Customer's bank account. This creates control in Creditor (*see supra*, §219). If Customer deposits cash proceeds belonging to some other secured party with an interest in the account, Creditor has priority over these cash proceeds. [U.C.C. §9-327(1)] If Customer takes out a loan from American Bank and fails to pay it, American Bank's right of setoff against the account is superior to the rights of Creditor. [U.C.C. §9-327(4)] However, if Creditor had achieved control by taking Customer's name off of the account completely and substituting its own name as the owner of the account, American Bank's right of setoff against Customer would have been junior to Creditor's. [U.C.C. §9-327(4)]

---

3. Priority in Letter of Credit Rights [§403]

There are two ways of getting a perfected security interest in a letter of credit right: getting *control* (*see supra*, §220), and perfecting a security interest in the *account* that the letter of credit backs up, in which case there is automatic perfection in the letter of credit right (as a "supporting obligation," *see supra*, §205). In this case the creditor having *control* has priority over all other creditors. [U.C.C. §9-329] As is the case with investment property and deposit accounts, if more than one creditor obtains control over the same letter of credit rights, the *first party to gain control* has priority. [U.C.C. §9-329(2)]

---

e.g. **Example:** Seller gave a perfected security interest in all its accounts receivable to First Bank (which perfected First Bank automatically in any supporting obligations, such as a letter of credit backing up the accounts receivable). When Buyer ordered $10,000 worth of goods from Seller, Seller demanded that Buyer get a letter of credit naming Seller as the beneficiary of the letter of credit (so that Seller could get payment directly from the bank issuing the letter of credit). Second Bank issued such a letter of credit to Seller. Seller, needing to borrow money to run its operation, went to Third Bank and asked to borrow the needed sum, using the letter of credit rights as collateral. Third Bank achieved control over the letter of credit rights by getting Second Bank to agree to pay the letter of credit's proceeds directly to Third Bank. Third Bank has priority over First Bank in the proceeds, since it has control and First Bank does not.

EXAM TIP **gilbert**

When deciding which party has priority in investment property, deposit accounts, or letter of credit rights, always remember the general rule that applies to all three types of collateral: **The creditor with control prevails** over creditors without control. There is also a general rule (with some exceptions, depending on the type of collateral) for situations in which more than one creditor has control of investment property, deposit accounts, or letter of credit rights: **The first creditor to gain control wins**.

G. Priority Among Perfected Creditors— As Affected by Terms of Security Agreement

1. Future Advances [§404]

Under section 9-204(c) of the Code, a security agreement can create security interests in the collateral covering not only the current loan but also future loans by the same creditor. In this case, a new security agreement is not needed when the future loan is made. The filed financing statement will then perfect the security interest both as originally made *and as expanded* by later advances to the debtor, thereby continuing the original priority. [U.C.C. §9-323]

Example: Creditor A loans Debtor $10,000 and takes a security interest in Debtor's machinery. The security agreement provides that the machinery is to be collateral not only for this loan but also for any future loans made by A to Debtor. A files a financing statement on January 1. On February 1, Debtor borrows money from Creditor B, who takes a security interest in the same machinery and files a financing statement. On March 1, Creditor A makes another loan to Debtor under the original security agreement. A's security interest in the machinery for the March 1 loan is covered by the original financing statement and so is perfected when the loan is made. Thus, A has priority over B as to both the January and March advances because A filed first.

a. **Distinguish—advances under later security agreements [§405]**

Sometimes the original security agreement *fails to cover future loans* to the debtor, and the question may arise whether the secured party's priority extends to loans made under *later* security agreements where there are other intervening security interests involved.

(1) **General rule [§406]**

As long as a secured party had priority over later creditors by *filing or possession*, that party will also prevail as to advances pursuant to a *later* security agreement. This is true even where other Article 9 creditors perfected their security interest in the same collateral *between* the advances. [U.C.C. §9-324, Comment 3]

Example: Sporting Goods Store used its inventory as collateral for a loan of $5,000 from Bank A, which filed a financing statement on March 1, in the proper place. Store repaid this debt in full on September 1. On September 10, Store borrowed $3,000 from Bank B, which also took a security interest in the inventory and filed a financing statement in the proper place. On October 1, Store again borrowed $5,000 from Bank A pursuant to a new security agreement, and again the inventory was used as collateral. As long as Bank A's *original* financing statement is *still on file* (*i.e.,* no termination statement was filed when Store paid off the first loan), Bank A *still* has priority over Bank B—even though its loan was second in time—because Bank A was the first to file.

(a) **Rationale—second creditor had notice [§407]**

The second creditor (such as Bank B in the above example) has little to complain about: It should have known of Bank A's *superior position* since Bank A's financing statement was still on file when it made its loan; the purpose of a financing statement is to give other creditors *notice* that the secured party claims some interest in the named collateral. (Specific information about the *details* of the underlying agreement—*e.g.,* amount of loan, payment schedule, after-acquired property, etc.—are found in the *security agreement*, which a later creditor can find out about through the debtor.)

(b) **Note—second creditor can protect itself [§408]**

The second creditor can always protect itself against future advances by the first creditor to the common debtor, either by insisting that the first creditor's financing statement be removed from the files (a "termination statement"; *see supra,* §292) or by obtaining a *subordination* agreement from the first creditor (*see supra,* §110).

(c) Limitation—filing or possession required [§409]

The first creditor prevails only if its later advance of funds was made while the original security interest was perfected by *filing or possession*. If its interest was perfected in any other way (*e.g.,* "temporary perfection" under section 9-312, *see supra,* §206), the later advance would be junior to a perfected interest arising beforehand. [*See* U.C.C. §9-323, Comment 3]

2. Dragnet Clauses [§410]

A security agreement sometimes provides that the collateral will be security not only for repayment of this loan but also for *any other debts* owed by the debtor to the creditor now or in the future. Such a provision is called a "dragnet clause."

a. Validity [§411]

Although section 9-204 (and particularly its Comment 5) would appear to authorize dragnet clauses, in the past courts have refused to enforce them if the other debt is completely *unrelated* to the original transaction so that the parties probably did not intend it to be covered by the dragnet clause, because it drags all debts into the same transaction. [*In re* **Wollin**, 249 B.R. 555 (Bankr. D. Or. 2000)]

Example: To finance new purchases of cattle for his herd, Farmer borrowed $10,000 from Farmers Friend Bank, giving the bank a perfected security interest in his livestock. The parties signed a security agreement containing a dragnet clause. Six months later, Farmer failed to pay a bill for $300 worth of Christmas presents he had purchased using the credit card Farmers Friend Bank had issued him years before. The bank repossessed his cattle. Some courts would hold Farmers Friend Bank guilty of conversion since the *probable intention* of the parties was to have the dragnet clause operate only to secure transactions of the *same class* as the first transaction (*i.e.,* livestock loans). Whether courts will reach this result under the 1999 revision is unclear.

---

b. Consumer laws [§412]

A number of states have enacted special consumer protection statutes designed to prohibit or regulate dragnet clauses and other "cross-collateralization" clauses in consumer transactions. [*See, e.g.,* Uniform Consumer Credit Code §3.303 (1974 version)]

3. Consent Clauses and Waiver of Security Interests [§413]

Security agreements often provide that the debtor may not sell the collateral without the written consent of the secured party. Just as frequently, the debtor continues to sell the collateral on a regular basis anyway. If the secured party finds out about the sales but says nothing and the debtor later defaults on the loan, the question arises as to whether the secured party may follow the collateral into the hands of the debtor's buyer and repossess it, or whether the silence of the secured party constitutes a waiver of the security interest.

a. **Finding of waiver [§414]**

Many courts have followed the common law doctrine of waiver (typically defined as "voluntary relinquishment of a known right") and have held that the failure of the secured party to enforce the terms of the security agreement results in a *waiver* of the security interest. [**Clovis National Bank v. Thomas**, 425 P.2d 726 (N.M. 1967)]

Example: Bank held a perfected security interest in Farmer's cattle. The security agreement provided that the cattle could not be sold by Farmer without Bank's written consent (which it never gave). Nonetheless, over a period of years, Farmer frequently sold the cattle to a meat packing plant, remitting the proceeds of the sales to Bank. Bank knew of all the sales. When Farmer missed three debt repayments in a row, Bank brought a conversion action against the meat packing plant. In jurisdictions following *Clovis, supra*, Bank would probably be held to have waived its security interest in the cattle, and the meat packing plant would win.

---

(1) **Statutory basis for waiver [§415]**

This result is supported by U.C.C. section 9-315(a)(1), which states that a security interest continues in collateral notwithstanding the debtor's sale, unless the disposition was authorized by the secured party.

b. **No waiver—"course of dealing" theory [§416]**

Some jurisdictions refuse to find waiver in the above situation on grounds that by the time the bank learns of the sales, its only recourse is in the proceeds of sale anyway. Therefore, by allowing the security interest to continue in the collateral, such interest also attaches to proceeds of the sale, which the creditor can then claim to satisfy the debt. [*See, e.g.,* **Wabasso State Bank v. Caldwell Packing Co.**, 251 N.W.2d 321 (Minn. 1976)]

(1) **Statutory support? [§417]**

Courts following this approach purport to base their finding of no waiver on the language of section 1-205(4) of the Code, which provides that a "course of dealing" between the parties (*i.e.*, the creditor's unspoken acquiescence in the debtor's sales) cannot change the express terms of the security agreement.

(a) **Criticism**

This is an unsound theory. The language of section 1-205 refers to a "course of dealing" occurring *prior* to the agreement. Furthermore, this approach ignores the basic rule of contract law that written conditions in an agreement can be waived by the conduct of the parties (*see* Contracts Summary). [*See* U.C.C. §2-208(3)]

c. **"Conditional consent" theory [§418]**

Finally, some jurisdictions have developed a "conditional consent" test, whereby the alleged "waiver" is ineffective to destroy the creditor's security interest if the debtor failed to comply with the implied *condition* in the security agreement that the proceeds of the sale be used to repay the debt to the creditor. If the proceeds are so used, the security interest is waived; if not, the creditor has the option of repossessing the collateral from the buyer or suing the buyer in conversion. [*See* **Baker Products Credit Association v. Long Creek Meat Co.,** 513 P.2d 1129 (Or. 1973)]

H. Priority Among Perfected Creditors and Other Claimants

1. Buyers of the Collateral—General Rule [§419]

As discussed earlier (*supra,* §322), a buyer of collateral that is subject to an *unperfected* security interest almost always acquires the property free of the creditor's right to reclaim it. However, with the exceptions listed below, a buyer of collateral covered by a *perfected* security interest generally takes the collateral *subject* to the security interest.

a. Exception—buyers in the ordinary course of business [§420]

A buyer who purchases goods in the *ordinary course of business* from a dealer's *inventory* takes free of perfected security interests held by the dealer's creditors in the inventory. This is true even though the buyer *knows* that the inventory is covered by a security interest, as long as the buyer does not know that the sale is in *violation* of the terms of the security agreement. [U.C.C. §9-320(a)] *Rationale:* The dealer's creditor has a "floating lien" over the inventory. All parties to the transaction (dealer, creditor, and consumer) *expect* that the particular item sold will be freed from the inventory lien.

Example: Consumer buys a watch from Jeweler knowing that Jeweler's inventory is subject to a perfected security interest in favor of Bank. At the moment of sale, the Bank's security interest *detaches* from the particular watch sold and is transferred to the "proceeds" of the sale (*i.e.,* the money paid by Consumer to Jeweler), and Consumer takes free of the security interest. [U.C.C. §9-315] *Note:* The result is the same even if the security agreement between Jeweler and Bank stated that Jeweler was forbidden to sell this particular watch, unless Consumer knew of this particular limitation in the security agreement (most unlikely). [U.C.C. §9-320, Comment 3]

(1) Special rules for farm products [§421]

Under U.C.C. section 9-320(a), a buyer of farm products from a farmer does *not* take free of existing perfected security interests in the farm products held by the farmer's creditors. *Rationale:* Farmers have so much trouble getting financing that lenders willing to extend credit to farmers are given extra protection. However, the federal Food Security Act of 1985 (below) preempts this rule.

(a) Federal Food Security Act of 1985 [§422]

Under section 1324 of the Food Security Act of 1985 [7 U.S.C. §163], farmers are required to furnish their creditors with a list of buyers of their products. The secured parties then send a notice to these buyers telling them how payment should be made. A buyer who complies with these instructions takes free of the perfected security interest. The Act also encourages the states to set up a central filing system for registry of all the restrictions imposed on selling farmers by their creditors, so that compliance with the central registry restrictions would also protect the buyers of the farm products. Farmers who fail to inform their creditors of the identities of the potential buyers of the farm products are subject to a fine of at least $5,000. [*See* 9 C.F.R. 10795—U.S.D.A. regulations on point]

Example: Farmer gave a perfected security interest in his crop to Big Bank and also gave Big Bank a list of buyers to whom Farmer planned to sell his crop. Big Bank sent a letter to all the buyers on the list, telling them that payments for the crop should be made by checks payable to both Farmer *and* Big Bank. Betty Buyer received one of these letters and when she bought part of Farmer's crop, she dutifully made out the check as directed. Paul Purchaser was not on the list, and even though he knew about Big Bank's security interest in the crop, when he bought part of Farmer's crop, he paid cash directly to Farmer. Both buyers take free of Big Bank's security interest (Betty, because she followed instructions, and Paul, because he received none). Big Bank's rights are against Farmer alone. [**Farm Credit Bank of St. Paul v. F & A Dairy,** 477 N.W.2d 357 (Wis. 1991)]

---

(2) Buyer must be "in the ordinary course of business" [§423]

The rule of section 9-320(a), above, protects only "buyers in the ordinary course of business," and then only if the security interest in the inventory was "created by the buyer's seller." The elements qualifying a buyer for freedom from the security interest in the inventory come from sections 1-201(9) (defining "buyer in the ordinary course of business") and 9-320(a) itself. They are:

(a) Ordinary purchase [§424]

The buyer must buy goods out of *inventory* in the "ordinary course of business"—*i.e.,* the transaction must be a "run of the mill" purchase and not an extraordinary sale. However, " bulk sales" do *not* qualify for section 9-320(a) protection. A "bulk sale" occurs when the buyer buys a "major part" of the dealer's inventory. [U.C.C. §6-102(1)]

(b) New value [§425]

The buyer must give *new* value and not just cancel out an old indebtedness. [**Chrysler Credit Corp. v. Malone**, 502 S.W.2d 910 (Tex. 1973)—holding insurance salesperson's purchase of car from dealer subject to prior security interest because payment for car was cancellation of old insurance debt dealer owed him]

(c) No knowledge [§426]

The buyer must buy in *good faith* and not know that the sale is in violation of the terms of a security agreement between the seller and the seller's creditor. [**International Harvester Co. v. Glendenning**, 505 S.W.2d 320 (Tex. 1974)—no protection to buyer of tractor who went along with dealer's lie to dealer's creditor that buyer had traded in an old tractor as partial payment]

(d) Interest created by seller [§427]

Finally, the security interest in the item sold must have been *created by the buyer's seller.*

---

e.g. **Example:** Bank had a perfected purchase money security interest in Sailor's yacht. Sailor sold the yacht to Used Boats, Inc., which resold it to Consumer. Consumer does *not* take the yacht free from Bank's security interest because it was not created by Consumer's "seller" (*i.e.*, Used Boats, Inc.). [**Security Pacific National Bank v. Goodman**, 24 Cal. App. 3d 131 (1972)]

---

1) Rationale

If a creditor takes a security interest in inventory, it expects the collateral to be sold and can police the disposition of the proceeds. However, if the debtor sells the collateral to someone who puts it into inventory, as in the last example, the creditor will not know that this has happened and ought not to lose its interest in the collateral simply because the collateral was sold to an innocent buyer. The issue arises most often in the sale of used goods. The disappointed buyer gets relief by suing the used-goods seller for breach of the warranty of good title. [U.C.C. §2-312; *and see* Sale & Lease of Goods Summary]

(e) Secured party in possession trumps buyer in the ordinary course of business [§428]

If the secured party keeps possession of the collateral, the secured party has priority over even a buyer in the ordinary course of business. [U.C.C. §9-320(e)]

> **Example:** A manufacturer sold goods on credit to a processing company, which in turn sold them to a buyer on the open market on credit. The goods remained in the manufacturer's warehouse. The manufacturer's purchase money security interest in the goods it sold will prevail over the rights of the ultimate buyer in the ordinary course of business as long as it keeps possession of the goods. (This reverses the rule of a famous case, **Tanbro Fabrics v. Deering Milliken,** 39 N.Y.2d 632 (1976).)

(3) Distinguish—other collateral [§429]

Note that a security interest in goods *other than inventory* continues in the collateral even in the hands of a good faith buyer for value. [U.C.C. §9-315(a)(1)]

> **Example:** Bank held a perfected security interest in all the *equipment* in Jack's Bar. One night, Jack sold the painting hanging over the bar to a patron. Bank's security interest remains attached to the painting, and if Jack defaults on his loan to the bank, the painting can be repossessed from the patron's home. [**I.T.T. Industrial Credit Co. v. H. & K. Machine Service,** 33 U.C.C. Rep. 400 (E.D. Mo. 1981)]

REQUIREMENTS FOR BUYER IN ORDINARY COURSE OF BUSINESS STATUS — **gilbert**

A BUYER OF GOODS QUALIFIES AS A BUYER IN THE ORDINARY COURSE OF BUSINESS AND THUS TAKES THE GOODS FREE OF ANY SECURITY INTERESTS IN THEM IF:

- ☑ The purchase is an "ordinary" purchase of the seller's *inventory*;
- ☑ The buyer purchased the goods for *value*;
- ☑ The buyer purchased the goods in *good faith* and *without knowledge of a violation* of the security agreement; and
- ☑ The security interest was created by the *buyer's seller*.

---

b. Exception—buyers not in the ordinary course of business—future advances [§430]

If a buyer does *not* qualify for protection against prior security interests under section 9-320(a), the question arises as to what extent the buyer is subject to expansion of the prior security interest due to future advances.

(1) Forty-five-day rule [§431]

The U.C.C. provides that a buyer *not* in the ordinary course of business (*e.g.*, a purchaser of non-inventory) takes *free of increases* in the security interest due to future advances, *unless* the advances are made by the creditor in the **45 days** following the sale and are made either *without knowledge* of the sale or "pursuant to a commitment" that was entered into without such knowledge. [U.C.C. §9-323(d) - (e)]

---

e.g. **Example:** On September 30, Lawyer Jones sold a grandfather clock that had been sitting in his office for years to Client who much admired it. He failed to mention to Client that all his equipment (worth $50,000) was covered by a perfected security interest in favor of Lawyers Finance Co. ("LFC"), which had loaned Jones $25,000. On October 10, LFC loaned Jones an additional $25,000 (a future advance), which was also collateralized by the office equipment. If LFC had no knowledge of the clock sale at the time of the second loan, *or* if it had such knowledge, but prior to learning of the sale, it had made a commitment to Lawyer Jones to make the second loan, Client would hold the clock subject to LFC's expanded security interest since the sale was within the 45-day period.

(a) "Pursuant to commitment" [§432]

"Pursuant to a commitment" means pursuant to an agreement by the secured party to loan money to the debtor in the future. A loan remains "pursuant to a commitment" even if there is an escape clause in the agreement (*e.g.*, "no loan shall be made if the debtor cannot produce financial records demonstrating solvency"), unless the condition excusing the loan promise is completely at the whim of the secured party. [U.C.C. §9-102(a)(68)]

c. Exception—buyers of consumer goods from other consumers [§433]

U.C.C. section 9-320(b) provides that a consumer buying consumer goods from another consumer for value takes free of a perfected security interest in the goods unless the buying consumer *knows* of the security interest, or a financing statement covering the goods has been *filed.* Since PMSIs in consumer goods are automatically perfected without filing (*see supra,* §182), it would be a rare case in which a filing would exist. [U.C.C. §9-311(b)] *Note:* If the consumer goods are motor vehicles, notation on certificate of title is equivalent of filing.

---

e.g. **Example:** Department Store sold Alice a refrigerator on credit, keeping a PMSI therein. Three months later, Alice sold the refrigerator to her next-door neighbor, Betty. Betty gets the refrigerator free of Department Store's security interest unless she knows of the interest, or unless Department Store took the unusual step of filing a financing statement.

An easy way to remember this exception is to think of a typical *garage sale*. At most garage sales, consumers buy goods from sellers who themselves used the goods as consumers. For example, Sarah might go to a garage sale and buy a lamp to use in her home from David, who also used the lamp in his home. In this scenario, even if David bought the lamp on credit and still owed money on it, Sarah would take the lamp free of any security interests David created in the lamp.

d. Exception—buyers of quasi-tangible collateral [§434]

Under other Articles of the U.C.C., certain buyers of quasi-tangible paper collateral (instruments, documents, and chattel paper) are given the freedom to purchase such property free of the claims of others—including perfected Article 9 security interests in the paper. [U.C.C. §9-331]

(1) Who is protected [§435]

The protected buyers are *"holders in due course"* of negotiable instruments [*see* U.C.C. §3-302, *and see* Commercial Paper Summary]; buyers of instruments who give value and take possession in good faith and without knowledge that the purchase violates a security agreement [U.C.C. §9-330(d)]; "holders to whom a negotiable *document of title* has been duly negotiated" [U.C.C. §§7-501, 7-505; *and see* Sale & Lease of Goods Summary]; and "bona fide purchasers" with control of *investment property* [U.C.C. §8-303].

> **Example:** Karate School pledged all the promissory notes its students had signed to Merchant Finance. When one of the notes fell due, Karate School asked for it back from Merchant Finance so the school could present it to the maker for payment. Merchant Finance released the note to the school, relying on its temporary 20-day period of perfection without possession. [U.C.C. §9-312(a); *see supra*, §209] Instead of presenting the promissory note to the maker, Karate School sold it. If the purchaser qualifies as a holder in due course, it takes the note free of Merchant Finance's security interest.

2. Statutory Lien Holders [§436]

Article 9, for the most part, excludes coverage of "statutory" liens (such as tax liens, artisan's liens, etc.). [U.C.C. §9-109(c), (d)(1) - (2); *see supra*, §314] However, priority between Article 9 perfected security interests and *possessory* statutory liens (*i.e.,* those arising when the statutory lien holder gets and maintains possession of the collateral) is regulated by Article 9. [U.C.C. §9-333]

a. Only possessory liens covered [§437]

The priority rule of section 9-333 applies only to *possessory* statutory liens. When a statute creates a statutory lien that does *not* require the lien claimant to maintain possession of the collateral to keep the lien, the priority between the nonpossessory statutory lien and an Article 9 security interest is governed by non-U.C.C. law. [**Leger Mill Co. v. Kleen-Leen, Inc.,** 563 P.2d 132 (Okla. 1977)]

b. General rule of priority [§438]

Under section 9-333, a person who acquires (under separate state law) a lien on goods in that person's possession as a result of materials or services furnished (*e.g.,* repairing a car) *prevails* over a prior perfected security interest in the goods.

Example: Consumer financed the purchase of a car through Consumers Credit Union, which held a perfected PMSI therein. The car broke down, and Consumer took it to Al's Repair Shop. Consumer failed to pay the repair bill, leaving the car at Al's. Consumer then missed two payments to the credit union, which tried to repossess the car. As long as Al's Repair Shop maintains possession of the car, its artisan's lien has priority over the credit union's interest.

---

(1) Liens covered [§439]

This is true whether the "statutory" lien arises from a statute or the common law (which gave "artisans" a lien for their labors). [**National Bank v. Bergeron Cadillac, Inc.,** 361 N.E.2d 1116 (Ill. 1977)]

(2) Consent irrelevant [§440]

It is also true even if the Article 9 secured creditor did not *consent* to the repair work giving rise to the statutory lien. [**General Motors Acceptance Corp. v. Colwell Diesel Service & Garage,** 302 A.2d 595 (Me. 1973)]

c. Exception—statutory priority [§441]

The only exception to the general rule of priority is where the statute creating the lien *expressly* makes the statutory lien junior to prior security interests, which such statutes rarely do. [U.C.C. §9-333(b)]

d. Distinguish—consensual liens [§442]

In addition to the statutory lien that arises by operation of law, the lien holder sometimes makes the debtor sign an agreement giving the lien holder a *nonpossessory* consensual lien on the debtor's collateral. This agreement *is* an Article 9 security agreement and should be perfected under the Article 9 procedures to be valid against other creditors. However, even if the lien holder fails to perfect, the *statutory lien* may still be available if the lien holder has possession of the collateral.

Example: Suppose that when Consumer in the above example took his car in for repair, Al's Repair Shop made him sign a security agreement giving Al's a security interest in the car. A state statute provides that consensual liens are invalid unless noted on the certificate of title; thus, Al's security interest is unperfected. Nonetheless, Al's may still have the benefit of the state's statutory artisan's lien if Al's maintains possession of the car. [*See, e.g.,* **Bank of North America v. Kruger,** 551 S.W.2d 63 (Tex. 1977)]

3. Federal Tax Lien

a. In general [§443]
When a taxpayer fails to pay federal taxes, the Internal Revenue Service ("I.R.S.") has the benefit of a federal statute creating a tax lien on *all* of the taxpayer's property, real and personal, now owned or after-acquired, exempt or nonexempt (*i.e., **everything the taxpayer owns or hopes to own***). [26 U.S.C. §§6321 - 6323]

(1) Creation of lien [§444]
The federal tax lien ("FTL") arises at the moment of "assessment"—*i.e.,* the I.R.S.'s determination that the tax is owed, as manifested by a notation of tax liability on a list in the I.R.S.'s district director's office. If the taxpayer does not pay the taxes due, the government will sell the property subject to the lien and pay the taxes from the proceeds.

b. Priorities [§445]
The FTL is valid against the taxpayer and most other parties at the moment of assessment, even though only the I.R.S. knows about it (*i.e.,* the FTL is a "secret" lien). However, its validity against Article 9 security interests depends on whether such interests are *perfected* before notice of the lien is *filed* in the state. [26 U.S.C. §6323(a); **Sams v. New Kensington City Redevelopment Authority,** 261 A.2d 566 (Pa. 1970)] The Federal Tax Lien Act ("FTLA") provides that a "security interest" in existence before an FTL is filed prevails over the FTL. "Security interest" is defined in such a way that only *perfected* Article 9 security interests qualify. [26 U.S.C. §6323(a), (h)(1); **Aetna Insurance Co. v. Texas Thermal Industries, Inc.,** 591 F.2d 1035 (5th Cir. 1979)]

(1) Unperfected security interests [§446]
If an Article 9 security interest is unperfected at the time the FTL notice is filed, the federal government has priority over the unperfected creditor. [**Fred Kraus & Sons, Inc. v. United States,** 369 F. Supp. 1089 (N.D. Ind. 1974)]

(2) Perfected security interests [§447]
If an Article 9 security interest is perfected at the time the FTL notice is filed, the secured creditor has priority over the federal government.

(3) Subsequent PMSIs [§448]
Although the FTLA is silent on the point, the I.R.S. has ruled that the government lien is *subordinate* to a perfected PMSI in property acquired by the taxpayer *after* the FTL filing. [Rev. Rul. 68-57, 26 C.F.R. 301.6321-1 (1968)]

(4) Security interests in after-acquired property [§449]

In addition, the FTLA gives limited recognition to security interests that arise automatically in after-acquired property of the debtor ("floating liens"). Such after-acquired security interests in inventory, chattel paper, instruments, and accounts that come into existence within the **45 days** after the FTL is filed are senior to the FTL, while those arising after the 45-day period are junior to the filed tax lien.

Example: Shoe Store borrowed money from Bank, giving Bank a security interest in the store's inventory. Bank filed a financing statement in the proper place. One year later, on June 15, the I.R.S. filed an FTL against Shoe Store, which had not been paying its taxes. Thereafter, Store received two shipments of new shoes: one on June 20, and the other on September 25. Bank would have priority as to the inventory acquired by the June 20 shipment (within 45 days of the FTL filing), but the I.R.S. would have priority as to the second shipment (which arrived after the 45-day period had expired).

(a) Note

In the example above, Bank's knowledge of the tax lien filing is *irrelevant* to its priority as to the collateral acquired during the 45-day period. [Treas. Reg. §301.6323(c)(1), (d)]

(5) Future advances [§450]

Where the security agreement covers future advances as well as the original loan (*see supra,* §404), a perfected security interest takes priority over the FTL to the extent enlarged by a future advance only if the advance was made **without knowledge** of the FTL during the 45 days after the FTL filing. [26 U.S.C. §6323(d)]

Example: Bank loaned Smith Machine Co. $20,000, taking a security interest in all of Smith's equipment. The security agreement provided that the equipment would be collateral not only for this loan, but also for any future loans made to Smith by Bank. Bank filed a financing statement in the proper place. One year later, on May 2, the I.R.S. filed an FTL against all of Smith Machine Co.'s property. On May 10, Bank loaned Smith Machine another $20,000. Bank's security interest is superior to the FTL as to all $40,000, as long as Bank did not know of the filed FTL at the time of the second loan. (If it did, Bank's security interest is superior only as to the first $20,000.)

(a) Other applications of 45-day rule [§451]

Similar "45-day" periods apply in determining priorities of future advances over buyers of the collateral [U.C.C. §9-323(d); *see supra,* §404] and judicial lien creditors [U.C.C. §9-323(b), *infra*].

4. Judicial "Lien Creditors"

a. General rule of priority [§452]

While a judicial lien creditor is senior to an unperfected security interest (*see supra*, §320), a judicial lien creditor is junior to a *perfected* security interest in the collateral. [U.C.C. §9-317(a)(2)]

b. Priority of future advances [§453]

This general rule is modified somewhat where the Article 9 perfected creditor makes future advances to the debtor. In this case, the future advances *retain priority* if made: (i) *within 45 days* after the judicial lien is acquired (whether or not the Article 9 creditor knows of the lien); *or* (ii) *after* the 45 days if the creditor either has *no knowledge* of the judicial lien or the advance is made "pursuant to a commitment which was entered into without knowledge of the lien" (*supra*, §432). [U.C.C. §9-323(b)]

> **e.g. Example:** Debtor's unsecured creditor wins a lawsuit against Debtor and sends out the sheriff, who levies on (seizes) property subject to a *perfected* Article 9 security interest in favor of Lender. The next day, Lender loans Debtor more money, knowing of the judicial lien but relying on their security agreement stating that the collateral secures future advances as well as the original loan. The second loan (the "future advance") is superior to the judicial lien because the future advance was made within 45 days after the judicial lien was acquired.

> **e.g. Example:** Bank perfects a security interest in factory equipment used by Smith Machine Co. as collateral for a series of loans from Bank. The parties' security agreement provides that the collateral will also secure future advances made to Smith by Bank and obligates Bank to make loans for one year as long as Smith Machine Co. makes regular repayments of part of the loaned amounts. Pursuant to its "commitment," Bank loans Smith $5,000 on the first of every month starting on January 1. On August 1, Smith Co.'s equipment is seized by the sheriff as part of a judicial action brought against Smith Machine Co. by an unpaid supplier of raw materials. *All* of Bank's loans for the whole year (even those after August 1) are protected by its superior security interest in the equipment because these future advances were made "pursuant to a commitment entered into without knowledge of the lien." [U.C.C. §9-323(b)(2))]

5. Article 2 Claimants to the Collateral—Buyers and Sellers [§454]

Article 2 of the U.C.C. (the Sales Article) creates rights in sellers and buyers of goods that can cause priority problems when those goods are also subject to Article 9 security interests.

a. Automatic Article 2 security interest [§455]

On the happening of certain events (below), Article 2 of the U.C.C. creates possessory "security interests," or rights very much like security interests, in favor of buyers and sellers of goods.

(1) Interests of buyers [§456]

Under Article 2, a buyer has the right to *reject* defective goods tendered by the seller; or, if a substantial defect is discovered only after "acceptance" of the goods, the buyer may *revoke* acceptance and demand a refund. Upon exercise of either of these rights, the buyer obtains a *possessory* security interest in the goods to secure the return of the price paid for them and other incidental damages. [U.C.C. §§2-602, 2-608, 2-711(3); *and see* Sale & Lease of Goods Summary]

(2) Interests of seller [§457]

Similarly, a seller's Article 2 "security interest" arises upon exercise of the seller's right to order a carrier of goods sold to stop delivery of the goods (a "stoppage in transit"), or the right of an unpaid seller (or someone in the same position, such as a bank assigned the seller's rights) to *resell* goods the buyer will not accept and *sue* the buyer for the difference between the contract price and the resale price (plus incidental damages, such as the cost of the resale). [U.C.C. §2-706]

EXAM TIP   **gilbert**

Notice that to perfect these Article 2 security interests, all that the Article 2 claimant must do is retain *possession* of the goods; no security agreement or filing is required. *Rationale:* The Article 2 security interests arise by operation of law. They are not *consensual*, as are Article 9 security interests, and hence no security *agreement* is possible. Furthermore, no filing is required since (as under Article 9) possession fulfills the function of giving notice to others of the Article 2 claimant's interest.

---

b. Priorities between Article 2 claimants and Article 9 creditors [§458]

The same goods subject to an automatic Article 2 security interest may also be subject to security interests held by Article 9 creditors. Article 9 gives priority to the Article 2 claimant as long as the Article 2 claimant has *possession* of the goods. [U.C.C. §9-110]

Example: Seller's equipment was subject to a perfected security interest in favor of Bank. Without the permission of Bank, Seller sold one of its computers to Buyer on credit. When the computer proved defective, Buyer used section 2-608 of the Code to *revoke its acceptance* of the computer and then used section 2-711(3) to claim a security interest in the computer (*see supra*, §456). As long as Buyer keeps possession of the computer, Buyer has an interest therein that is superior to that of Bank, and this is true even though Bank perfected first. *Note:* If Bank's interest had been in "inventory" collateral, and the computer had been part of Seller's inventory, a sale of the computer to a buyer in the ordinary course of business would have freed the computer from Bank's security interest. [U.C.C. §9-320(a); *see supra*, §420]

Example: Buyer ordered goods from Seller. Even before delivery, Buyer gave a security interest in the goods to Bank, which filed a financing statement in the proper place. Before delivery, Buyer repudiated the sale, and Seller resold the goods pursuant to the procedure specified in U.C.C. section 2-706 (*supra*, §457). Seller's interest in the goods would be senior to that of Bank because the goods never left Seller's possession. By the time Bank filed its financing statement and the goods were "identified" so that Buyer had rights in them (a requisite for "attachment"; *see supra*, §151), Seller's possessory rights under Article 2 already existed.

(1) Special priority rule where buyer insolvent

(a) Seller's interest [§459]

An insolvent buyer who orders goods on ***credit*** commits an act regarded as common law ***fraud***. Therefore, under the U.C.C., if a seller discovers that the buyer is insolvent, the seller has ***10 days*** following delivery of the goods to make a demand for their return. However, if the buyer has sent the seller a written misrepresentation of solvency within the three months before delivery, the 10-day limitation does not apply. [U.C.C. §2-702; *and see* Sale & Lease of Goods Summary]

(b) Article 9 creditor prevails [§460]

However, Article 2 states that the seller's right to reclaim goods from an insolvent buyer is subject to the rights of a "good faith purchaser." Since "purchaser" is defined by the Code to include an Article 9 secured creditor, such a creditor's perfected security interest attaching to goods in the hands of the insolvent buyer is ***superior*** to the rights of an unpaid seller trying to reclaim the goods under section 2-702. [***In re* Samuels & Co.**, 510 F.2d 139 (5th Cir. 1975)]

Example: Bank held a perfected security interest in all of Buyer's Clothing Store's inventory "now owned or after-acquired." Buyer, while insolvent, ordered new inventory from Seller, who failed to take a security interest in the merchandise it shipped to Buyer's Clothing Store. The day the goods arrived, Seller learned of Buyer's insolvency and demanded return of the goods. Because Bank qualifies as a "good faith purchaser," its interest in the goods is superior to the reclaiming seller.

1) "Cash sales" [§461]

Note that the same rule applies even where the buyer pays by check in a transaction that was meant to have ***no credit*** involved (at common law, a "cash sale"). Thus, if the buyer's check bounces, the seller still loses to the buyer's perfected creditors. [*In re* **Samuels & Co.**, *supra;* U.C.C. §2-403(a)]

a) Statutory exception—livestock [§462]
An amendment to the federal Packers & Stockyards Act creates an exception to this rule. If a seller of livestock to a meat packer receives a bad check in return, the *seller prevails* over the packer's creditors if the seller acts quickly after the check is dishonored. [7 U.S.C. §206]

(c) Buyer's bankruptcy [§463]
Under section 546(c) of the Bankruptcy Code, the buyer's trustee in bankruptcy is *subject* to the seller's written demand for return of the goods made within *20* days after their delivery (not just 10, as in U.C.C. section 2-702).

1) Exception [§464]
The Bankruptcy Court may refuse to permit reclamation by the seller if it protects the seller's interest either by giving the seller a priority payment as an administrative expense or by granting the seller a lien in the property.

2) No three-month exception [§465]
The U.C.C. provision on which the bankruptcy rule is based [U.C.C. §2-702] provides that the seller is not limited to the 10-day period if the buyer has made a written misrepresentation of solvency within the three months before delivery. The Bankruptcy Code has no such three-month rule; thus, the seller must always make a written demand within 20 days of delivery to prevail over the buyer's bankruptcy trustee.

Chapter Seven: Bankruptcy Proceedings and Article 9

CONTENTS

Chapter Approach

A.   Debtor's Bankruptcy   §466

B.   After-Acquired Property in Bankruptcy   §507

Chapter Approach

If the debtor suffers financial death and files for bankruptcy, the Bankruptcy Code and Article 9 of the Uniform Commercial Code combine to regulate the division of the debtor's property. The key thing to watch for is whether the creditor *perfected* a security interest. If the creditor has done all that the U.C.C. requires to perfect a security interest in the collateral, the collateral can be reclaimed from the bankruptcy estate and used to satisfy the debt. If, however, the creditor has done something wrong, the trustee in bankruptcy will be able to avoid the security interest, add the property to the bankruptcy estate free and clear of the creditor's interest, and relegate the creditor to the pool of "general" (uncollateralized) creditors, who rarely get paid anything.

Even if you find a valid security interest, it may still be subject to attack as a *fraudulent conveyance*. If there has been fraud as to any existing creditor, the trustee in bankruptcy can set aside the transfer. Similarly, the interest may be attacked as a *preference*. To determine whether there has been a preference, look at *when* the interest was perfected (including the grace period), and whether sufficient *value* was given (remember the special rule as to PMSIs).

A. Debtor's Bankruptcy

1. Introduction [§466]

The acid test of the validity of a security interest is its ability to withstand attack by a trustee in bankruptcy if the debtor goes bankrupt, because a trustee in bankruptcy can assert the rights of almost everyone who can challenge the validity of a security interest. Of course, even if the secured party's interest in the collateral withstands such attack, this is no assurance that the debt will be paid in full. The debtor may have disposed of part of the collateral elsewhere; or, even if the collateral is surrendered intact, its resale may not repay the debt, and a discharge in bankruptcy frees the debtor from further *personal* liability for the deficiency (the amount still owed).

2. Bankruptcy Proceedings [§467]

Bankruptcy is a *federal* procedure for the relief of debtors. It is initiated by the filing of a voluntary or involuntary *petition* in bankruptcy in the local federal district court. Bankruptcy proceedings are tried before a bankruptcy judge. Appeal from the bankruptcy judge's decision is to the federal district court, and from there, through the federal appellate process. In many federal circuits, the appeal from the bankruptcy court skips the district courts and goes directly to a Bankruptcy Appellate Panel ("BAP"), made up of actual bankruptcy judges (who have a greater understanding of how the Bankruptcy Code works than do ordinary federal trial court judges). Appeals from the decision of a BAP are to the appropriate Circuit Court of Appeals.

a. Note—bankruptcy relief limited

The Bankruptcy Code was substantially rewritten in 2005 to make it harder for debtors to discharge unsecured debts (such as those owed on credit cards) and to force those with large unsecured debts (and some ability to pay them) into Chapter 13 proceedings, a form of bankruptcy where the debtor engages to repay a portion of what is owed over a three- to five-year period. Note, however, that the bankruptcy provisions discussed below will also apply to Chapter 13 proceedings.

b. Bankruptcy petition [§468]

Along with the petition, which acts as a request for a discharge from the debts, the debtor files schedules of assets, liabilities, and creditors. The creditors are then notified by the court of the need to file a "proof of claim."

(1) Timing crucial [§469]

The moment of filing of the bankruptcy petition is crucial, because many key bankruptcy issues focus on the status of the parties as of that moment. In addition, control of the debtor's estate passes to the bankruptcy court at the moment of filing the petition.

c. Interim trustee [§470]

If the debtor's property needs care and management until a trustee can qualify (*see* below), an interim trustee will be appointed. The interim trustee takes *temporary* custody of the debtor's property.

d. Trustee [§471]

At the first meeting of the debtor's creditors, the creditors elect a representative called the "trustee." Once the trustee has *qualified, title* to all of the bankrupt's property is vested in the trustee and relates back to the filing of the petition. [Bankruptcy Code §541]

e. Distribution of debtor's assets [§472]

The trustee's first duty is to *marshal* (gather) the debtor's property, *inventory* it, and *investigate* the validity of any claims asserted by the debtor or any third party for release of the property.

(1) Exempt property released [§473]

The trustee is under a duty to release promptly any asset that is exempt from creditor process under section 522 of the Bankruptcy Code (the Code allows the debtor to keep a certain amount of specified property, such as clothes, tools, household goods, etc.).

(2) Property subject to lien or security interest [§474]

Collateral subject to any kind of lien or security interest (whether perfected Article 9 types, real property mortgages, or judicial or statutory liens) that the trustee determines was valid *as of the moment of the filing of the bankruptcy petition* is generally released by the trustee to the lien creditor. Thus, lien creditors get their property *intact*—without any charge or expense of the bankruptcy proceeding being deducted.

(3) Remaining property sold and proceeds distributed [§475]

The debtor's nonexempt property that is free from valid creditor liens or interests is then sold and the proceeds applied as follows:

(a) "Special" (priority) creditors [§476]

The first monies go to any "special" creditors (*i.e.*, those listed in Bankruptcy Code section 507) to cover costs of the bankruptcy proceeding, wages and retirement benefits owing to employees of the bankrupt, alimony, certain creditor expenses, and some tax debts. These are priority debts and must be paid *in full* before any funds are paid to the "general" (unsecured) creditors.

(b) "General" (unsecured) creditors [§477]

Finally, after the priority claims are fully paid, the remaining proceeds are distributed pro rata among the "general" (unsecured) creditors. Often, of course, there is little or nothing left for these creditors.

f. Discharge [§478]

In return for surrendering all nonexempt property, the debtor is usually granted a discharge (a judicial forgiveness) of further personal liability for most debts. [*See* Bankruptcy Code §§523-524]

RIGHTS OF PERFECTED CREDITOR VS. UNPERFECTED CREDITOR UPON DEBTOR'S BANKRUPTCY — gilbert

	PERFECTED CREDITOR	UNPERFECTED CREDITOR
CAN CREDITOR REPOSSESS DEBTOR'S PROPERTY COVERED BY SECURITY INTEREST?	Yes, on getting relief from the automatic stay, *unless* there has been a fraudulent transfer or a preference.	No.
CAN CREDITOR RECOVER MONEY OWED BY DEBTOR (OR DEFICIENCY IF COLLATERAL REPOSSESSED)?	Yes, but creditor must file claim with bankruptcy trustee and typically will receive only small portion of amount owed.	Yes, but creditor must file claim with bankruptcy trustee and typically will receive only small portion of amount owed.

3. Effect of Bankruptcy on Secured Party's Rights—the Automatic Stay [§479]

The above discussion makes it clear why it is important for a creditor to have a secured interest in the debtor's property. Even if the secured interest is fully perfected, however, the debtor's bankruptcy may interfere with the secured party's right to enforce the security interest according to the terms of the contract. The reason is that once a petition in bankruptcy has been filed and the property of the debtor passes into the possession and control of the trustee, a secured creditor *must seek permission* of the court or the trustee to enforce any rights. The filing of the bankruptcy petition creates an *automatic stay* against any creditor collection activity, violation of which leads to contempt of court and damages under Bankruptcy Code section 362.

4. Trustee's Powers [§480]

The trustee in bankruptcy not only succeeds to all of the debtor's rights and interests, but in addition is given various statutory powers under the Bankruptcy Code that enable the trustee to invalidate security interests that would be completely secure outside of bankruptcy.

a. All rights and powers of debtor [§481]

Upon appointment, the trustee is vested by operation of law with the full *title* the debtor had in the property at the time the petition was filed, *including all rights of action* the debtor had. The trustee also has the benefit of all *defenses* available to the debtor as against third persons. [Bankruptcy Code §541]

Example: The trustee in effect "steps into the shoes" of the debtor. If the debtor could have asserted a right to have a security interest set aside—*e.g.*, for violation of the Statute of Frauds—the trustee may also assert its invalidity.

---

b. Power to set aside fraudulent interests [§482]

The trustee can also assert the invalidity of any security interest that is fraudulent as against *any* existing unsecured creditor, or that is otherwise voidable by any creditor under any federal or state law. [Bankruptcy Code §544(b)]

(1) "Creditor" defined [§483]

The "creditor" must be an *actual* unsecured creditor with a claim provable under the Bankruptcy Code; hypothetical creditors are ignored. [*But see* Bankruptcy Code §544(a)—discussed *infra*, §489]

(2) Effect of setting aside [§484]

If a security interest is subject to attack as fraudulent against *any* creditor, then the *entire* security interest is invalid and can be upset by the trustee—thereby benefiting not only the actual creditor as to whom the transaction was fraudulent, but *all creditors*. [**Moore v. Bay**, 284 U.S. 4 (1931)]

(3) "Fraud" defined [§485]

The concept of fraud under the Bankruptcy Code is given form by several provisions of the Code. Generally, "fraud" encompasses all transactions that limit a creditor's remedies in an *unlawful manner*.

(a) Uniform Fraudulent Transfer Act [§486]

The Uniform Fraudulent Transfer Act, in effect in many states, defines some forms of fraud. Bankruptcy Code section 548 is a short form of the Act.

(b) Presumption of fraud [§487]

Transfers of property (including creation of security interests) made within two years of the filing of the bankruptcy petition by an *insolvent* debtor for less than "fair consideration" are *presumed* fraudulent. [Bankruptcy Code §548(a)(2)]

(c) Intent to defraud [§488]

In other cases, the concepts of fraud generally apply only if there is *actual intent* to defraud other creditors of the debtor. [Bankruptcy Code §548(a)(1)]

c. "Strong arm clause" [§489]

The trustee also has whatever powers *could have been exercised* by a creditor with writ of execution returned unsatisfied, or a creditor with a lien on all property of the debtor at the moment the petition for bankruptcy was filed (whether or not such a creditor actually exists), and, for real property (other than fixtures), the trustee also has the rights of a bona fide purchaser of the property. Thus, the trustee is given the powers of real *or hypothetical* creditors. [Bankruptcy Code §544(a)] This provision of the Bankruptcy Code is known as the "strong arm clause."

Example: Big Bank took a security interest in Sue Seller's inventory, but due to malpractice by its attorney, failed to file its financing statement in the appropriate place. Sue filed for bankruptcy, and her trustee in bankruptcy seized and sold the inventory. Under the strong arm clause, the trustee gets whatever rights a levying judicial lien creditor would have, and since such a creditor's levy would cut off unperfected security interests under U.C.C. section 9-317, the trustee has the same ability to take free of Big Bank's security interest.

EXAM TIP   **gilbert**

Note that the strong arm clause gives the trustee an automatic judicial lien on all property of the debtor, so that if a judicial lien creditor **could have had priority** over an Article 9 security interest as of the filing of the bankruptcy petition, the trustee has such priority on behalf of *all* the creditors filing claims. In other words, the trustee will prevail against any claims, liens, or interests that are **not fully perfected** (under applicable state law) **at the time of bankruptcy**. *Note:* Sometimes even a perfected security interest may be defeated by the trustee if "perfection" occurred within the 90-day period preceding the filing of the petition (*see* "preferences," below).

WAS TRANSFER OF DEBTOR'S PROPERTY A VOIDABLE PREFERENCE?

gilbert

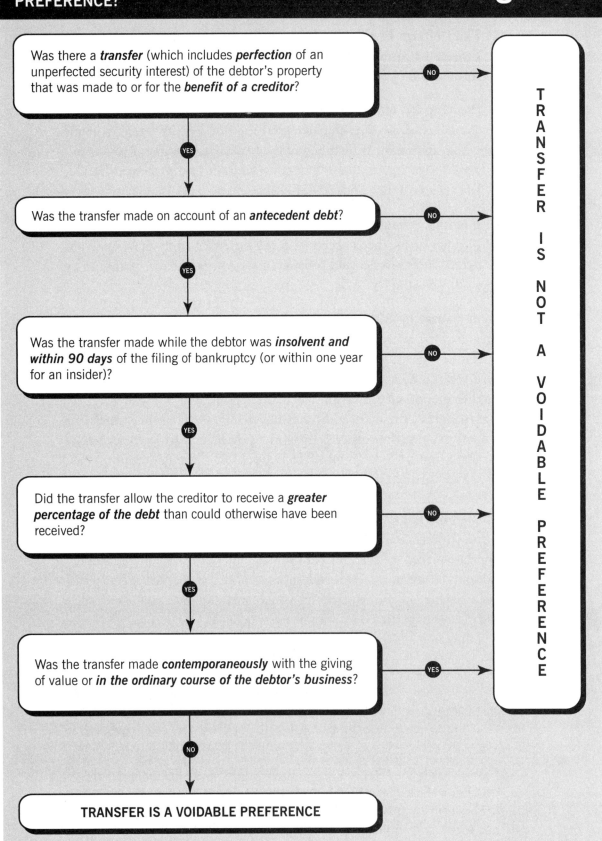

Was there a *transfer* (which includes *perfection* of an unperfected security interest) of the debtor's property that was made to or for the *benefit of a creditor*? → **NO** →

YES ↓

Was the transfer made on account of an *antecedent debt*? → **NO** →

YES ↓

Was the transfer made while the debtor was *insolvent and within 90 days* of the filing of bankruptcy (or within one year for an insider)? → **NO** →

YES ↓

Did the transfer allow the creditor to receive a *greater percentage of the debt* than could otherwise have been received? → **NO** →

YES ↓

Was the transfer made *contemporaneously* with the giving of value or *in the ordinary course of the debtor's business*? → **YES** →

NO ↓

TRANSFER IS A VOIDABLE PREFERENCE

TRANSFER IS NOT A VOIDABLE PREFERENCE

5. Preferences [§490]

A security interest that is neither fraudulent nor attackable by the trustee asserting the powers of real or hypothetical creditors (above) may still be vulnerable if the perfection of the security interest constitutes a preference.

a. What constitutes a "preference" [§491]

A "preference" is:

(i) *A transfer* of any property of the debtor (including the *perfection* of an unperfected security interest),

(ii) *Made to or for the benefit of a creditor,*

(iii) *On account of an antecedent debt,*

(iv) *Made by the debtor while insolvent and within 90 days before the filing* of the bankruptcy petition,

(v) *The effect* of which transfer is to allow the creditor *to obtain a greater percentage of the debt* than the creditor could otherwise have received in the bankruptcy proceeding,

(vi) And, in a consumer case only, the *aggregate value of all affected property is greater than $600.*

[Bankruptcy Code §547(b), (c)(8)]

(1) Result of finding preference [§492]

If a challenged transaction meets *all* of these qualifications, it is *voidable* by the trustee in bankruptcy. This means that the "preferred" creditor must repay the money to the trustee; or, where *perfection* of a security interest is held "preferential," that the security interest is simply invalid and the creditor becomes a "general" (unsecured) creditor.

Example: Lawyer learned that one of her former clients, Spendthrift, was planning to file a bankruptcy petition. Before filing, Spendthrift paid Lawyer $700 that he owed Lawyer for past services rendered. If Spendthrift then filed a petition within the next 90 days, Lawyer would have to give back the $700 to Spendthrift's trustee and file a proof of claim for $700 as a general creditor.

Example: If Spendthrift had long ago given Lawyer a security interest in his business equipment, but Lawyer had failed to take steps to perfect the interest until the 90-day period before bankruptcy, perfection within that period would be a preferential transfer of property and therefore void. Lawyer would then be an unperfected creditor whose interest is wiped out by the trustee's status as a judicial lien creditor under Bankruptcy Code section 544(a) (*supra,* §489).

EXAM TIP	gilbert

Remember that your analysis of the rights of a bankruptcy trustee against a secured party *does not end* once you find that the creditor had a perfected security interest at the time the debtor's bankruptcy petition was filed (thus giving the creditor superior rights over the bankruptcy trustee). You must *then* determine whether the creditor acted *fraudulently* or was given a *preference*, because the bankruptcy trustee has the power to make such security interests *invalid*.

(2) Nonpreferential payments [§493]

Payments for *value* and payments made to a *fully secured creditor* (*i.e.*, with collateral worth as much or more than the debt owed) are *not* voidable as "preferences" even if made on the eve of bankruptcy.

Example: Spendthrift bought $80 worth of groceries the day before filing his petition. This payment is *not* preferential because it is not on account of an "antecedent" (old) debt. Rather, it was a *contemporaneous* exchange (*infra*, §498).

Example: Bank held a *perfected* security interest in Spendthrift's car. The amount Spendthrift owed was $1,500, and the car is now worth $3,000. On the day before Spendthrift filed his petition, he paid Bank $200 on the loan. This payment is *not* preferential because it does not diminish Spendthrift's estate. As Spendthrift pays off the debt, the bank's security interest goes down accordingly, and thus more of the car's value is available to the other general creditors.

(3) Insolvency required [§494]

A transfer is preferential only if it was made while the debtor was insolvent. [Bankruptcy Code §547(b)(3)]

(a) Presumption of insolvency [§495]

The trustee must *demonstrate* that the debtor was insolvent at the time of the transfer, but this task is made easier by the Code's *presumption* that the debtor was insolvent during the 90 days preceding the filing of the petition. [Bankruptcy Code §547(f)]

(b) "Insolvency" defined [§496]

The term "insolvency" in a bankruptcy sense means *more debts than assets*. [Bankruptcy Code §101(26)]

(4) Certain preferences excused [§497]

Even if a transfer qualifies as a preference, the trustee may not avoid it if it falls into one of the following categories:

(a) Substantially contemporaneous exchange [§498]

If the parties *intended* a contemporaneous exchange or the transfer was in fact substantially contemporaneous, no preference occurs. [Bankruptcy Code §547(c)(1)]

Example: Bank loaned debtor money and *two hours* later, the debtor signed the security agreement giving the bank a security interest in the debtor's inventory. There is no preference.

(b) Routine payments [§499]

Payments made in the ordinary course of the debtor's business or financial affairs (if made according to ordinary business terms) are not preferential. [Bankruptcy Code §547(c)(2)] This would exempt routine payments made to all *secured or unsecured creditors*.

Example: The day before she went bankrupt, debtor paid her monthly phone bill. This is not a preference.

(5) Special rules for transfers to an "insider" [§500]

Where the preferred creditor was an "insider" who received a preferential transfer in the period between *90 days and one year before the filing* of the petition, the trustee can recover the property transferred *if* the insider had reasonable cause to believe the debtor was insolvent at the time of transfer. [Bankruptcy Code §547(b)(4)(B)]

Example: On January 10, Debtor, who owed $5,000 to Granny, his grandmother, gave her a security interest in his car (worth $2,500). On May 10, he gave her another security interest in his boat (worth $2,500). He was insolvent on both occasions and filed his bankruptcy petition on June 1. His trustee can avoid the May 10 transfer as a preference regardless of Granny's knowledge of Debtor's financial condition, but to avoid the January 10 transfer, the trustee will have to establish that Granny had at that time reasonable cause to believe her grandson was insolvent.

(a) "Insider" defined [§501]

An "insider" is someone having a *close connection with the debtor*, such as a spouse, a relative, a partner, a corporate director, or anyone in control of the debtor. [Bankruptcy Code §101(25)]

b. When "transfer" complete [§502]

In determining whether a voidable preference has been created, the first thing to focus on is the time of "transfer." For personal property, transfer is complete *when a general creditor of the debtor could no longer have secured a superior lien* to the property by suing the debtor on the debt and levying an attachment on the collateral. For real property, the test is whether a *bona fide purchaser of the property could have obtained rights superior* to those of the secured party. [Bankruptcy Code §547(e)(1)]

(1) Hypothetical creditor or purchaser [§503]

Again, there is no requirement that such a general creditor or bona fide purchaser actually exists—only that a hypothetical one *could* have achieved a higher priority within 90 days of bankruptcy.

(a) Note

The lien of the hypothetical general creditor must be a judicial lien that could be obtained in *the course of proceedings on a simple contract*. It does *not* include statutory liens given preference over earlier security interests; *e.g.*, a mechanic's lien does not qualify.

(2) Grace periods for transfers of security interests

(a) Purchase money security interests [§504]

Where a purchase money secured creditor (*see supra*, §184) perfects within 30 days after the debtor receives possession of the property, no preference occurs even if the creditor gave value prior to the debtor's possession (so that the attachment of the security interest now protects an antecedent debt). [Bankruptcy Code §547(c)(3)]

---

e.g. **Example:** On November 1, Bank loaned Debtor $5,000 to buy a boat, making Debtor sign a security agreement. On December 15, Debtor bought the boat, and Bank filed a proper financing statement on December 20. Even though the *transfer* takes place on December 15 (when attachment occurred because Debtor then acquired rights in the collateral) and, measured at that moment, it secures a loan made *prior in time* (and hence is a preference), because this is a purchase money transaction, no preference occurs.

---

1) Preference excused [§505]

Note that in the last example the transfer *is* a "preference" under the usual test. Even the "relation back" to December 15 does not help, since measured as of that date, the transfer is on account of a debt incurred on December 1. The Bankruptcy Code arbitrarily *excuses* this transaction from classification as a "preference" in order to give increased protection to purchase money creditors.

(b) Other thirty-day grace periods [§506]

The Bankruptcy Code gives *all* creditors a 30-day grace period—running from the time the transfer takes effect between the parties—in which to perfect. If perfection is had in that period, the transfer then is judged as of the moment it became effective between the parties (typically the moment of attachment). [Bankruptcy Code §547(e)(2), (3)] Notice that this rule would not help in the last example (*supra*,

§504) had the security interest there not been of the purchase money variety, for the reason stated *supra,* §505.

B. After-Acquired Property in Bankruptcy

1. Introduction [§507]

The major problem encountered in handling security interests in bankruptcy proceedings occurs when the security interest involves **after-acquired collateral** or a **floating lien** on the inventory or accounts receivable of the debtor. The issue arises if inventory or accounts receivable first come into existence and become covered by the perfected security interest within the 90-day period prior to bankruptcy, so that the attachment of the security interest to them is arguably "preferential."

2. No Preference [§508]

Under section 547(c)(5) of the Bankruptcy Code, accounts receivable or inventory falling under a perfected creditor's floating lien are **not** preferential even though first acquired in the 90 days (or one year for insiders) prior to the petition.

Example: Big Bank took a security interest in Retailer's inventory "now owned or after acquired" in return for a loan made on January 3; a proper financing statement was filed on that date reflecting the bank's floating lien on the inventory. On September 8, Retailer purchased new inventory, and since Retailer would not have "rights in the collateral" until then (*see supra,* §147), the bank's security interest could not attach until that time. On September 10, Retailer filed a petition in bankruptcy. Because of the section 547(c)(5) exemption, the September 8 "transfer" of an interest in Retailer's property to the bank is **not** a "preference."

a. Exception—"build-up" prohibited [§509]

If in the 90-day period (one year for transfers to insiders), the secured party has the debtor acquire **more** inventory or accounts receivable than were present at the start of the period (or the bank's first loan if within the period), a preference occurs to the extent of the build-up if unsecured creditors are hurt thereby. [Bankruptcy Code §547(c)(5)]

Example: Bank had a perfected security interest in Debtor's inventory. On January 10, the inventory was worth $20,000. On April 10, when Debtor filed a bankruptcy petition, the inventory was worth $25,000. Bank has received a $5,000 preference. If the bank had loaned the debtor money for the first time on February 10, when the inventory was worth $25,000, no preference would have occurred.

Chapter Eight:
Default Proceedings

CONTENTS

Chapter Approach

A.	Introduction	§510
B.	Occurrence of Default	§512
C.	Remedies—In General	§527
D.	Right of Possession upon Default	§531
E.	Realizing on the Collateral	§550
F.	Debtor's Right of Redemption	§603
G.	Effect of Failure to Comply with Default Provisions	§607
H.	Nonwaivable Rights Under the Security Agreement	§615
I.	Special Default Rules for Intangibles and Fixtures	§623

Chapter Approach

If the debtor cannot pay the debt, the creditor must look to the collateral for at least some satisfaction. Debtors, understandably, are reluctant to surrender their property, and heated battles can ensue when the creditor attempts repossession.

This chapter looks at the rights and duties of the parties when repossession threatens. Analyze a question in this area by asking:

1. Has a *default* occurred?

2. What remedies are provided by the *security agreement*?

3. What remedies are provided by the *U.C.C.*?

   (i) The creditor may *sell* the collateral; if so, discuss the notice requirements, the right of the secured party to bid, the debtor's right to an accounting and to the proceeds after disbursement, and whether the debtor is liable for any deficiency.

   (ii) The creditor may *retain* the collateral in *full or partial satisfaction* of the debt, but remember the notice requirements and the limitations as to consumer goods.

   (iii) The creditor may ignore the collateral *and sue on the debt.*

   Watch for any *breach of the peace* by the creditor in taking the property. If there has been such a breach, the creditor loses U.C.C. authorization and is in effect stealing the goods.

4. Has the debtor *redeemed* the collateral?

5. What is the effect of the secured party's *failure to comply* with the U.C.C. provisions on disposing of collateral?

A. Introduction

1. Default [§510]

Regardless of how careful a secured party is in choosing credit risks, there are bound to be cases in which the debtor is unable to meet the obligation set under the security agreement and thereby defaults. Article 9 does not purport to establish what *conditions* constitute a default; rather, this is to be determined by the provisions of the *security agreement*. The Code does, however, specify certain *remedies* for the creditor, although the parties are free to provide other remedies if they choose. [U.C.C. §9-601]

2. Consumers and Article 9 [§511]

Consumer advocates worried that Article 9 would reduce consumer protection and therefore decided that they were happier leaving most consumer issues to resolution of law outside of Article 9 (*see, e.g., supra,* §196). Thus many of the Code's provisions expressly state that they are not applicable to consumer transactions, allowing non-Code law to fill in the gaps. Article 9's default rules do contain some very definite rules protecting the consumer as debtor, but at key moments they defer to common law or other statutes (*see, e.g., infra,* §578).

B. Occurrence of Default

1. In General [§512]

As noted above, the conditions or events that constitute a default are left to the parties' security agreement. Within limits, the parties are free to establish any conditions that they like. The following clauses, frequently included in such agreements, merit special attention.

2. Acceleration Clauses [§513]

An acceleration clause gives the secured party the option of declaring the *entire unpaid balance* of the obligation *immediately due* upon the occurrence of some default. The Code specifically authorizes such clauses [U.C.C. §1-208], but limits the secured party's right to accelerate to cases "in which he in *good faith* believes that the *prospect of payment or performance* is impaired." Thus, the secured party is prevented from accelerating for trivial or inconsequential defaults. In any event, however, the burden is on the *debtor* to show that the secured party was not acting in good faith. [U.C.C. §1-208; **Brown v. Avemco Investment Corp.**, 603 F.2d 1367 (9th Cir. 1979)]

3. Insecurity Clauses [§514]

Security agreements often accord the secured party the right to *declare the entire obligation due "at will"* or in the event the *secured party "deems himself insecure."* Even so, the standards of *good faith* applicable generally to acceleration apply here as well; *i.e.,* the secured party can accelerate or demand more collateral only if that party in good faith believes the prospects for payment have become impaired. [U.C.C. §§1-208, 1-203]

a. Meaning of "good faith" [§515]

Courts are split as to the standard for deciding whether the creditor exercised "good faith" in accelerating the debt or in "deeming himself insecure."

(1) Subjective test [§516]

Since "good faith" is defined in section 1-201(19) of the Code as meaning *"honesty in fact,"* some courts have adopted a purely *subjective* test. Under this approach, the creditor who *in fact* feels "insecure" may accelerate the debt even though no reasonable person in the creditor's position would feel insecure, and even though the creditor is proceeding on the basis of erroneous information that he has made no attempt to verify. [**Van Horn v. Van De Wol, Inc.,** 497 P.2d 252 (Wash. 1972)—creditor who negligently relied on false rumor that debtor had been denied bank loan allowed to accelerate]

(2) Objective test [§517]

Other courts, following the common law maxim that the "law abhors a forfeiture," do not allow repossession unless the creditor has made a diligent and honest *effort to check* the grounds of insecurity, *and* a reasonable person in the same circumstances would repossess (an "objective" standard). [**Black v. Peoples Bank,** 437 So. 2d 26 (Miss. 1983)]

4. Waiver of Defenses Against Assignees [§518]

To facilitate financing and negotiability, security agreements frequently contain provisions by which the borrower or buyer agrees to "waive," as against any assignee of the seller or lender, whatever defenses the borrower might have if the seller or lender sued directly. This is to assure that the assignee will be able to invoke default remedies if the debtor fails to make the payments due. Otherwise, the debtor could claim there was no default because the debtor's claims against the seller offset any payments due, and the assignee would have "bought a lawsuit" instead of an enforceable security agreement.

a. Validity of waiver [§519]

Except as to consumer goods (*see* below), the Code provides that such waivers are *valid* if the assignee purchased the agreement in *good faith* and *without notice of any defenses* that the buyer or borrower might have against the assignor-seller. [U.C.C. §9-403]

(1) "Good faith" [§520]

"Good faith" is construed narrowly so as to disqualify assignees who are in *collusion* with the assignor. The closer the business dealings between the assignor (*e.g.*, seller) and assignee (*e.g.*, finance company), the more likely the assignee will be denied the "good faith purchaser" status. [**Unico v. Owen,** 232 A.2d 405 (N.J. 1967)]

(2) "Real defenses" not affected [§521]

And note that even an otherwise valid "waiver" of defenses does not cut off so-called real defenses—defenses that could be raised against a holder in due course of a negotiable instrument (*e.g.*, forgery or unauthorized signatures, fraud as to nature of instrument). [U.C.C. §§9-403(c), 3-305; *and see* Commercial Paper & Payment Law Summary]

b. Consumer goods limitation [§522]

The validity of waiver of defenses against assignee provisions in the sale or lease of *consumer goods* must be determined by *other* statutes or decisional laws. [U.C.C. §9-403(e)]

(1) Some states uphold [§523]

Some states uphold such waivers in favor of "good faith" assignees (*see* above) *provided* the assignee has first *notified* the debtor of the assignment and given the debtor a stated period of time (*e.g.*, 10 days) within which to advise the assignee of any defenses to the assigned account.

(2) Most states prohibit [§524]

Most states prohibit such waivers altogether in the sale or lease of consumer goods. [*See, e.g.,* Cal. Civ. Code §1804.2—providing that buyer can assert defenses against the seller's assignee "notwithstanding any agreement to the contrary"]

(a) Note

The above California statute has been read very broadly so as to permit the buyer not only to defend any action by the assignee, but also *to sue the assignee affirmatively* (for rescission and restitution of the purchase price), at least where the assignee had knowledge of the seller's fraudulent practices. [**Vasques v. Superior Court**, 4 Cal. 3d 800 (1971)]

(3) Federal statutes [§525]

Moreover, agreements with "waiver of defenses" clauses and the use of a negotiable note to cut off the borrower's defenses are now ineffective under a Federal Trade Commission ("FTC") regulation: Contracts signed by consumers in credit sales or in loans closely connected to those sales *must* contain a statement preserving the ability of the consumer to raise defenses against a later assignee of the contract. [16 C.F.R. 433 (1976); *and see* Commercial Paper & Payment Law Summary] Even if the required FTC statement is omitted from the agreement, U.C.C. section 9-403(d) *automatically adds it,* thus allowing consumers to raise all defenses against remote assignees of the contracts they sign.

5. Time Is of the Essence Clauses [§526]

The security agreement frequently states that the debtor must pay the debt on the days stated in the agreement and that *"time is of the essence"* in making such payments, which means that failure to make any payment on time is so serious that the secured party may declare a *default* and repossess the collateral. Since this is a *condition* as that term is used in Contracts law (*see* Contracts Summary), it can be *waived* by the creditor's conduct in routinely accepting late payments. To combat this possibility, the security agreement often will contain a warning (called an *"anti-waiver" clause*) that specifically states that the acceptance of late payments will *not* result in a waiver of the right to declare a default and repossess without warning. While some courts enforce anti-waiver clauses, most courts hold that a course of performance [*see* U.C.C. §2-208] of accepting late payments *waives the anti-waiver clause*, which can only thereafter be reinstated by a warning that the waiver has ceased and payments now must be made on time. [**Moe v. John Deere,** 516 N.W.2d 332 (S.D. 1994); U.C.C. §2-209(5)] *Rationale*: This protects the *reliance interest* the debtor develops in the ability to make late payments without default occurring, regardless of what the fine print in the contract says about the issue.

C. Remedies—In General

1. Cumulative Remedies [§527]

The Code eliminates common law doctrine that required a secured party to make an *election of remedies* between repossession of the goods and an action on the obligation in default. In contrast, the U.C.C. declares that the secured party's rights and remedies are *cumulative*. [U.C.C. §9-601(c)]

2. Three Basic Remedies [§528]

The three remedies set out in the Code, each of which will be discussed in detail *infra* (§§550 *et seq.*) are:

(i)   *Retention* of the collateral [U.C.C. §§9-620 - 9-622];

(ii) *Sale or other disposition* of the collateral [U.C.C. §9-610]; and

(iii) *An action for the debt* [U.C.C. §9-601(a)].

The Code does not allow the secured party to make a profit at the expense of the debtor by compounding remedies, but the pursuit of one remedy does *not* bar pursuit of a subsequent remedy until the secured party is made whole. [**Olsen v. Valley National Bank,** 234 N.E.2d 547 (Ill. 1968)]

EXAM TIP   **gilbert**

Remember that the creditor's remedies above are *cumulative*. Therefore, if a creditor repossesses and sells the debtor's collateral for less than the amount the debtor owes (*e.g.,* if the debtor's car sold for $8,000, but the debtor owed the creditor $12,000), the creditor *also may sue* the debtor for the amount still owed after the sale (*i.e.,* the "deficiency"). However, as stated above, the creditor *cannot recover more than what is owed him* (*e.g.,* if the debtor's car sold for $8,000 and the debtor owed the creditor $8,000, the creditor could not both receive the $8,000 sale proceeds and recover $8,000 in an action for the debt).

---

3. Documents as Collateral [§529]

In the event that the collateral consists of documents of title (*e.g.,* a warehouse receipt or a bill of lading), the secured party may proceed against either the documents or the underlying goods. [U.C.C. §9-601(a)(2)]

4. Collateral Involving Real Property Interests [§530]

When a security interest applies to collateral that involves both real and personal property—*e.g.,* a security interest in a factory (real property) and its inventory (personal property)—the secured party may proceed against the entire collateral under the procedures governing real property, in which case, the Code does not apply. Alternatively, the secured party may exercise Code remedies with respect to that portion of the collateral that consists of personal property. [U.C.C. §9-604]

D. Right of Possession upon Default

1. In General [§531]

The Code grants the secured party the right to take possession of the collateral upon default, provided that the parties have not agreed otherwise. [U.C.C. §9-609] Repossession of the collateral sets the stage for other remedies, such as sale of the collateral to satisfy the debtor's obligation or extinguishing further rights through continued possession. The provisions for taking possession—often referred to as "self-help measures"—present several innovations.

2. Is Judicial Process Necessary?

a. No breach of peace [§532]

The Code stipulates that as long as possession of the collateral can be obtained *without a breach of the peace*, the secured party may proceed to *seize* it without judicial process (*i.e.,* this is *"self-help" repossession*). Otherwise, legal proceedings are required. [U.C.C. §9-609(b)]

(1) Rationale—lower costs with self-help measures [§533]

Forcing the secured party to go to court in every case merely runs up costs, which in turn will be passed on to the debtor. Also, there is no real justification for legal proceedings if the debtor will voluntarily relinquish the collateral or allow the secured party to reclaim it peacefully. Presumably, the fear of a tort action will keep the secured party from taking the collateral by force.

(2) What constitutes "breach of the peace"

(a) Violence or disturbance not required [§534]

A repossession made over *any protest* by the debtor or anyone present constitutes a "breach of the peace," even though no violence or significant disturbance occurs. [**Morris v. First National Bank**, 254

N.E.2d 683 (Ohio 1970)—repossession of lawn mower from front yard over protest of debtor's son held to be breach of peace and trespass]

1) Subsequent attempts not prohibited [§535]

However, where an attempted repossession is halted upon protest by the debtor, nothing in the Code forbids the creditor from making second, third, or more attempts at repossession. [**Ford Motor Credit Co. v. Cole,** 503 S.W.2d 853 (Tex. 1974)]

(b) Constructive force [§536]

A "peaceful" repossession by a creditor with a *weapon* (*i.e.,* the weapon is not used or even unholstered) constitutes a "breach of the peace," as does a phony show of legal authority (*e.g.,* dressing up as a sheriff). Such actions contain *implied threats* ("constructive force") and hence are not considered "peaceful" repossessions. [**Stone Machinery Co. v. Kessler,** 463 P.2d 651 (Wash. 1970)—repossession improper if creditor accompanied by off-duty sheriff wearing uniform]

(c) Breaking and entering [§537]

Many, but not all, courts hold that breaking and entering the debtor's property is a breach of the peace (and a trespass) even if the security agreement authorizes the same. *Rationale:* Debtors cannot contract away the rights of their families and neighbors to the quiet enjoyment of their surroundings. [*See* **Davenport v. Chrysler Credit Corp.,** 818 S.W.2d 23 (Tenn. 1991)]

1) Distinguish—simple trespass [§538]

However, if the creditor comes onto the property but does not have to "break and enter," most courts hold that the mere technical trespass is *not* a "breach of the peace." [*See* **Raffa v. Dania Bank,** 321 So. 2d 83 (Fla. 1975)]

(d) Trickery allowed [§539]

Repossessing under false pretenses (*e.g.,* creditor calls debtor to "bring your car in because it's been recalled and we want to fix it up") is perhaps unfair, but the courts have usually held such repossessions valid. [**Cox v. Galigher,** 213 S.E.2d 475 (W. Va. 1975); *but see* **Ford Motor Credit Co. v. Byrd,** 351 So. 2d 557 (Ala. 1977)]

EXAM TIP   **gilbert**

Because the Code does not define "breach of the peace," court decisions offer the only guidance for determining whether a breach of the peace has occurred. Thus, on an exam you must make a *fact-based determination* of whether there has been a breach of the peace, using the above cases as guidelines.

(3) Effect of breach of peace [§540]

If the repossessing creditor does breach the peace, the creditor loses the authorization of section 9-609 to repossess without the aid of the courts. Such a creditor is, in effect, *stealing* the debtor's property and is no longer authorized by law to repossess. The debtor may *sue for conversion* and recover actual (and frequently punitive) damages. [*See* 35 A.L.R.3d 1016]

b. Requirement of notice [§541]

Absent a provision in the security agreement to the contrary, the creditor is *not* required to give the debtor *notice* of a planned repossession. *Rationale:* A debtor given notice might hide the collateral.

(1) Exception—provision requiring notice [§542]

However, if the language of the security agreement *expressly or impliedly* requires the secured party to give a pre-repossession notice, a creditor who seizes the property without first complying is subject to an action for *conversion* and possibly punitive damages. [**Klingbiel v. Commercial Credit Corp.**, 439 F.2d 1303 (10th Cir. 1971)—security agreement providing for repossession only "on demand" held to require notice]

(2) Distinguish—post-repossession notice of resale [§543]

After repossession, the creditor may wish to resell the collateral and sue the debtor for the amount still due (the "deficiency"). In this situation, the U.C.C. *does require notice* of the time and place of resale. [U.C.C. §9-611; *see infra*, §563]

c. Unconscionability [§544]

Debtors may attack the provisions of the security agreement authorizing repossessions on grounds of *"unconscionability"*—at least where they involve an unreasonable forfeiture of the debtor's equity. [**Fontane v. Industrial National Bank**, 298 A.2d 521 (R.I. 1973)—where creditor repeatedly accepted debtor's late payments, repossession was not allowed without prior notice; **Guzman v. Western State Bank**, 540 F.2d 948 (8th Cir. 1976)—punitive damages awarded debtors under Federal Civil Rights Act for repossession of mobile home by creditor using obviously unconstitutional state procedures]

3. Right of Assemblage [§545]

The security agreement may require the debtor, upon default, to assemble the collateral at a specified place, reasonably convenient to both parties. Such provisions indicate the parties' intent that the secured party be afforded access thereto in event of default, and are specifically enforceable. [U.C.C. §9-609(c); **Clark Equipment Co. v. Armstrong Equipment Co.**, 431 F.2d 54 (5th Cir. 1970)—mandatory injunction requiring debtor to assemble and turn over collateral]

4. Disabling Equipment [§546]

When the collateral consists of equipment, the secured party may render the equipment unusable (*e.g.*, by removing a necessary part) on the debtor's premises and then may dispose of the collateral (*e.g.*, sell it) on the same premises. [U.C.C. §9-609(a)(2)]

a. Limitation—reasonableness [§547]

In exercising this right, however, the secured party is still bound by the standard of *commercial reasonableness* (*see infra*, §560). In addition, although section 9-603 allows the parties to set standards measuring the fulfillment of the rights and duties of the parties, the standards *cannot be "manifestly unreasonable."* Parties also may not contract away the requirement that a creditor not commit a *breach of the peace* when repossessing (*see supra*, §532).

5. Duties of Secured Party in Possession [§548]

After taking possession, the secured party assumes the same duties as a party who perfects by possession; *i.e.*, the possessor must take *reasonable care* of the collateral, maintain it, insure its upkeep, etc. [U.C.C. §9-207; *see supra*, §§169-180]

a. Duty to return personal items repossessed with collateral [§549]

If, in repossessing the collateral, the creditor comes into possession of other personal property (*e.g.*, golf clubs in the trunk of a repossessed car), the debtor may be able to sue for conversion. To avoid this problem, most security agreements contain clauses authorizing the secured party to repossess "the collateral and all property contained therein, the property not covered by the security interest to be returned promptly." Recall that U.C.C. section 9-603 generally allows the parties to set their own standards, as long as they are not manifestly unreasonable (*see supra*, §547).

(1) Note

If the creditor follows this procedure and behaves fairly, most courts refuse to find the creditor liable for conversion. [**Jones v. General Motors Acceptance Corp.**, 565 P.2d 9 (Okla. 1977)] However, other courts disagree. [**Ford Motor Credit Co. v. Cole**, *supra*, §535—clause void as against public policy and creditor liable for conversion of debtor's other property]

E. Realizing on the Collateral

1. Strict Foreclosure [§550]

In lieu of other remedies, the creditor who repossesses goods may elect to *keep* them and forget the rest of the debt. This procedure, commonly called *strict foreclosure* (though the Code never uses this phrase), is authorized by section 9-620 of the Code. For obvious reasons, it is used only if the collateral is appreciating in value (*e.g.*, a famous painting) or if the cost of further action is prohibitive.

a. Exception for consumer goods [§551]

If the repossessed collateral constitutes consumer goods, and the debtor has already *repaid at least 60%* of the cash price or loaned amount, the creditor *must* resell the collateral within 90 days of repossession (or within a longer period agreed to by the debtor) and turn over any excess to the consumer. Otherwise, the creditor will be liable to the consumer either for *conversion* or, at the consumer's option, *actual damages plus punitive damages* in the amount of either: (i) the finance charge plus 10% of the loan amount; or (ii) the time-price differential plus 10% of the cash price. [U.C.C. §§9-620(e), 9-625(c)]

(1) Rationale—to ensure debtor reimbursement [§552]

In this case, the consumer has substantial equity in the collateral, and the value of the collateral may often exceed the balance on the debt. Hence, the Code ensures payment of the surplus to the debtor without requiring the debtor to take any further action.

(2) Waiver after default [§553]

If, however, it is to the debtor's advantage that the secured party keep the collateral in satisfaction of the debt, section 9-624 allows the debtor to *waive* the right to sale—but only *after* default has occurred. A waiver contained in the security agreement would therefore have no effect. [**Kruse, Kruse & Miklosko, Inc. v. Beedy,** 353 N.E.2d 514 (Ind. 1976)]

b. General notice requirement [§554]

If consumer goods are *not* involved (or where the consumer has not paid 60% of the original amount), the creditor electing strict foreclosure must *send an authenticated notice* to the debtor of the creditor's intention to keep the collateral in satisfaction of the debt. The creditor must also send such a notice to other creditors having an interest in the collateral if those creditors themselves have previously sent an authenticated notice to the repossessing creditor of their interests or filed a financing statement. [U.C.C. §9-621]

(1) Duty fulfilled when notice sent [§555]

Note that the secured party's duty is fulfilled when the notice is *sent.* The risk of nondelivery of the mails is on the debtor or other secured party. [U.C.C. §1-201(38)]

(2) Waiver of notice requirement forbidden [§556]

Note also that the debtor may *not* waive this notice requirement. [U.C.C. §9-602(10)]

c. Effect of objection [§557]

If, within *20 days* after the notice is sent, any person entitled to notice (above) *objects* to the secured party's proposal to retain the goods in satisfaction of the debt, the secured party *must* dispose of the collateral by sale. [U.C.C. §9-620]

d. Strict foreclosure in partial satisfaction of the debt [§558]

Article 9 makes it clear that the secured party may propose that the debtor surrender the collateral in *partial satisfaction* of the debt, with the rest of the debt *still owing*. A partial strict foreclosure occurs if: (i) the secured party gives the same authenticated notice to the debtor and other secured parties as that required for a full strict foreclosure (*see supra,* §554), (ii) the debtor *consents* in an authenticated record, and (iii) no other perfected secured parties object within 20 days after the authenticated notice was sent. [U.C.C. §9-620] Worried that consumer debtors would too easily agree to such a partial strict foreclosure, the drafters provided that *it is not allowed if the collateral is consumer goods*. [U.C.C. §9-620(g)]

Example: Business Corporation bought a computer on credit from Computer Sales, Inc., but had trouble paying for it after it was delivered. When Business Corporation still owed Computer Sales, Inc. $10,000 on the debt, Computer Sales, Inc. repossessed the computer and then sent Business Corporation an authenticated notice stating that an appraisal evaluated the current value of the used computer as only $2,000, and proposing that the debtor agree that Computer Sales, Inc.'s retention of the computer would reduce the debt owed only by that amount. If Business Corporation agrees to this in authenticated record and no other secured parties having an interest in the collateral object within 20 days of authenticated notice of this being sent to them, the partial strict foreclosure has occurred. Thus Computer Sales, Inc. can keep the collateral without the necessity of the foreclosure sale, and it can still sue Business Corporation for the $8,000 deficiency.

Example: When Consumer bought a car on credit from Fast Eddie's Auto but failed to make payments, Fast Eddie's repossessed the car. While Fast Eddie's may propose to accept the car as *full payment* for the outstanding amount due (a strict foreclosure) as long as Consumer has not yet paid 60% of the original debt (*see supra,* §551), because the car is consumer goods Fast Eddie's may *not* propose to accept it as only a partial reduction of the amount due.

EXAM TIP — **gilbert**

Remember the key difference between partial and full strict foreclosure: If *partial* strict foreclosure is used, a creditor may *sue* the debtor for the amount owed beyond the agreed value of the collateral; if *full* strict foreclosure is used, the debt is *completely discharged*, and the creditor cannot thereafter sue for a deficiency, even if the market value of the collateral is much lower than the debt.

2. **Disposition of the Collateral by Sale [§559]**

The U.C.C. provides a great deal of flexibility in the rules governing disposition of collateral by sale. First, under section 9-610, the secured party is not restricted to sale, but is permitted to "*sell, lease, license, or otherwise dispose* of the collateral." Even so, disposition by sale is by far the most common method of realizing on the collateral—particularly because the Code permits either *public or private* sale, and because after sale, the secured party may pursue the debtor for any amount remaining unpaid (the "deficiency").

a. Commercial reasonableness standard [§560]

The only real limitations on the power to sell are that the secured party must act in *good faith* and in a *commercially reasonable manner*. Every aspect of the disposition, including the method, manner, time, place, and terms of sale must be *completely reasonable*. [U.C.C. §9-610(b)] *Note:* In any ensuing *litigation*, the secured party has the *burden* of proving that the sale was commercially reasonable. [U.C.C. §9-626(a)(2)]

(1) Time within which sale must occur [§561]

No specific time is set within which the secured party must make a disposition of the collateral. The U.C.C. merely requires that the collateral be sold within a "commercially reasonable" time after repossession.

(a) Note

A repossessing creditor will not be subject to damages or waive its right to any remedy by retaining possession of the collateral long enough to explore all available avenues for collection of the debt. It need *not* proceed immediately to sell the collateral.

(b) Distinguish

On the other hand, a prolonged interval between the repossession and sale raises at least an inference of commercial *unreasonableness* so that the burden of proof is on the secured party to establish a valid reason for the delay. [**Farmers State Bank v. Otten,** 204 N.W.2d 178 (S.D. 1973)—13-month delay]

(c) And note

In the past, some courts held that an unreasonable delay in reselling the repossessed collateral resulted in the loss of the option to do so—in effect a forced "strict foreclosure." [**Moran v. Holman,** 514 P.2d 817 (Alaska 1973)—creditor's use of repossessed truck for personal business for four months held to be an election of strict foreclosure] However, Article 9 specifically provides that strict foreclosure must be *elected* by the creditor, and therefore it cannot be forced on the creditor by simple inaction. [U.C.C. §9-620(b) and Comment 5]

(2) Preparation for sale [§562]

Although the Code makes no reference to a duty on the part of the secured creditor to *advertise or solicit purchasers* for the sale, failure to do so evidences a *lack* of "commercial reasonableness." [**Dynalectron Corp. v. Jack Richards Aircraft Co.,** 337 F. Supp. 659 (W.D. Okla. 1972)] In addition, although section 9-610 allows resale of the collateral "in its present condition," courts have required creditors to take reasonable steps to make the collateral presentable. [**Weiss v. Northwest Acceptance,** 546

P.2d 1065 (Or. 1976)—repossessed logging equipment must have mud washed off prior to sale]

b. Notice requirement [§563]

Authenticated notice of the sale of the collateral must be given to the debtor and certain other persons (below), except where the collateral is *perishable* (*i.e.,* likely to decline speedily in value) or is of a type sold in a *recognized market* (*e.g.,* stocks and bonds). [U.C.C. §9-611(d)]

(1) Contents of notice [§564]

Under U.C.C. section 9-613, the authenticated notice is sufficient if it contains the following information:

(i) A *description of the debtor and the secured party;*

(ii) A *description of the collateral;*

(iii) The *method of sale* (*i.e.,* public or private);

(iv) The *time and place of a public sale* or the *time after which a private sale will be made* (in case the debtor wants to redeem the collateral); and

(v) A *statement that the debtor is entitled to an accounting* for the unpaid indebtedness and the *charge* for performing the accounting. [*See* **Coxall v. Clover Commercial Corp.,** 4 Misc. 3d 654 (2004)—improper notice when statement not made]

(a) Additional notice requirements for consumer goods [§565]

If the collateral consists of *consumer goods,* the notice must meet the above standards, and it also must:

(i) Describe the *liability for a deficiency* (the amount still due after the resale);

(ii) Contain a *telephone number* to find out the amount that must be paid to the secured party to *redeem* the collateral (*see infra,* §§604-606); and

(iii) Contain a *telephone number or mailing address* from which *additional information* concerning the disposition and the obligation secured is available.

[U.C.C. §9-614]

(b) Safe harbor forms [§566]

While the Code does not require any particular phrasing in these notices, the drafters have helpfully provided *sample forms* to send in each case, and stated that using these forms will protect the creditor from arguments about noncompliance with the notification rules (*i.e.*, they are "*safe harbor*" forms). [U.C.C. §§9-613, 9-614 and Comment 3]

(c) Improper notice [§567]

The creditor must take reasonable steps to make sure the notice is actually *received* by the debtor. [*See* **R & J of Tennessee, Inc. v. Blankenship-Melton Real Estate, Inc.,** 166 S.W.3d 195 (Tenn. 2005)—notice sent to wrong address not sufficient]

(2) Persons to be notified

(a) Debtor [§568]

Notice of the intended sale is required to be sent by the secured party to the debtor.

1) Waiver of right to notice before default [§569]

Any provision in the original security agreement by which the debtor purportedly waives notice of sale is *void as a matter of law*. Public policy strongly favors the protection of the debtor's rights through such notice. [U.C.C. §9-602]

2) Waiver after default [§570]

The Code specifies that the debtor, *after default*, may sign a statement renouncing or modifying the debtor's right to notice of sale. In such a case, the debtor may be able to extract some concessions from the secured party in exchange for the waiver. [U.C.C. §9-624]

(b) Sureties [§571]

Co-signers, sureties, and guarantors of the debtor's obligation are also entitled to notice. [U.C.C. §6-111(c)(2)]

(c) Other creditors of record [§572]

If the collateral is *nonconsumer goods*, the secured party must also send a notification to all creditors who have *filed a financing statement* as to this collateral in the 10 days before notice is required to be sent, and also to any other person from which the secured party has received, before the notification date, an *authenticated notification of a claim of an interest* in the collateral. [U.C.C. §9-611(c)]

This will allow other creditors to protect their interests by objecting to or policing the resale or other disposition of the collateral.

(3) Exception as to goods sold in "recognized market" [§573]

As indicated above, notice is not required if the collateral is sold in a "recognized" market. [U.C.C. §9-611(d)] However, courts have limited the concept of a "recognized market" to *auction markets*, such as grain markets or stock exchanges, where goods are *fungible*. [*See, e.g.,* **Layne v. Bank One, Kentucky, N.A.**, *supra*, §172—sale of stock on NASDAQ commercially reasonable as a matter of law]

(a) Automobiles [§574]

The courts are unanimous in holding that automobiles are *not* sold on a "recognized market" because there are so many variables in automobile sales. [*See, e.g.,* **Norton v. National Bank of Commerce**, 398 S.W.2d 538 (Ark. 1966); **Nelson v. Monarch Investment Plan**, 452 S.W.2d 375 (Ky. 1970)]

(b) Caution [§575]

If a secured party mistakenly determines that the sale is in a "recognized market" and it is not, the secured party may be liable in damages to the debtor. [*See* U.C.C. §9-625; *and see infra,* §608] Or, the creditor may even be barred from recovering any deficiency against the debtor (*see infra,* §592). The safest course, therefore, is to send the notice.

(4) Timing of notice [§576]

The notice must be sent *after default* and a *reasonable time* before the date of disposition of the collateral. [U.C.C. §9-612(a)] Thus the notice cannot be in the original security agreement (since no default has yet occurred).

(a) Safe harbor rule—ten days for nonconsumer transactions [§577]

In nonconsumer transactions, if the secured party sends the notice at least 10 days before the earliest possible disposition of the collateral, the notice is timely sent and cannot later be attacked on this basis—creating a "*safe harbor*" for the creditor to rely on. [U.C.C. §9-612(b) and Comment 3]

(b) No safe harbor rule—consumer transactions [§578]

The above safe harbor rule does *not* apply if the collateral is consumer goods. In that case, the courts would have to decide the reasonableness of the notice as a matter of fact on a *case by case basis* (*see supra,* §511). [U.C.C. §9-612(a); *see* **Coxall v. Clover Commercial Corp.**, *supra,* §564—11 days too short in consumer case]

NOTICE OF DISPOSITION OF COLLATERAL BY SALE— A SUMMARY — **gilbert**

WHEN REQUIRED	Required when the seller wishes to dispose of repossessed collateral by sale, *unless* the goods are perishable or of a type sold in a recognized market
WHO RECEIVES	The *debtor* (unless, after default, the debtor waives the right to notice), any *sureties*, and *other creditors* who filed a financing statement at least 10 days before notice was sent or who gave the repossessing creditor authenticated notice of their claims
CONTENTS	The notice must contain: (i) Descriptions of the *debtor*, the *secured party*, and the *collateral*; (ii) The *method* of sale and the *time and place* (public sale) or time *after* which sale will occur (private sale); and (iii) A statement that the debtor is entitled to an *accounting* for the unpaid indebtedness and the *charge* for this service. *Note:* If collateral is *consumer goods*, the notice must also (i) describe the liability for a *deficiency*; (ii) contain a phone number to call about *redemption* of the collateral; and (iii) contain a phone number or address from which to obtain *additional information*.
WHEN TO SEND	Must be sent within a *reasonable time* before disposition of the collateral (10-day safe harbor period for nonconsumer goods)

c. Secured party's right to bid for collateral

(1) At public sale [§579]
The secured party has the right to purchase the collateral at a public sale. [U.C.C. §9-610(c)(1)] Indeed, the secured party is often the only bidder.

(2) At private sale [§580]
Where a *private* sale is involved, the secured party is entitled to bid for the goods only if they are of a type customarily sold in a *recognized market* or are of a type subject to *standard price quotations*. [U.C.C. §9-610(c)(2)]

d. Application of proceeds [§581]
The Code establishes a strict priority for application of the proceeds of a sale of collateral. In general, proceeds are applied in turn to (i) the *expenses* of the secured party in connection with the default; (ii) the *debt owed* the secured party; and (iii) the indebtedness owed to *junior creditors* having interests in the collateral. [U.C.C. §9-615]

(1) Expenses [§582]
The secured party is first reimbursed for the expenses incurred in the

sale, including legal expenses and reasonable attorneys' fees (*if* provided for in the security agreement) and any costs in taking or holding the collateral. Also, the secured party is entitled to be reimbursed for any improvements in or processing of the collateral undertaken to make it more marketable. [U.C.C. §9-615(a)(1)]

(2) Debt [§583]

After initial expenses, the proceeds are applied to the obligation upon which the debtor has defaulted and under which the disposition of the collateral is made. [U.C.C. §9-615(a)(2)]

(3) Junior creditors [§584]

Creditors who are *junior* to the repossessing creditor get paid only after the debt to the repossessing creditor is paid in full, and then only if they send an *authenticated demand* for such a payment to the repossessing creditor. [U.C.C. §9-615(a)(3)(A)] They are paid in order of their priority.

Example: Business Corporation used its equipment as collateral for loans from Creditor B and Creditor C. Creditor B filed and perfected before Creditor C. Business Corporation defaults on the loans and Creditor B repossesses and sells the equipment. Creditor C gets paid from the proceeds of Creditor B's resale only if there is a surplus after Creditor B is paid in full and if Creditor C sends a notice to Creditor B requiring payment of this surplus to be made to it.

(a) What does senior creditor recover? [§585]

Where more than one creditor has an interest in collateral, prior law did not say what happened if the *junior* creditor repossessed first and sold the collateral. Did the proceeds belong to the senior creditor? Article 9 answers this question: The cash proceeds generated on disposition by the junior creditor need *not* be paid to the senior creditor as long as the junior creditor proceeds in good faith and is "without knowledge that the receipt violates the rights of the senior interest." [U.C.C. §9-615(g)] The commentators are clear that *mere knowledge* of the senior interest does not necessarily violate this standard. This has led to speculation about the wisdom of including in the original financing statement a warning that the senior creditor objects *in advance* to any retention of proceeds by a foreclosing junior creditor (the so-called *bulletin board* financing statement). This may all be less important than it sounds, since the resale notice must be sent to all creditors of record (*see supra*, §572), and alert senior creditors can jump in prior to the foreclosure sale and protect their interests. Note however that the senior creditor's security interest continues in the collateral notwithstanding foreclosure and resale by junior creditors (*see infra*, §599). Buyers at such a foreclosure sale should be aware of this cloud on their title, and bid accordingly.

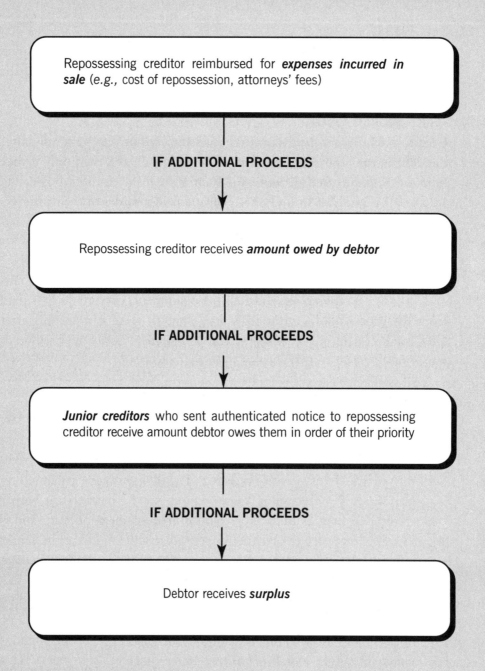

Repossessing creditor reimbursed for **expenses incurred in sale** (*e.g.,* cost of repossession, attorneys' fees)

IF ADDITIONAL PROCEEDS

Repossessing creditor receives **amount owed by debtor**

IF ADDITIONAL PROCEEDS

Junior creditors who sent authenticated notice to repossessing creditor receive amount debtor owes them in order of their priority

IF ADDITIONAL PROCEEDS

Debtor receives **surplus**

Example: Same facts as in the previous example, except Creditor A files and perfects its security interest in Business Corporation's equipment before Creditors B and C. When Creditor B repossesses the equipment, Creditor B must notify the other creditors of record, but can sell the collateral and keep the cash proceeds of the sale unless Creditor A objects (or pre-objected in its filed financing statement—the bulletin board financing statement mentioned above). If Creditor A does not object, Creditor A may still repossess the collateral from the buyer at Creditor B's foreclosure sale in the event that Business Corporation defaults on its debt to Creditor A.

---

e. **Surplus and deficiency [§586]**

The secured party must give the debtor any surplus proceeds that are left *after* the above disbursements. Conversely, the debtor will be liable for any *deficiency*—the amount by which the proceeds failed to cover the expenses of sale and the indebtedness. [U.C.C. §9-615]

(1) Computing amount of surplus or deficiency

(a) Sale price [§587]

Absent fraud in the sale, the amount bid or received on the sale of the collateral is usually accepted as the basis for determining the amount of the surplus or deficiency. [**Schabler v. Indianapolis Morris Plan,** 234 N.E.2d 655 (Ind. 1968)]

1) Low price not determinative [§588]

The mere fact that the amount realized at the sale is substantially below the fair market value of the collateral is *not enough* by itself to render the sale commercially *unreasonable*—at least where the secured party has otherwise acted reasonably to attract prospective purchasers and bidding. [**Sierra Financial Corp. v. Brooks-Farrer Co.,** *supra,* §76—where collateral worth $27,000 sold to secured party for $500, sale upheld; *see* U.C.C. §9-627(a); *but see* **Coxall v. Clover Commercial Corp.,** *supra,* §578—in consumer case, suspiciously low price requires creditor to prove commercial reasonableness of the resale]

EXAM TIP	gilbert

If an exam question indicates that collateral was resold for an amount much lower than its market value, remember that low price alone does *not* make the sale commercially unreasonable. However, you *can* point to the low price as *one of several factors* (*e.g.,* poor advertising, inadequate upkeep of collateral) indicating that the sale was commercially unreasonable.

2) Collusive sales [§589]

The surplus and deficiency provisions were drafted in response to the rather common practice of a repossessing creditor reselling the collateral either to itself or a confederate (or the debtor's surety) at a very low price, so that the debtor still owes a huge deficiency, and then having the buyer at the resale turn around and sell the collateral for a much greater amount.

Example: Secured Party repossessed Debtor's car, which Debtor thought was worth around $8,000. Debtor was therefore surprised to learn that the car only brought $2,000 at the foreclosure sale and that Secured Party was now demanding $6,000 as still due (the "deficiency"). Debtor did some investigating and learned that Secured Party sold the car to one of its subsidiary companies, which then resold the car on the open market for $8,000. If Debtor is forced to pay the $6,000 deficiency, Secured Party and its subsidiary will make quite a profit.

---

a) Presumption that collateral worth what independent buyer would pay—Rapson rule [§590]

If the buyer in the resale is the *secured party*, a person *related* to the secured party, or a party owing a *supporting obligation* (*i.e.*, a surety), and the amount of proceeds of the resale is *significantly below* the range of proceeds that a complying disposition to an *independent person* would have brought, the Code presumes that the surplus or deficiency is to be calculated based on the amount of proceeds that would have been realized in a proper disposition to such an independent party. [U.C.C. §9-615(f)—the "*Rapson rule*," after its drafter] In *nonconsumer goods transactions*, the *debtor* has the burden of proving this amount. [U.C.C. §9-626(a)(5)]

b) Accounting to consumers [§591]

Before making a demand for payment of a deficiency or payment of any surplus of the resale (and in any event within 14 days of the debtor's demand therefor), in *consumer transactions* the secured party must send out a complete *explanation* of how the deficiency or surplus was calculated, including such things as the creditor's expenses, required rebates (*e.g.*, the creditor cannot collect unearned interest), etc. [U.C.C. §9-616] If the secured party does not plan to collect any deficiency from the consumer debtor/obligor, no such accounting need be sent. [U.C.C. §9-616, Comment 2] However, the secured party must send the consumer a statement *waiving* the right to the deficiency within 14 days of the debtor's request for such a statement. [U.C.C. §9-616(b)(2)] Failure to send the notice of accounting makes the secured party liable for *actual damages plus $500 in punitive damages.* [U.C.C. §9-625(b), (e)]

SELLER'S RETENTION VS. SALE OF COLLATERAL—A COMPARISON		**gilbert**
	RETENTION OF COLLATERAL	SALE OF COLLATERAL
IS DEBTOR'S CONSENT (OR LACK OF OBJECTION) NEEDED?	Yes	No
MUST NOTICE BE GIVEN TO DEBTOR?	Yes	Yes (debtor may waive requirement after default)
MUST SECURED PARTY ACT WITH "COMMERCIAL REASONABLENESS"?	No	Yes
CAN SECURED PARTY SUE FOR DEFICIENCY?	No (unless collateral retained only in *partial* satisfaction of debt)	Yes

(2) Possible loss of deficiency in noncomplying resale [§592]

If the secured party fails to conduct a commercially reasonable resale or send out the required notices, Article 9 specifies the penalty in nonconsumer transactions: It adopts the *"rebuttable presumption"* rule (which the majority of courts had already followed). Under the rule, in *nonconsumer transactions,* failure of the secured party to follow the rules on default results in a *rebuttable presumption* that a foreclosure sale following the rules would have brought the amount still due, so there is *no deficiency* and the debtor owes nothing further. [U.C.C. §9-626 and Comment 4] Therefore, if someone objects to a sale, the secured party has the *burden of proving* compliance with the Code. [U.C.C. §9-626(a)(2)] If the secured party cannot meet this burden, section 9-626 presumes that a proper foreclosure sale would have paid everything that is still due on the debt, unless the secured party can show what amount would have been brought by a proper sale.

Example: When Bank repossessed the logging equipment that was the collateral for a loan on which Debtor still owed $80,000, it sold the equipment without cleaning off the mud that caked it completely and made it hard for prospective buyers to examine. The logging equipment, which everyone agreed should have brought around $50,000, only sold for $12,000. Assuming that Bank's sale was commercially unreasonable (*see supra*, §560), there is a rebuttable presumption that a sale that had been commercially reasonable would have completely paid the $80,000 outstanding debt, leaving to Bank the burden of establishing what the logging equipment would have sold for if properly cleaned (probably the estimated $50,000 that everyone agreed was the likely value).

---

(3) No statutory rule in consumer cases [§593]

The rebuttable presumption rule of section 9-626 does not apply in consumer cases, and the Code gives no guidance as to what rule should be used when the creditor misbehaves (*i.e.,* when sale is not commercially reasonable or notice is not properly given). Under prior law, the courts split, with a majority finding that the creditor forfeited the right to any deficiency (the *"absolute bar"* rule), but with many jurisdictions adopting the *rebuttable* presumption rule even for consumer cases. Those older cases are still likely to dictate the outcome. [*See* **Coxall v. Clover Commercial Corp.,** *supra*, §588—absolute bar rule applied in consumer cases, so that creditor could not recover anything from the consumer if the sale did not comply with Article 9's resale rules]

(a) Statutory damages under Article 9 [§594]

In any event, a consumer may recover *punitive damages* for creditor noncompliance in the amount of the finance charge (*i.e.,* the interest owed on the original debt) *plus* 10% of the total amount of the principal. [U.C.C. §9-625(c)(2); *see* **Coxall v. Clover Commercial Corp.,** *supra*—awarding statutory damages while at the same time forbidding the creditor any right to a deficiency]

(4) Exception as to sales of accounts, chattel paper, payment intangibles, and promissory notes [§595]

If the collateral in question consists of *accounts, chattel paper, payment intangibles, or promissory notes* in the possession of the secured party, unless the security agreement states otherwise, the *debtor is neither entitled to any surplus, nor liable for any deficiency*, regardless of whether the resale was commercially reasonable. [U.C.C. §9-615(e)]

(a) Rationale

The collateral here involves rights to *payments owed by a third person,* and the price that a purchaser is willing to pay upon sale of these rights may reflect the *willingness of the seller to guarantee* and make good the performance of the third party in the event that party defaults.

1) *When accounts, chattel paper, payment intangibles, or promissory notes are sold,* they are sold either "with recourse" or "without recourse." (If no mention, it is presumed they are sold "without recourse.")

2) *When sold "with recourse,"* the seller *guarantees* the obligation in the event the account-debtor fails to pay, thus allowing the creditor *recourse* to the seller. If the sale is made *"without recourse,"* there is no such guarantee.

3) *Since a sale "without recourse" is generally more risky* for the purchaser, that party usually pays a somewhat *lower price* for the rights involved than would have been paid if the seller had been willing to sell "with recourse."

4) *In any event, because the purchase price depends on the seller's* (secured party's) willingness to guarantee the obligations, the U.C.C. rule is to *exclude* any right to either surplus *or* deficiency—unless the parties *expressly* provide otherwise.

f. Rights of purchaser of collateral [§596]

The purchaser of the collateral at the secured party's sale takes *all rights* the debtor had in the collateral, together with the interest of the secured party and *all interests subordinate thereto.* [U.C.C. §9-504(4)]

(1) As to junior creditors [§597]

This means that the purchaser takes *free* from the secured interests of all creditors lower in priority than the seller; *i.e.*, the purchaser "steps into the shoes" of the secured party with respect to all other security interests in the collateral.

(2) As to senior creditors [§598]

The purchaser at the resale takes subject to the security interest of the senior creditor, who would have to be paid off by the purchaser; otherwise the senior creditor could repossess the collateral from the purchaser. This possibility will also depress the amount paid by the purchaser. [U.C.C. §§9-615(g), 9-617, *and see* §9-610, Comment 5]

(3) Effect of defects in sale [§599]

Even if the secured party has failed to comply with the default provisions of Article 9, at least with respect to junior interests, the purchaser's interest is still protected as long as the purchaser was acting in *good faith*. [U.C.C. §9-617(b)]

(4) Warranties on resale [§600]

The sale by the repossessing creditor gives rise to *all the usual warranties* that arise in the sale of any item, most particularly the warranty of title found in section 2-312 of the Code, and, if the sale is of goods, all the usual quality warranties found in Article 2 of the Code. [U.C.C. §9-610(d); *and see* Comment 11] This is a change from prior law, which typically did not create a warranty of title in the sale of repossessed goods. To protect the repossessing creditor from liability in this situation, section 9-610 allows the creditor to disclaim the warranty of title, and gives sample language for doing so. [U.C.C. §9-610(e), (f)]

3. Allowing Debtor to Retain Collateral and Suing on Debt [§601]

The secured party may allow the collateral to remain with the debtor and sue on the debt, thereby reducing the claim to a judgment. Any lien that the secured party subsequently acquires through a levy on the collateral (*e.g.*, by writ of execution) *dates back to the date of perfection of the original security interest*. [U.C.C. §9-601(e)]

Example: Creditor perfected a security interest in Debtor's factory equipment on May 1. Debtor defaulted in loan repayment on September 1. Creditor did not repossess the collateral, but instead *sued* Debtor and recovered a judgment in the amount owed. The sheriff, pursuant to writ of execution, levied on (seized) Debtor's factory equipment on October 1. Debtor filed a bankruptcy petition the next day. Creditor's lien on the factory equipment dates from May 1, *not* October 1—an important distinction since the trustee in bankruptcy can attack liens arising in the 90-day period prior to bankruptcy as preferences (*see supra*, §§490-492).

---

a. Judicial sale [§602]

In most jurisdictions, the secured party may purchase at a *judicial sale* (*i.e.*, one conducted under court supervision), in which event that party takes the collateral free from any provisions of the U.C.C. *Note:* Sales approved by a court are conclusively deemed to be reasonable. [U.C.C. §627(c)]

EXAM TIP   **gilbert**

Keep in mind that if a creditor decides to obtain a judgment against the debtor rather than using self-help repossession and sale/retention of the collateral, many of the above requirements (*e.g.*, no breach of the peace, commercial reasonableness) do not apply. Therefore, a *uniformed sheriff's deputy* may seize the collateral and the judicial sale is *conclusively deemed to be reasonable*.

F. Debtor's Right of Redemption

1. In General [§603]

The fact that the debtor has defaulted does not irreversibly set in motion the provisions for the disposition and retention of collateral by the secured party under the Code. The debtor may exercise the *right of redemption* at any time prior to the time the secured party has disposed of the collateral or entered into a contract for its disposition, or before the debtor's obligation has been discharged by the secured party's retention of collateral. [U.C.C. §9-623]

2. Tender [§604]

To redeem, the debtor must tender the debt owed at the time of redemption (*i.e.,* payment of delinquent installments), *plus* any expenses incurred by the secured party in taking or caring for the collateral, along with any expenses already incurred in connection with the sale of the collateral. [U.C.C. §9-623]

a. Acceleration clause [§605]

If the agreement contains an acceleration clause, the debtor must be prepared to tender the *entire* debt, not just the delinquent installments. However, courts *may* read in "unconscionability" or "public policy" limitations to prevent unjust results so that the debtor need do no more than pay the expenses of repossession and the debt currently due *without acceleration.* [*Compare* U.C.C. §9-623, Comment 2, *with* **Urdang v. Muse,** 276 A.2d 397 (N.J. 1971); **Robinson v. Jefferson Corp.,** 4 U.C.C. Rep. 15 (N.Y. 1967); **Street v. Commercial Credit Corp.,** 281 P. 46 (Ariz. 1929)]

3. No Waiver Prior to Default [§606]

A debtor *cannot* validly waive the right of redemption *prior* to default. This is specifically prohibited in the Code [U.C.C. §9-602; *see infra,* §619] and reflects basic public policy of protecting debtors' rights [**Indianapolis Morris Plan v. Karlen,** 28 N.Y.2d 30 (1971)]. The common law maxim is that "nothing can clog the equity of redemption."

a. Note

The right of redemption may be waived *after* a default (*see infra,* §620).

G. Effect of Failure to Comply with Default Provisions

1. In General [§607]

If the secured party does not comply with the default provisions of the Code in proceeding against the debtor, the debtor may seek *judicial direction* as to the type of disposition or may wait until after the goods have been disposed of and then proceed against the secured party for *damages.* [U.C.C. §9-625(a)]

2. Penalties for the Secured Party's Noncompliance [§608]

Failure to comply with the default rules of Article 9 exposes the secured party to *actual damages*, including the debtor's loss of the surplus that the secured party should have realized on a proper sale. If the collateral is *consumer goods*, the debtor's minimum recovery is either (i) the finance charge plus 10% of the loan amount, or (ii) the time-price differential plus 10% of the cash price. [U.C.C. §9-625(b) - (d)]

3. Punitive Damages [§609]

In the situations below, the noncomplying secured party must pay *punitive* damages of *$500* (which the Code's comments call "statutory damages") in addition to any actual damages the debtor suffered. [U.C.C. §9-625]

a. Secured party improperly retains control [§610]

A secured party must pay punitive damages if the secured debt has been paid, but the secured party *fails to relinquish control* over deposit accounts, investment securities, electronic chattel paper, or letter of credit rights. [U.C.C. §9-208]

b. Secured party improperly accepts payments from account debtors [§611]

If a secured party has notified account debtors that their payments should be made directly to the secured party rather than the debtor (who is the creditor of the account debtors), once the debtor pays its indebtedness to the secured party, the secured party must then tell the account debtors to resume making their payments to the debtor. [U.C.C. §9-209; *see infra*, §624]

Example: Wonder Spa used the consumer accounts that its spa customers owed it by contract as collateral for a loan from Finance Company. Finance Company sent all these consumer customers a notice that future monthly payments on their spa contracts should be made to it until further notice. Once Wonder Spa pays its debt in full to Finance Company, Finance Company must send the spa's customers a notice to resume paying the spa directly, or it will have to pay actual damages plus the $500 penalty.

---

c. Secured party does not properly file [§612]

If a secured party makes a *bogus filing* [U.C.C. §9-509(a); *see supra*, §296] or fails to file or send a *termination statement* when required [U.C.C. §9-513(a), (c); *see supra*, §292], the secured party will be liable for punitive damages.

d. Secured party fails to notify of deficiency or waiver of deficiency [§613]

A secured party must pay punitive damages if, as part of a pattern of noncompliance, it fails to send an explanation of the deficiency/surplus to a consumer when required to do so. [§9-616(b)(1); *see supra*, §591] The secured party is also liable if it fails to inform the consumer obligor of its waiver of the right to a deficiency within 14 days of the obligor's inquiry. [U.C.C. §9-616(b)(2); *see supra*, §591]

4. Attorneys' Fees [§614]

The Code does *not* authorize the recovery of attorneys' fees for either party, but the right to attorneys' fees can be obtained by contract or awarded by other statutes (as consumer protection statutes often do).

H. Nonwaivable Rights Under the Security Agreement

1. **In General [§615]**

    As has been stressed, the default provisions of the Code invite flexibility, and the parties are encouraged to tailor their security agreement to the facts of their case. However, this is not an invitation for the parties to evade the Code through clever private draftsmanship, because the standards specified by the parties cannot be manifestly unreasonable. Moreover, the Code declares that a number of rights may *not* be waived, although parties may specify their own standards for the performance of these rights (*see* below). [U.C.C. §§9-602, 9-603]

2. **Accounting for Surplus [§616]**

    When the security agreement secures an indebtedness, the parties may not dispense with the obligation to account for any surplus that accrues from the disposition of the collateral. [U.C.C. §9-602(5)]

3. **Notice Requirements [§617]**

    The secured party must comply with the notice requirements for disposition and/ or retention of the collateral (above). These *cannot be waived.* [U.C.C. §9-602(7)] *Note:* The debtor may, *after* default, effectively waive the right to notice of *disposition* of the collateral (*see supra,* §570).

4. **Discharge Upon Retention [§618]**

    The secured party's retention of the collateral in full or partial satisfaction of the debt under section 9-620 discharges the debtor's obligation to the extent it is satisfied (*see supra,* §550), and the parties may not contract otherwise. [U.C.C. §9-602(10)]

5. **Right of Redemption [§619]**

    The parties may not contractually eliminate the debtor's right to redeem the collateral under section 9-623 (*see supra,* §606). [U.C.C. §9-602(11)]

    a. **Waiver after default [§620]**

       However, section 9-624(c) *allows* the debtor to waive the right to redemption *after default.* At this point, the secured party theoretically has no advantage over the debtor, and the debtor may be willing to sign a waiver if the debtor does not intend to redeem in order to give the secured party more flexibility in his disposition arrangements. Also, the debtor may be able to bargain for a release of personal liability on any deficiency.

6. **Liability for Failure to Comply [§621]**

    The secured party may not disclaim or reduce liability under section 9-625 for failing to comply with the default provisions of the Code. [U.C.C. §9-602(13)] Here again, the Code protects a debtor in a weak bargaining position from negotiating away essential rights in order to obtain credit.

7. **Waiver of Rights by Guarantor [§622]**

    The common law clearly allowed guarantors of the debt to sign a guarantee agreement in which the right to object to improper resales of the collateral was waived. Article 9 clearly gives *all supporting obligors—e.g.,* sureties, guarantors, and co-signers—the *same nonwaivable rights* as the debtor. [U.C.C. §9-602 and Comment 4]

I. Special Default Rules for Intangibles and Fixtures

1. Intangibles [§623]

If the financing transaction involves accounts or chattel paper—either through the sale of such rights or through their use as collateral—the secured party may wish to collect directly from the underlying obligors, rather than by taking payment through the debtor or seller of the rights. Where the debtor-seller's financing arrangements are kept concealed from the debtor's customers, the customers may not know that the right to their payments has been assigned; they will continue to pay the debtor, who then remits to the secured party. This is known as *"nonnotification financing"* of accounts receivable (*see supra*, §28).

a. Rights of notification [§624]

In the event of default, the secured party is *entitled* to notify the underlying account debtors or obligors of the secured party's interest and to collect directly from them. [U.C.C. §9-607(a)]

(1) Note

Of course, if the parties agree, the secured party may also exercise the right of notification prior to any default. [U.C.C.§9-607(a)]

(2) And note

If the financing is on a "with recourse" basis (the debtor being liable for any ultimate deficiency; *see supra*, §595), the secured party may charge the debtor for the *reasonable expenses* incurred in notifying the debtor's customers and collecting the accounts. [U.C.C. §9-607(d)]

b. No rights to surplus or deficiency [§625]

Remember the special rules governing *surplus and deficiency* on sale of accounts, chattel paper, payment intangibles, and promissory notes. The debtor is neither entitled to any surplus nor liable for any deficiency. [U.C.C. §9-604(e); *see supra*, §595]

2. Fixtures and Related Interests [§626]

In the case of fixtures and accessions, there is an obvious problem in taking the collateral for retention or sale since it is attached either to real property or to other goods. The Code protects the rights of the secured party in fixtures and accessions by declaring that *when the secured party has priority* over other interests in the real property or the mass of goods (*see supra*, §§351, 358, 362), the secured party is entitled *to remove* the collateral. [U.C.C. §§9-335(e), 9-604(c)]

a. **Damages caused by removal [§627]**

The secured party must reimburse the encumbrancer or owner of the underlying property (*other than the debtor*) for any *damages or repair* necessitated by the removal. The owner or encumbrancer may demand adequate security of such reimbursement before allowing removal. However, the secured party is *not* liable for any diminution in the value of the property caused by removal. [U.C.C. §§9-335(f), 9-604(d)]

---

e.g. **Example:** Secured Party has a perfected interest in Debtor's built-in television and decides to remove the television upon default. It costs $100 to repair the hole in the wall, but the house is worth $500 less without the built-in television. If the only person suffering a loss here is Debtor, Secured Party owes nothing and may repossess freely (Debtor has only himself to blame if repossession causes damage). But if another creditor has an interest in the realty (*e.g.*, a mortgage), Secured Party is responsible to the other creditor for the $100 repairs but not for the diminution in the value of the underlying property.

---

b. **Foreclosure by other parties—rights of fixture creditor [§628]**

The secured party having a security interest in a fixture is not limited to recovering the fixture if law other than Article 9 gives the fixture creditor greater rights. [U.C.C. §9-604(b)]

---

e.g. **Example:** Debtor failed to pay the mortgage on her home, which was located in State X, and Finance Company (the mortgagee) seized the home and sold it at a sheriff's auction. State X's real property law provides that if realty is foreclosed upon and sold, the proceeds must be paid to creditors in the order of their priority. If Frankie's Furnace Co. has a PMSI in the home's furnace (a fixture) that has priority over Finance Company under the priority rules of section 9-334 (*see supra*, §351), Frankie's Furnace Co. will be paid *first* out of the proceeds of the sheriff's sale.

Review Questions
and Answers

Review Questions

COVERAGE OF ARTICLE 9

1. Farmer executes a chattel mortgage on his crops to Bank as security for a loan. Is the transaction subject to Article 9? _____

2. Architect has a contract under which she is to receive $25,000 from Builder upon completion of a design for a new office building. Because she is short of funds, she borrows money from Lender and, as security for repayment, assigns the fee that she is to receive. Is the transaction subject to Article 9? _____

   a. Assume Architect also delivered to Lender as security the research studies, blueprints, and preliminary design work she had done on the building. Would this transaction be subject to Article 9? _____

3. Professor assigns to Lender, as security for a loan, the salary that he is to earn from University during the forthcoming year. Is the transaction subject to Article 9? _____

4. Manufacturer sells to X all of his outstanding accounts receivable, for which X pays face value less 10%.

   a. Assume the purpose of the sale was to enable Manufacturer to raise needed cash for expansion purposes. Is the transaction subject to Article 9? _____

   b. Assume the assignment was part of Manufacturer's sale of his entire business (along with his equipment, inventory, etc.). Would the transfer of his accounts be subject to Article 9? _____

   c. Assume the assignment was made to satisfy a *preexisting* indebtedness owed by Manufacturer to X (rather than for new consideration). Would the assignment be subject to Article 9? _____

5. As security for a loan, Manufacturer executes a promissory note and assigns to Lender his leasehold interest in the premises where he conducts business. Is the transaction subject to Article 9? _____

   a. Assume that Lender, to secure its own line of credit, then assigns Manufacturer's note and the assigned leasehold interest to Bank. Is the transaction between Lender and Bank subject to Article 9? _____

CREATION OF SECURITY INTEREST

6. Debtor executed a valid security agreement with Bank covering Debtor's machinery and equipment. However, Bank failed to perfect its security interest by filing or in any other manner. If Debtor defaults, can Bank enforce the interest? _____

7. Jeweler pledges a bag of diamonds worth $50,000 as security for repayment of a loan from Lender. Assume no authenticated security agreement is ever executed and no financing statement is ever filed. Does Lender have an enforceable security interest in the diamonds? _____

8. If a security agreement describes the collateral as "all machinery and equipment located at . . . [debtor's address]," is the description sufficient to create a security interest in machinery and/or equipment having license or serial numbers for identification? _____

9. As security for a loan, Merchant conveys to Lender a security interest in his "inventory and stock on hand" at a designated location.

   a. Does such description confer upon Lender a security interest in the cash and accounts that Merchant will obtain when he sells the inventory? _____

   b. Is the description sufficient to confer upon Lender a security interest in items that become part of Merchant's inventory *after* the date of the security agreement, in the absence of any "after-acquired property" clause? _____

   c. Assume Merchant has signed the security agreement. Must it also sign the financing statement? _____

10. Debtor executes a security interest on certain collateral in reliance on Lender's promise to loan $10,000. Can Lender claim an enforceable interest in the collateral *before* paying over the $10,000? _____

11. Printer borrows $50,000 from Bank to purchase a printing press to be manufactured to his specifications by Pressco. The security agreement describes the press as being in the process of manufacture. Does Bank have any security interest in the press during the several months that it takes to complete manufacture and prior to its delivery to Printer? _____

PERFECTION

12. As security for a loan, Debtor delivers to Lender several bags of "junk silver coins." No financing statement is filed but Lender has signed a receipt for the coins, stating that they will be returned on repayment of the loan.

   a. Does Lender have a perfected security interest in the coins? _____

   b. Is Lender entitled to add insurance and storage costs to the amount of the loan and retain the coins until these are paid? _____

c. If the coins are stolen from Lender and insurance does not cover the full loss, who bears the loss? _____

d. If Lender fails to exercise reasonable care for the coins, does Lender lose the security interest? _____

13. Circuit Buy Store sells and delivers a $5,000 stereo system to Buff, who pays $2,000 down and agrees to pay the balance in monthly installments plus interest. Buff subsequently defaults.

a. Buff did not authenticate a security agreement. If Store's invoice to Buff states, "Seller reserves title to all merchandise sold until paid in full," can Store assert a valid security interest against Buff? _____

b. Assume there is a valid authenticated security agreement, but no financing statement is ever filed. Can Store assert a security interest in the stereo system against *other creditors* of Buff? _____

c. Assume that Store did not finance the purchase. Rather, Buff went to Bank, where he borrowed the $3,000 necessary to pay off Store and executed a valid security agreement. Can Bank assert a security interest in the stereo system against Buff's other creditors *without filing* a financing statement? _____

d. Same facts. Assume that Buff's authenticated security agreement with Bank expressly stated that the interest would extend to "all debts and obligations now or hereafter owed" to Bank. Assume further that Buff then owed Bank $2,000 on an *unrelated* debt. Can Bank assert a perfected security interest as to the $2,000 debt *without filing* a financing statement? _____

14. Grimm is in the business of buying hard-to-collect accounts at a discount. Grimm purchases from Manufacturer all of its "bad" accounts (those 180 days or more past due) at 50% of face value. Grimm neither notifies the account-debtors nor files a financing statement as to his purchase. Does Grimm have a perfected security interest in the accounts (so as to be protected against later assignments by Manufacturer)? _____

15. Bank lends money to Processor to enable it to purchase a boatload of raw material. As security for the loan, Processor signs a security agreement with respect to the shipment and assigns to Bank the bill of lading covering the shipment. Before the shipment arrives, Bank releases the bill of lading to Processor to enable it to make arrangements for delivery. If Other Creditor levies a writ of attachment while the bill of lading is in Processor's possession, who prevails? _____

16. Bank lends money to Printco, a corporation registered in State X, to enable Printco to purchase a new printing press, which is installed in Printco's plant in State X. Printco signs a security agreement covering the press, and Bank's interest is perfected by filing in State X. Later, however, Printco moves the press to a new

plant site in State Y, without Bank's knowledge or consent. Would the unauthorized removal of the press operate to jeopardize Bank's perfected security interest? _____

    a.   If Printco changes its location by registering in State Y without Bank's consent or knowledge, how long does Bank's original perfection in State X last? _____

17.   Coyote owns some securities accounts and wishes to use them as collateral for a loan from Acme Bank. Pursuant to Acme's security interest, Acme gets the name on Coyote's securities accounts changed from "Coyote" to "Acme Bank." Does Acme have a perfected security interest in the securities accounts? _____

18.   Sly purchases a used car from Seller in State A on a conditional sale contract. Seller's interest is noted on the car's certificate of title as required by State A law, and Seller retains the certificate. Sly moves his residence to State B without advising Seller and makes no further payments on his contract.

    a.   If it takes Seller *six months* to locate Sly in State B, can Seller still claim an enforceable security interest in the car? _____

    b.   Would the answer be the same if, in the interim, Sly had registered the car in State B (which does not require the surrender of the certificate of title) and had obtained a clean certificate showing him as the sole owner? _____

    c.   Would the answer be the same if, after obtaining the clean certificate in State B, Sly had sold the car to Dealer in State B, who had no knowledge of Seller's interest? _____

FILING

19.   A filed financing statement lists the debtor as "Impecunious, Inc." but the debtor's real name is "Impecunious National, Inc." Is the secured party still perfected in spite of this mistake? _____

20.   Which, if any, of the following facts *must* be shown in the financing statement to perfect the security interest? _____

    a.   The amount of the debt or obligation.

    b.   Due date of debt or obligation.

    c.   Intended use of collateral.

    d.   Whether after-acquired collateral is also covered.

    e.   Whether proceeds are covered.

21.   A filed financing statement lists the debtor as "Minerva Schwartz." Several months later, the debtor marries and changes her name to "Minerva Jones." Is the filed statement effective to perfect the secured party's interest in *after-acquired collateral*? _____

a. Is it effective to perfect a security interest in the original collateral a year after the name change? _____

22. To cause trouble for her ex-husband, Billy, Mary filed a phony financing statement that supposedly covered all his assets, listing herself as the secured party. Is this financing statement effective to perfect a security interest in these assets? _____

23. A filed financing statement describes Manufacturer's collateral as "machinery and equipment located at 407 Fillmore Street, San Francisco." Later, the Manufacturer acquires *other* machinery and equipment at a *different* address in the same city. Is the filed statement effective to perfect the secured party's interest in the other collateral? _____

a. If Manufacturer pays off the debt, must the secured party file anything? _____

24. Regardless of the nature of the collateral, is a secured party automatically protected by filing the financing statement in the appropriate *state* office (as opposed to any local or county filing)? _____

25. Lender filed a copy of the security *agreement* in lieu of a financing statement. The agreement shows that the loan is due in 12 months. For how long a period is the filing effective? _____

26. If a loan remains unpaid at the end of the effective period of the original filing, can the secured party *unilaterally* obtain an extension of the effectiveness of the financing statement? _____

27. Can a prospective lender force the secured party to divulge the amount and extent of its interest in order to evaluate whether to make a further loan to the debtor? _____

PRIORITIES

28. On March 1, Lender A files a financing statement covering Jeweler's inventory, but does not actually make the loan until March 15. Meanwhile, on March 10, Jeweler pledges a bag of diamonds to Lender B, who advances funds immediately. Who is entitled to priority as to the bag of diamonds? _____

29. Lender A advances funds to Debtor on April 1, but inadvertently fails to file a financing statement until April 10. Meanwhile, on April 5, Lender B advances funds and takes possession of the collateral. Who is entitled to priority? _____

a. Would it make any difference whether Lender B *knew* of Lender A's interest when Lender B made the loan on April 5? _____

30. Bank loans money to Debtor on May 1 to enable Debtor to purchase a new stereo: Debtor signs a security agreement with Bank covering the stereo but no financing statement is ever filed. On June 1, Debtor borrows money from Lender,

signing a security agreement and financing statement covering the same stereo. Lender's financing statement is promptly filed. Who is entitled to priority? _____

31. On January 1, Computer Store borrows from Bank and executes a security agreement and financing statement. The security agreement creates an interest in Computer Store's "existing inventory of office machines, as well as any and all such items hereafter acquired." When Bank files the financing statement, it describes the collateral only as "inventory located at . . . [store address]."

    a. Is the filing sufficient to constitute a lien on office machines later acquired by Computer Store as part of its inventory? _____

    b. Assume that on June 1, Computer Store borrowed from Lender and gave a security interest on its entire inventory as of that date. Who would be entitled to priority as to office machines acquired after June 1? _____

32. Bank has a perfected security interest in Printer's machinery and equipment, pursuant to a security agreement that expressly covers "all items of press equipment now located at [printing plant] as well as any such equipment hereafter acquired and installed at such location." Printer buys a new press from Press Co., which immediately perfects a security interest in the press to secure payment of the purchase price. Who is entitled to priority in the new press—Bank or Press Co.? _____

33. Bank loans Printer funds on May 1 to purchase a new printing press. Printer signs a security agreement with Bank covering the printing press, but no financing statement is ever filed. On June 1, Printer borrows money from Lender, signing a security agreement and financing statement covering the printing press. Lender's financing statement is promptly filed. Who is entitled to priority? _____

34. On May 1, Bank loans Printer funds to purchase a new printing press, and Printer obtains delivery of the press on the same date. On May 3, Printer borrows from Lender, who immediately files a financing statement covering the press. On May 8, Bank files a financing statement covering the press. Who is entitled to priority? _____

    a. Would the result be the same if Lender had perfected its interest by obtaining *possession* of the printing press on May 3? _____

    b. If Printer sold the press for cash, who would have priority as to the cash proceeds? _____

35. On May 1, Bank loans Liquor Distributor funds to purchase a truckload of liquor, which is to be received on May 5. Bank is *aware* that Lender has previously filed a security interest covering all of Liquor Distributor's existing and after-acquired inventory. Can Bank attain priority over Lender's interest as to the truckload of liquor? How? _____

36. Homeowner purchases a new furnace from Appliance Co., and the furnace is installed in Homeowner's house. Appliance Co. has retained a security interest in

the furnace to secure payment of the purchase price. Homeowner's house is already subject to a mortgage that constitutes a lien on any fixture therein. As between Mortgage-Holder and Appliance Co., who is entitled to priority with respect to the furnace?

_____

37. Business Corporation borrowed money from Lender and gave Lender a security interest in the bank account it had at Octopus National Bank. To perfect its interest, Lender had Octopus National agree to follow its instructions without Business Corporation's consent.

  a. Will this perfect a security interest in the bank account?

_____

  b. If Business Corporation owes Octopus National money because of a series of bounced checks, which creditor has priority in the bank account: Octopus or Lender?

_____

38. Produce Co. supplies a carload of potatoes to Chip Co. and perfects a security interest in the shipment to secure payment of the purchase price. Chip Co. uses the potatoes to manufacture 500 cases of potato chips. At all times, Chip Co.'s finished goods inventory was subject to a perfected security interest held by Lender, which covered both its existing and after-produced inventory for regular financing purposes.

  a. Does Produce Co. have any enforceable interest in the potato chip inventory?

_____

  b. As between Produce Co. and Lender, who is entitled to priority?

_____

39. Lender has filed a financing statement perfecting its security interest in the inventory of Steve's Sound Systems Store. Steve's sells a stereo set for $5,000 to Purchaser, who pays for it as follows: $1,000 credit for trade-in on old equipment (added to the store's inventory); $1,000 cash, balance of $3,000 to be paid on a "conditional sale" installment contract.

  a. Does Lender have a security interest in the stereo system sold to Purchaser?

_____

  b. Does Lender have a security interest in the old equipment traded in by Purchaser and added to the store's inventory?

_____

  c. Does it make any difference that *neither* the security agreement nor the financing statement filed by Steve's Sound Systems Store mentioned any security interest in "proceeds"?

_____

  d. Does it make any difference that Steve's Sound Systems Store's sale of the stereo system *violated* a term of the security agreement (which provided that no system selling for more than $1,000 would be sold without Lender's express consent)?

_____

e. Assume that Steve's deposited the $1,000 down payment received from Purchaser in its checking account, along with other funds. Will Lender's security interest continue in Steve's Sound Systems Store's checking account for any amount? _____

f. Assume that Steve's discounted and assigned Purchaser's $3,000 installment contract to Bank, who is *aware* that Lender had a security interest in the store's inventory. As between Lender and Bank, who is entitled to priority in Purchaser's obligation? _____

g. Assume that Purchaser returned the stereo system to Steve's because the system was defective. As between Lender and Bank, who is entitled to priority in the returned stereo system? _____

40. On October 1, Jeweler borrows $10,000 from Bank and executes a security agreement and financing statement covering Jeweler's entire inventory. Bank files the financing statement immediately. On October 15, Jeweler takes from inventory a bag of diamonds and pledges this to Lender as security for a $25,000 loan. On November 1, Bank lends Jeweler an additional $50,000 without knowledge of the interim transaction with Lender. Who is entitled to priority and in what amount? _____

a. Would the answer be the same even if the financing statement filed by Bank made *no mention* of the fact that future advances would be made? _____

b. Would the answer be the same if Bank was *not obligated* under the security agreement to make the $50,000 loan on November 1? _____

c. Would the answer be the same if Bank *knew* about the intervening transaction with Lender? _____

41. Lender has a perfected security interest in Manufacturer's machinery and equipment to secure repayment of a loan. Manufacturer sells its entire business, including the machinery and equipment, to Purchaser. Purchaser paid full value and had no knowledge of Lender's security interest. Manufacturer's loan from Lender remains unpaid.

a. Assume that Manufacturer had falsely stated to Purchaser that there were no security interests outstanding in its machinery and equipment and Purchaser relied in good faith in purchasing the equipment. Does the sale to Purchaser cut off Lender's security interest? _____

b. Assume that Purchaser, as security for its own financing, conveys a security interest in the machinery and equipment to Bank. Is Bank's interest subject to Lender's security interest? _____

42. Lender has a perfected security interest in the inventory of Liquor Distributor. Distributor makes an unauthorized sale of 200 cases of whiskey to Purchaser, who

pays full value, and who has no knowledge of Lender's security interest. Does Purchaser take subject to Lender's interest? _____

    a.   Would Purchaser take subject to Lender's interest if Purchaser *knew* of Lender's interest when the purchase was made? _____

43.   Lender has filed and perfected a security interest in the inventory and equipment of Liquor Distributor. Included in its equipment is an expensive camera that Distributor uses for advertising purposes. Distributor makes an unauthorized sale of the camera to Purchaser, who buys the camera for personal use, pays full value therefor, and has no knowledge of Lender's security interest. Does Purchaser take subject to Lender's interest? _____

44.   On June 1, Jeweler borrows $10,000 from Bank and executes a security agreement and financing statement covering Jeweler's entire inventory. Bank files the financing statement immediately. On June 15, in an effort to streamline inventory, Jeweler sells to Liquidator all silverware and related items in inventory. Liquidator paid $25,000 (a fair price) and had no knowledge of Bank's interest. On October 1, Bank loaned Jeweler an additional $50,000 without knowledge of the intervening sale of the silverware inventory. What is the extent, if any, of Bank's security interest in the silverware following the sale? _____

    a.   Could Bank also claim a security interest in the $25,000 received by Jeweler from Liquidator? _____

45.   Carl became insolvent and could not afford to get his car out of We-Fix-It Auto Shop where he had taken it for repairs. A month later, Carl persuaded We-Fix-It to let him borrow his car for a few hours to visit his father in a local hospital. While the car was parked at the hospital, it was seized by the county sheriff, who was executing a judgment acquired by Carl's landlord for $460 back rent owed by Carl. Both Crunch Credit Union (which had a perfected security interest in the car when it was seized) and We-Fix-It Auto Shop seek to have the car turned over to them. Who wins? _____

46.   Bank has a perfected security interest in Jeweler's inventory to secure payment of a $10,000 loan. Creditor levies a writ of execution on the inventory, which is actually worth $50,000. The following day, Bank loans Jeweler an additional $40,000 pursuant to the security agreement and files a third-party claim proceeding for release of the inventory, asserting the amount of its lien as $50,000. Creditor resists on the ground that Bank's lien is limited to $10,000. In whose favor should the court rule in the third-party claim proceeding? _____

BANKRUPTCY PROCEEDINGS

47.   Lender loaned money and obtained a valid security interest on Debtor's inventory one week before Debtor filed for bankruptcy. Debtor was adjudicated a bankrupt

before Lender filed its financing statement. Will Lender's security interest be set aside because it was not fully perfected at the time of bankruptcy?

_____

48. On June 1 and while clearly insolvent, Debtor gives a security interest in Debtor's inventory to Lender as security for an account past due. Lender delays filing the financing statement until June 9. On October 15, Debtor files bankruptcy. Can Lender's security interest be set aside as a "preference"?

_____

49. On June 1, Lender loans money to Debtor whom Lender knows is insolvent, and obtains a security interest in Debtor's inventory. On July 9, Lender files a financing statement. On August 1, Debtor files bankruptcy. Can Lender's security interest be set aside as a "preference"?

_____

50. On March 1, Lender perfects a security interest in Debtor's "existing and after-acquired" inventory as security for a loan made on that date. On August 1, Debtor makes a bulk purchase of a competitor's inventory assets and adds these to Debtor's own inventory, even though Debtor was then clearly insolvent. On September 1, Debtor files for bankruptcy. Lender claims an interest in the assets acquired by Debtor on August 1 as "after-acquired property." The trustee in bankruptcy moves to set aside the interest as a "voidable preference." Who wins?

_____

DEFAULT PROCEEDINGS

51. When Debtor failed to repay its debt to Bank, Bank declared a default and sent its repo man to Debtor's place of business to seize the computer that was collateral for the loan. Debtor's manager protested the repossession, but was brushed aside by the repo man, who took the computer and left. Is Bank's repossession valid?

_____

52. Pressco sells a printing press to Printer, retaining a valid security interest to secure payment of the purchase price, which is payable in installments over five years. Printer defaults in payment of one installment, whereupon Pressco enters Printer's plant and removes a key part of the press rendering it inoperative. Can Printer recover damages against Pressco?

_____

53. Jeweler pledges a bag of diamonds worth $100,000 with Lender as collateral for a $25,000 loan. If Jeweler fails to repay the loan within the time agreed, does Lender have the right to *retain* the diamonds in satisfaction of the loan (*i.e.,* without selling them and accounting to Jeweler for any excess)?

_____

    a. Assume that Jeweler had repaid all but $5,000 of the loan before defaulting. Would this affect Lender's right to retain the diamonds?

_____

54. Having perfected its security interest, Circuit Buy Store repossesses a stereo system upon default of Purchaser. After notifying Purchaser in writing of its intent to do so, it places the stereo on its showroom floor, and several days later sells it to another customer for $3,000, although it had been sold to Purchaser several months

earlier for $5,000. Purchaser sues for damages (amount of the down payment). Will Purchaser prevail? _____

a. Was notice to Purchaser required to be sent, since Circuit Buy intended to dispose of the goods at *private sale*? _____

b. Must Circuit Buy notify other secured parties who have filed a financing statement covering this same collateral? _____

55. Pursuant to its security agreement, Seller validly repossesses an auto following Purchaser's default in payment. Seller sends written notice to Purchaser that Seller intends to sell the automobile to itself at a designated time and place for "low blue book" price. Does Seller have a right to do so? _____

56. Collateral that has an actual fair market value of $100,000 is sold at a properly noticed public sale in good faith to an arm's-length purchaser for $10,000.

a. If the obligation in default is $25,000, is the secured party entitled to sue for a $15,000 deficiency? _____

b. In the absence of agreement, are expenses incurred by the secured party in *repossessing* the collateral proper charges in computing the amount of any deficiency? _____

c. If there was some defect in the notice or conduct of the sale, could Debtor move to set aside the sale to Purchaser? _____

57. Debtor defaults on an obligation for which a valid security interest is held by Secured Party. To facilitate immediate disposition of the collateral, Secured Party pays Debtor $100 to sign a document that purports to "waive" the following rights: (i) right to compel public sale of collateral; (ii) right to notice of public sale; (iii) right to any surplus from proceeds of public sale; and (iv) right to redeem collateral prior to public sale. Is the "waiver" valid in whole or in part? _____

58. Purchaser defaults on her contract to purchase a stereo system, upon which Circuit Buy Store has a perfected security interest. Circuit Buy repossesses and conducts a public sale, but fails to notify Purchaser in writing of the time and place of sale. The original cost of the stereo was $5,000, and Purchaser had paid $2,000 as down payment and signed a contract to pay $3,800 over three years (the $800 reflecting interest on the unpaid balance). What is the minimum amount of damages to which Purchaser is entitled? _____

Answers to Review Questions

1. **YES**   A security interest in any kind of "goods" is subject to the U.C.C. (and "goods" includes crops growing on land). [§57]

2. **YES**   A security interest can be created in "accounts." [§68]

  a. **YES**   As a pledge of "general intangibles." [§73]

3. **NO**   Assignment of wage claims is excluded from Article 9. [§102]

4.a. **YES**   The sale of accounts (or chattel paper, payment intangibles, or promissory notes) is as much a financing transaction as borrowing on the security of such accounts. It makes no difference whether the assignment is with or without reserve. [§§45, 104]

  b. **NO**   Here, it is clearly not for financing purposes and is covered by a specific exclusion. [§105]

  c. **NO**   Again, a specific exclusion applies. [§108]

5. **NO**   Leaseholds in real property are excluded from the U.C.C. [§97]

  a. **YES**   As a financing transaction involving *existing instruments*; it is immaterial that the original obligation giving rise to the instrument was exempt from the U.C.C. [§111]

6. **YES**   Failure to perfect a security interest does not affect the validity of the interest as against the debtor. [§§116-117]

7. **YES**   If collateral is in the *possession* of the secured party, no formal security agreement is required for the interest to attach, and the interest is perfected upon possession. [§§123, 158]

8. **YES**   A reasonable identification is all that is required; description by category and location is generally enough. [§§128-131]

9.a. **YES**   Unless otherwise agreed, proceeds of described collateral are covered as a matter of law. [§370]

  b. **YES**   Although there is some conflicting authority, the word "inventory" is usually sufficient to create an interest in after-acquired items. [§139]

  c. **NO**   The financing statement does not need to be signed, but it does need to be authorized. When the debtor authenticates the record of the security agreement, this automatically authorizes the secured party to file a financing statement. [§262]

10.	**YES**	The interest attaches when "value" is given, and the commitment to make the loan is "value" under the U.C.C. [§146]
11.	**PROBABLY**	A security interest attaches as soon as the debtor acquires rights in the collateral. [§145] Printer's right to possession (enforceable through replevin or specific performance) would arise as soon as goods had been *identified* to the contract. Bank's interest would attach at this time (subject to Pressco's right to withhold to complete production and to obtain payment, etc.). [§151]
12.a.	**YES**	The security interest was perfected by taking *possession*. [§§158-159]
b.	**YES**	Lender is entitled to reimbursement for reasonable expenses. [§174]
c.	**PROBABLY LENDER**	Debtor bears the loss unless it was attributable to Lender's failure to exercise reasonable care. Failure to insure to full value would probably constitute unreasonable care. [§§176-177]
d.	**NO**	The secured party is liable for any loss resulting from such breach of duty of care but does not forfeit the interest. [§169]
13.a.	**NO**	Where the debtor has possession of the goods, there must be an authenticated security agreement. [§125]
b.	**YES**	Because in consumer goods transactions, the seller can perfect a purchase money security interest without filing. [§182]
c.	**YES**	A purchase money security interest in consumer goods can be automatically perfected either by the seller or any lender who supplies the funds used to purchase the collateral in question. [§185]
d.	**NO**	A purchase money security interest in consumer goods can be perfected without filing only to the extent of the value advanced for the *purchase* of collateral. [§184]
14.	**DEPENDS**	On whether the "bad" accounts were a "significant portion" of Manufacturer's receivables. If not, no filing is required; the interest is perfected on sale or assignment. [§§198-201]
15.	**DEPENDS**	On whether Bank filed a financing statement within 20 days after release of the bill of lading. Having possession of the bill of lading, Bank's interest was perfected *without filing*; but upon releasing the bill of lading (a negotiable document), Bank's interest would become unperfected *after 20 days* unless Bank filed a financing statement in the interim. If Bank failed to do so, Other Creditor would prevail. [§§208-210]
16.	**NO**	The movement of the collateral is irrelevant to Bank's continued security interest therein. A nonpossessory security interest in equipment is governed by the

law of the state in which the *debtor* is located. Printco, a corporation, is located in the place of its incorporation—State X. Therefore, Printco's filing in State X is still effective. [§§227, 229]

a. **FOUR MONTHS** — The original perfection only lasts for four months unless the creditor reperfects in State Y within that period. [§243]

17. **YES** — Acme obtained perfection through *control* of the securities accounts when it had its name placed on the account. [§216]

18.a. **YES** — The rule requiring a reperfection within four months does not apply to a security interest in an automobile that has been perfected by notation on the certificate of title until a new certificate of title that does not contain the notation is obtained in a new state. [§§254-255]

b. **YES** — As long as no innocent purchaser is involved, Seller's interest would still be enforceable. [§255]

c. **NO** — After the vehicle moves and is covered by a new certificate of title, the Code protects later purchasers whose interests arise more than four months after the issuance of the new certificate. [§255]

19. **MAYBE** — A minor error that is not seriously misleading is not fatal to perfection, and the Code uses the test of whether a search under the incorrect name using the filing office's search engine logic would find the original financing statement. [§268]

20. **NONE** — A financing statement is effective if it contains the names and addresses of the debtor and secured party and a description of the collateral. No further details are required. [§261]

21. **DEPENDS** — A new filing within four months is required whenever debtor's name is changed so as to be "seriously misleading." (Note that this impairs only after-acquired collateral, however.) [§274]

a. **YES** — A name change does not affect perfection of an interest in the original collateral. [§274]

22. **NO** — A *bogus* filing (*i.e.*, a filing made by a person who is not entitled to file) does not result in perfection. Billy is entitled to a termination statement and may recover actual damages and $500 punitive damages from Mary. [§297]

23. **NO** — The designation of location would not constitute reasonable notice of interest claimed at other locations. [§275]

a. **YES** — The debtor is entitled to have a termination statement filed within 20 days of authenticated demand. [§292]

24.	**NO**	Only a *local* filing will perfect a security interest in fixtures, minerals, and timber to be cut. [§281]
25.	**5 YEARS**	The loan period (if shown) is irrelevant. [§287]
26.	**YES**	Secured party may file a **continuation** statement for an additional five years. The continuation statement must be filed within six months prior to expiration. [§291]
27.	**NO**	No third party has the right to compel the secured party to release this information, but the secured party must give an authenticated statement upon request of the *debtor*. [§§303-304]
28.	**LENDER A**	The first to file or perfect wins. Filing on March 1 protects Lender A even though his interest was not actually perfected until he made the loan (March 15). *Rationale:* Lender B could have protected himself by checking the filings before lending money. [§§325-326]
29.	**LENDER B**	Lender B is first to file **or perfect**. (Lender A's interest **attached** first, but that does not count.) [§§325-326]
a.	**NO**	Where interests have been perfected, priority is **not affected** by actual knowledge of competing interests. [§§325-326]
30.	**BANK**	A purchase money security interest in consumer goods is perfected **without** filing, and Bank is entitled to priority as the "first to file or **perfect**." [§§182, 325]
31.a.	**YES**	The financing statement need not mention the after-acquired property agreement. [§277]
b.	**BANK**	The after-acquired property clause in the security agreement gives Bank priority as to such property over subsequent interest holders. [§326]
32.	**PRESS CO.**	A properly perfected purchase money security interest in equipment takes priority over an after-acquired property clause. [§331]
33.	**LENDER**	A purchase money security interest in **nonconsumer** goods must be perfected by filing or possession. [§§182, 326]
34.	**BANK**	A purchase money security interest can be perfected **within 20 days** after the debtor obtains possession; if so perfected, it takes priority over any intervening interests. [§331]
a.	**YES**	The method by which the intervening interest was perfected is immaterial. [§333]
b.	**BANK**	The purchase money secured party is entitled to the same priority in proceeds as in the original collateral. [§331]

35.	**YES**	By giving Lender *authenticated notice* before the shipment is received that Bank expects to acquire a purchase money security interest therein, and by actually *perfecting* (*e.g.,* by filing) its interest *before* the shipment is received (no 20-day grace period). [§§336-341]
36.	**DEPENDS**	Appliance Co. would win as long as its security interest had *attached* before the furnace was installed, *provided* Appliance Co. *perfects* its interest through a special *fixture filing* (in real estate records) within 20 days after installation. [§351]
37.a.	**YES**	By requiring Octopus National to follow Lender's instructions, Lender has established control over the account and is thus perfected. [§219]
b.	**OCTOPUS**	Where the depository bank is owed money by a depositor, the bank prevails even over another creditor who has control. [§402]
38.a.	**YES**	As long as Produce Co.'s interest was *perfected* prior to processing, its interest continues in the finished product. [§365]
b.	**LENDER**	Produce Co. would prevail over Lender's perfected interest in the inventory only if it gave the section 9-324(b) notice and perfected prior to delivery. [§§336-341]
39.a.	**NO**	A sale in the ordinary course of business by Steve's Sound Systems Store cuts off the prior secured interest of Lender. [§§420-428]
b.	**YES**	The trade-in is "proceeds" of the inventory item sold. [§378]
c.	**NO**	The secured party's right arises by operation of law. [§376]
d.	**NO**	The fact that the "proceeds" were obtained in violation of the security agreement is immaterial. [§385]
e.	**POSSIBLY**	Where the proceeds are cash, the secured party's interest continues as long as the proceeds are "identifiable." [§382]
f.	**BANK**	A party who gives value and takes possession of chattel paper cuts off a security interest claimed merely as "proceeds" of inventory. Bank's knowledge of Lender's interest is immaterial. [§390]
g.	**BANK**	A purchaser of chattel paper (conditional sales contract) is entitled to priority over a financer of inventory as to returned goods. [§399]
40.	**BANK— $60,000**	Under the Code, future advances relate back to the date of original perfection (Bank filed October 1), so as to take priority over all later interests—even where the later interest is perfected by possession. [§§404-409]
a.	**YES**	This need not be disclosed in the financing statement. [§408]

b.	**YES**	Because the filing on October 1 constitutes constructive notice that Bank had some sort of interest; it would be up to Lender to find out. [§408]
c.	**YES**	Because the "first-to-file-or-perfect" rule applies regardless of knowledge of competing interests. [§326]
41.a.	**NO**	A perfected security interest in machinery and equipment is *not* cut off by a sale to a bona fide purchaser. Filing constitutes constructive notice. [§§419-429]
b.	**YES**	Lender's interest attaches to the *collateral* regardless of who is the owner. Bank is charged with notice of any interest conveyed by any prior owner in Purchaser's source of title. [§§325, 429]
42.	**NO**	A buyer *in the ordinary course of business* from a dealer in such goods cuts off even a perfected security interest. [§420]
a.	**NO**	Mere knowledge of Lender's interest would not invalidate the sale, but knowledge that the sale to Purchaser was *unauthorized* under the security agreement would. [§420]
43.	**YES**	Seller here was *not* a dealer in the goods sold, and hence the purchaser is not protected under U.C.C. section 9-320(a). [§§420-429]
44.	**ONLY $10,000**	Sale to Liquidator was *not* "in ordinary course of business" and hence did not cut off Bank's interest. But Bank's interest is limited to the original advance because the subsequent advance occurred *more than 45 days* following sale. [§§431-432]
a.	**YES**	As "proceeds" of the collateral originally covered. The fact that Bank's security interest also continued in the silverware (to the extent of $10,000) is immaterial; it *can claim both*. [§377]
45.	**CRUNCH CREDIT UNION**	We-Fix-It is a statutory lien holder with a possessory lien. [*See* U.C.C. §9-333] Since it parted with possession (regardless of how meritorious its reason for doing so), it lost its lien. [*See* §436] As between Crunch and the landlord, the former prevails since a judicial lien creditor (the landlord) is junior to a *perfected* security interest. [§452]
46.	**BANK**	Advances made within 45 days of levy by a lien creditor are protected even where secured party *had knowledge* of the lien. [§453]
47.	**YES**	Under the strong arm clause, the trustee in bankruptcy can avoid a security interest that is unperfected at the time of the filing of the bankruptcy petition. [§§489-492]
48.	**NO**	The Bankruptcy Code gives a secured interest holder 30 days within which to perfect by filing, in which event transfer dates from when interest was created

rather than from filing. Accordingly, Lender's interest dates from June 1, and the 90-day preference period expired September 1. [§§491, 506]

49. **YES**   Because filing occurred beyond the 30-day grace period. Hence, "transfer" took place only on July 9. At that time, it was for an *antecedent* debt (loan made June 1); hence, a preference. [§§490 *et seq.*]

50. **TRUSTEE**   The Bankruptcy Code condemns as a preference any *buildup* in inventory during the preference period, so the new inventory will go to the trustee and not Lender. [§509]

51. **NO**   Repossession must be done *without a breach of the peace*, and most courts hold that repossession over the debtor's slightest objection breaches the peace. A creditor who continues such a repossession is guilty of conversion. [§§532-540]

52. **PROBABLY NOT**   As long as a *default* exists (even one installment missed), the secured party is entitled to the remedies provided under the U.C.C. One of these is to *disable* the collateral on the debtor's premises, provided the secured party acts in a commercially reasonable manner. [§§546-547]

53. **YES**   If Lender sends out a notice of intention to do so, it can keep the collateral, but Jeweler can then object and force a resale. [§§554-555]

   a. **NO**   The "60%" rule applies only to consumer goods; Jeweler can force resale by objecting to strict foreclosure within 20 days after Lender's notice was sent. [§§554-557]

54. **PROBABLY NOT**   Assuming the repossession was proper, Circuit Buy was entitled to dispose of the collateral in any "commercially reasonable manner"—including private sale (especially since it was a dealer in such merchandise). Lower sale price is not enough by itself to show the resale was commercially unreasonable. [§§559-560, 587-588]

   a. **YES**   The notice requirement applies whether a public or private sale is contemplated. [§563]

   b. **NO**   Normally a secured party who repossesses must notify all secured parties who have filed a financing statement as to the same collateral, but not where the collateral is consumer goods. [§572]

55. **PROBABLY NOT**   A secured party is not entitled to sell to itself at a *private sale* except if the goods are of a type customarily sold in a recognized market or at widely distributed standard price quotations. "Low blue book" would probably *not* qualify. [§§574, 580]

56.a. **YES**   Absent fraud in the sale, the *sale price* (not market value) is used to compute any deficiency. [§587]

b. **YES**   All expenses incurred in good faith in retaking and disposing of the collateral may be included. [§582] Consumer debtors are entitled to an explanation of how the deficiency was calculated. [§591]

c. **NO**   The purchaser's title cannot be set aside for defects in the sale unless the debtor can prove that the purchaser was in collusion with the secured party or had knowledge of the defect. [§599]

57.   **IN PART**   (i), (ii), and (iv) *can* be "waived" by the debtor *after* default, as here. Not so, however, as to (iii). [§§615-620]

58.   **$1,300**   Consumer goods penalty measure: *i.e.,* the time-price differential ($800) plus 10% of the original cash price ($500). [§608]

Exam Questions and Answers

QUESTION I

Octopus National Bank ("ONB") loaned money to Luddite Technologies, Inc., with the latter signing a security agreement giving ONB a security interest in "the inventory of the debtor." ONB perfected this security interest by filing a financing statement in the proper place. A year later, Luddite ordered a shipment of abacuses from Voice of Japan, planning to add the abacuses to its inventory and resell them. To pay for the abacuses, Luddite sent Voice of Japan a check for the full amount, at which point Voice of Japan sent the abacuses to Luddite. When Luddite's check bounced, Voice of Japan investigated and discovered that Luddite was insolvent and had no money at all. At this same time, ONB repossessed the inventory since Luddite had defaulted and ceased making payment to ONB. Voice of Japan protested that the abacuses belonged to it because it still had title to them, that ONB's security interest never attached because Luddite had no rights in the abasuses, and that ONB's security agreement only covered Luddite's inventory that was in existence at the time of the loan because the security agreement only said "inventory," not "inventory now owned or after-acquired." Voice of Japan consults you for legal advice. Will these arguments prevail over ONB's floating lien? What should Voice of Japan do in the future to avoid this difficulty?

QUESTION II

Midway Attractions, a Delaware corporation, owned a huge carousel that was permanently installed in a park in Washington. It used the carousel as collateral for a loan from Last National Bank, located in Indianapolis.

(a) Midway has signed the bank's security agreement covering the carousel. Does it have to sign the financing statement, too?

(b) In what state should the bank file the financing statement?

(c) If Midway ceases to make payments and the bank must repossess the carousel, what law will apply to any repossession issues that arise?

QUESTION III

On a visit to Los Angeles, Alice bought a used car on credit from Fair Motors, which promptly obtained a California certificate of title, made sure its name was listed thereon as the lien holder, and kept the certificate at the dealership, telling Alice she could have it when she made all the required payments. Alice took the car back to her home state of Ohio, and then somehow obtained an Ohio certificate of title to the car that did not list Fair Motors as a lien holder. When she needed to borrow money from her mother, Alice's mother, Janice, had her sign a security agreement using the car as collateral, and Janice then had the Ohio certificate changed to reflect her lien on the car. Janice did not know about the Fair Motors lien. A month after she bought the car from Fair Motors, Alice sold it to Honest John's Used Cars in Cleveland. When Fair Motors finally found the car, it sued Honest John's to recover possession. Who has superior rights in the car?

QUESTION IV

The inventory of Arabian Rug Company "now owned or after-acquired" is subject to a perfected (filed) security interest held by Retailer Bank. Arabian Rug Company is contacted by Ornate Rugs of Persia, a rug manufacturer, which asks Arabian's owner if the company would be willing to act as Ornate's selling agent in the United States in return for a 30% commission on each rug sold. Ornate and Arabian sign a contract containing a clause providing that Arabian is only a selling agent and that title to the rugs will at all times remain in Ornate. Before shipping the rugs to Arabian, the president of Ornate seeks advice. Are there any other steps Ornate should take before shipment?

QUESTION V

In January, White Truck Ice Cream Company ("White Truck") granted a security interest in all its equipment to Tenacles National Bank ("TNB"), which perfected its interest by filing. TNB committed itself to loan White Truck $10,000 each month as long as White Truck repaid a certain portion of the debt monthly. These loans were made on the first of every month. On May 10, White Truck sold one of its ice cream making machines to a competitor, Blue Truck Ice Cream Company. TNB knew nothing about this sale. On September 1, TNB made its usual loan to White Truck. On September 25, the federal government filed a tax lien in the proper place against White Truck, which had somehow neglected to pay its taxes for the past year. On October 1, November 1, and December 1, TNB made its usual loans, but the day before Christmas, TNB discovered the tax lien. TNB wants to find out what its rights are against Blue Truck, and which, if any, of its loans to White Truck has priority vis-a-vis the government. Discuss.

QUESTION VI

Music, Music, Music Co. ("MMMC") sold musical instruments. Its inventory was subject to a security interest in favor of Local Bank, which had filed a financing statement in the proper place on April 1. When MMMC sold a piano on credit, it made the buyer sign a promissory note payable to MMMC, plus an agreement giving MMMC a security interest in the piano. MMMC never filed financing statements for these transactions. The resulting notes and security agreements were sold to Merchants Finance Company with an agreement to buy them back should they prove uncollectable. In January of the next year, MMMC contracted to buy 50 fancy black walnut pianos from Black Walnut Piano Company. Black Walnut agreed to sell them to MMMC on credit, reserving (pursuant to agreement) a security interest in the pianos to secure their purchase price. Prior to delivering the pianos to MMMC, Black Walnut filed a financing statement in the appropriate place and sent a letter to Local Bank (but not to Merchants Finance) describing the deal. Cathy Consumer bought a black walnut piano from MMMC on credit, signing the usual documents, which MMMC sold to Merchants Finance. Assuming MMMC repays none of its debts:

(a) Can Black Walnut or Local Bank get back the piano sold to Cathy Consumer?

(b) Which creditor, Local Bank or Black Walnut, has the superior interest in the black walnut pianos in MMMC's inventory?

(c) Which creditor, Local Bank, Merchants Finance, or Black Walnut, has the superior interest in the rights represented by the documents Cathy Consumer signed?

QUESTION VII

Helene Houseowner decided to build her dream house. To do the job, she borrowed $80,000 from Sharksteeth Finance Company ("SFC"), giving SFC a mortgage on the property and all additions thereto, which SFC properly recorded. When the dream house was almost complete, Helene bought a large exercise machine designed to be built into her exercise room from Muscles, Inc. on credit. Muscles, Inc. had Helene sign a security agreement and a financing statement.

Muscles, Inc. now seeks advice. On previous sales transactions, Muscles, Inc. was advised that it need not go through the expense of filing a financing statement to preserve its purchase money security interest in consumer goods. Is there any reason why it should file in this case? If so, where should it file? Are there any other steps it should take before installing the machine in Helene's exercise room?

QUESTION VIII

Farmer MacDonald put his crop in a grain elevator and received in return a negotiable warehouse receipt. MacDonald took the receipt to Antitrust National Bank ("ANB") and asked to borrow money on the strength of it. ANB loaned MacDonald $5,000 and had him sign a security agreement in its favor, but left the warehouse receipt with Farmer MacDonald. ANB filed the financing statement in the proper place. Farmer MacDonald then took the receipt to Farmers Friend State Bank ("FFSB") and pledged it to them for a loan of $7,000. Farmer told FFSB nothing about the ANB deal, and FFSB did not check the filing records. Two months later, when it came time to sell the grain, MacDonald retrieved the warehouse receipt from the possession of FFSB so that he could get the grain from the elevator. The next day, Farmer filed a voluntary bankruptcy petition and turned the receipt over to his trustee in bankruptcy. Both ANB and FFSB claim the receipt, and the bankruptcy trustee now seeks advice, stating that the financing statement filed by ANB failed to mention ANB's address. Who is entitled to the grain: the trustee or one of the banks?

QUESTION IX

On June 10, Mary Shrub borrowed $8,000 from Consumers Bank and signed a security agreement giving the bank a security interest in her very valuable china collection. On November 8, Mary bought furniture for her law office on credit, signing a security agreement in favor of the seller, Office Furnishings. On November 15, Mary filed a voluntary bankruptcy petition. On November 16, Office Furnishings filed its financing statement in the proper place, covering both the china and the furniture.

Which of these transactions is valid against Mary's bankruptcy trustee? Explain.

QUESTION X

After Tim Isle had paid back $900 of a $1,000 debt owed on his automobile to the Repossession Finance Company, he missed the final $100 payment. A clause in the security agreement gave Repossession the right to break into Tim's home to retrieve the car. Pursuant to this clause, Repossession sent out a repo-man named Sam Price, who jimmied open a window in Tim's garage, hot wired the car, and drove it off in the middle of the night. At the time of repossession, the car had several of its parts removed because Tim was tuning the engine. Four months after the repossession, the finance company sold the car for $40 to Sam Price, who paid this low amount because the car "wasn't running right." No one had checked the car to discover the source of its mechanical difficulties. Repossession gave no notice to Tim of the private sale to Price, so that the first Tim knew of the sale was when he received notice of a lawsuit Repossession was bringing against him for $360—the $60 remaining on the debt, plus the costs of repossession and resale. What arguments can Tim Isle raise in defense of this suit?

ANSWER TO QUESTION I

Voice of Japan will lose all of its arguments. First, title is not an important concept in the Uniform Commercial Code, and a reservation of title is limited to the reservation of a security interest in the collateral. [U.C.C. §1-201(37)] This means that Voice of Japan has a *purchase money security interest* in the abacuses, and should have taken the steps required of such a creditor to prevail over ONB's floating lien. [U.C.C. §§9-103, 9-324(b) - (c)] It is irrelevant that Voice of Japan did not mean to enter into a credit transaction with Luddite and thought of this as a "cash sale." [U.C.C. §2-403(a); *and see* §461] Second, as long as Luddite acquired possession of the collateral lawfully, it has sufficient rights therein for the security interest of ONB to attach and therefore prevail over Voice of Japan's unperfected security interest. ONB's security interest in the abacuses attached as soon as the abacuses were *identified* as belonging to this transaction [*see* §151], and Voice of Japan lost its priority as soon as it lost possession of the goods. [U.C.C. §9-320(e)] Finally, most courts have held that a reference to inventory includes both that currently in existence and that acquired in the future, since inventory necessarily turns over constantly. Therefore, ONB's security interest description reaches the after-acquired inventory of delivered abacuses. [*See* §139]

ANSWER TO QUESTION II

(a) It does not matter that Midway only signed the security agreement. The debtor's authentication of the security agreement also authorizes the filing of a financing statement, and the debtor's signature is not a requirement for the effectiveness of a financing statement. [U.C.C. §§9-502(a), 9-509(b); *and see* §§261, 266]

(b) If the carousel qualifies as a "fixture" (an issue to be determined by law other than the Uniform Commercial Code), the bank should make a fixture filing in the real property records in Washington, in the county where the carousel is located. [U.C.C. §§9-301(3)(A), 9-501(a)(1)(B); *and see* §§235, 281] If it is determined that the carousel is ordinary goods rather than a fixture, then the financing statement should be filed in the central state office in the state of the debtor's location. Corporations are located in the state of their incorporation, so the bank should file in Delaware. [U.C.C. §§9-301(1), 9-307(e), 9-501(a)(2); *and see* §§229, 281]

(c) The law of the *collateral's location* governs priority disputes and other issues involving rights in the collateral, so any repossession issues will be dealt with using the law of the state of Washington. [U.C.C. §9-301(3)(C) and Comment 7; *and see* §242]

ANSWER TO QUESTION III

Janice prevails over all other parties, with Fair Motors being second in line, and Honest John's Used Cars coming in last. Ordinarily, the notation of Fair Motors's security interest on the California certificate of title would remain effective for four months after the clean certificate of title was issued in Ohio. [U.C.C. §9-303(c); *and see* §255] However, Uniform Commercial Code section 9-337 protects some parties whose interests arise within the four-month grace period after the debtor obtains a clean certificate in a new state. One party so protected is a later secured party who is listed on the new certificate and who becomes a secured party without knowledge of the rights of the holder of the prior certificate. [U.C.C. §9-337(2); *and see* §257] Janice meets this requirement, so her interest is superior to that of Fair Motors. However, this section does not protect professional car buyers like Honest John's Used Cars, so Fair prevails over it. [U.C.C. §9-337(1); *and see* §257]

ANSWER TO QUESTION IV

This transaction is likely to qualify as a *consignment* pursuant to the definition of that term in Uniform Commercial Code ("U.C.C.") section 9-102(a)(20). [*See* §89] The U.C.C. treats the consignor (Ornate Rugs of Persia) as the holder of a purchase money security interest ("PMSI") in inventory. [U.C.C. §9-103(d)] For the consignor to prevail over a perfected floating lien covering the consigned goods in the consignee's inventory, the consignor must take the same steps as those required for a holder of a PMSI in inventory to gain super-priority: the consignor must make the debtor authenticate a security agreement covering the goods and perfect that interest before the debtor receives possession, and the consignor further must send a notice to the holder of the floating lien describing the goods involved and stating that it has a PMSI therein. [U.C.C. §9-324(b); *and see* §§336-341, 346] If the Article 9 definition of "consignment" does not cover the transaction (because, for example, the Arabian Rug Company is generally known by its creditors to be substantially engaged in the sale of goods belonging to another), Ornate Rugs of Persia will prevail over Retailer Bank since Article 9 no longer governs the transaction, and the common law of most jurisdictions allows a consignor to reclaim its goods over the rights of the consignee's creditors. [*See* §91]

ANSWER TO QUESTION V

Unless the secured party authorizes the sale or waives its security interest, the collateral is not freed from the security interest by the debtor's sale. [U.C.C. §9-315(a)] The buyer in the ordinary course of business exception does not apply because the sale of equipment is never in the ordinary course. Thus, Tenacles National Bank can repossess the truck from Blue Truck Ice Cream Company. (Blue Truck would, however, have an Article 2 breach of warranty of good title action against its seller, White Truck. [U.C.C. §2-312])

TNB's competition with the federal tax lien looks less promising. [*See* §443] Future advances by a creditor to a debtor are protected against a filed federal tax lien only if made without knowledge of the lien and within 45 days of the tax lien filing. Here, TNB's security interest protects the loans TNB made prior to 45 days after September 25 (when the tax lien was filed). Thus, the October and November loans (and the ones prior thereto) are superior to the I.R.S., but the December advance is not. [*See* §450]

ANSWER TO QUESTION VI

(a) No. Buyers of inventory who buy in the ordinary course of business are protected by U.C.C. section 9-320(a), which allows them to take the product they purchase free of preexisting security interests created by their seller. [*See* §420] Thus, Cathy Consumer gets the piano free of the security interests held by both Local Bank and Black Walnut.

(b) Black Walnut has the senior interest in the black walnut pianos since it complied with the steps that U.C.C. section 9-324(b) requires be taken by those creditors claiming a purchase money security interest in goods about to become part of the debtor's inventory—*i.e.*, perfection prior to debtor's possession and authenticated notice of the transaction to the existing inventory lienor. [*See* §§336-341]

(c) These documents (an instrument plus a security interest agreement) constitute "chattel paper." [U.C.C. §9-102(a)(11); *and see* §64] U.C.C. section 9-330 provides that a purchaser of chattel paper (here Merchants Finance Company) prevails over previous financers of the inventory who are claiming the chattel paper as proceeds of the inventory.

ANSWER TO QUESTION VII

A purchase money secured creditor usually does not have to file to perfect a purchase money security interest in consumer goods. [*See* §182] However, where, as here, the goods are to become *fixtures*, automatic perfection rules do not apply, and Muscles, Inc. must make a *fixture filing* of a financing statement in the county real estate records. [*See* U.C.C. §9-501(a)(1)(B); *and see* §§351-352] Moreover, even if Muscles, Inc. makes such a filing, it will still be junior to the preexisting perfected interest of Sharksteeth Finance Company which has a "construction mortgage" on the property. [U.C.C. §9-334(h); *and see* §355] Therefore, the best course for Muscles, Inc. to follow would be to get an agreement by SFC to *subordinate* its interest to Muscles, Inc. [U.C.C. §9-334(f)(1); *and see* §356]

ANSWER TO QUESTION VIII

The secured party's address is not required to be in the financing statement in order for perfection to occur by filing; it is only a ground for a filing office to *reject* the financing statement. [U.C.C. §§9-502, 9-516(b)(4)] If the filing office accepts the financing statement without such an address, the filing is effective. [U.C.C. §9-516, Comment 5; *and see* §269] Thus, ANB has a perfected security interest in the warehouse receipt.

FFSB's interest arose from a pledge of the warehouse receipt (a "document"). Under section 7-403(3) of the Uniform Commercial Code, a later good faith purchaser of a document qualifies as a "holder to whom a negotiable document of title has been duly negotiated" [U.C.C. §7-502], and such a party prevails over perfected Article 9 security interests [U.C.C. §9-331(a)]. [*See* §435] This means that ANB will lose to FFSB, which also beats out the trustee in bankruptcy since its interest was perfected when the bankruptcy was filed. FFSB is perfected even though FFSB surrendered the document to the debtor. U.C.C. section 9-312(f) continues FFSB's perfection for a 20-day period following the surrender, so that FFSB remains perfected against the debtor's trustee in bankruptcy whose interest arose in that period. [*See* §§208-209, 225]

ANSWER TO QUESTION IX

If Consumers Bank had filed its financing statement immediately after the loan (which it was required to do since it did not have a *purchase money* security interest in the china), it would have had no problems. Instead, however, it waited and filed after the debtor's filing of a bankruptcy petition. Thus, at the moment when the bankruptcy petition was filed, the bank was unperfected. Per the strong arm clause of section 544(a) of the Bankruptcy Code, the trustee has the rights of a judicial lien creditor, and such a creditor wipes out unperfected security interests per section 9-317 of the Uniform Commercial Code. [*See* §489] The trustee will have priority in the china.

In comparison, Office Furnishings *does* have a purchase money security interest in the furniture and, thus, has the benefit of a 30-day grace period after Shrub receives possession in which to file its financing statement. (Note that Office Furnishings must file since the collateral is not consumer goods.) [U.C.C. §9-317(e); *and see* §504] This 30-day period is *not* cut short by the filing of the bankruptcy petition, so the filing of the financing statement on November 16 perfected the interest against the attack of Shrub's bankruptcy trustee.

ANSWER TO QUESTION X

The actions of Repossession violated almost every relevant provision of Article 9 of the Uniform Commercial Code ("U.C.C."). Section 9-609(b)(2) permits self-help repossession of the sort undertaken here only if it can be accomplished without a "breach of the peace." Most courts would hold the peace breached by Price's breaking and entering, even though the security agreement gave the creditor this right. [*See* §537] A repossession without the authority of U.C.C. section 9-609 is *stealing*—the tort of conversion—for which the debtor may recover actual and punitive damages. (The latter may be measured by the U.C.C. section 9-625(c)(2) formula of 10% of the cash price plus the finance charges; *see* §609.)

In addition, the consumer-debtor who has paid 60% or more of the cash price (as Isle did here) is entitled by section 9-620(e) - (f) to have the collateral *resold* within 90 days of the repossession (here the creditor waited four months), or the debtor may sue in conversion or under section 9-625(c)(2). [*See* §§551-553]

Finally, U.C.C. section 9-610(b) requires that the resale be commercially reasonable in all aspects and that the debtor be sent a pre-sale notice. [*See* §560] Selling repossessed cars without repairing minor problems (like replacing engine parts that the debtor had removed for maintenance purposes) has been held to be commercially unreasonable. Of course, Isle received no notice here of the resale. In this situation, in addition to being liable for the damages listed above, Repossession may lose its right to sue for the deficiency (the amount still owing). Although the U.C.C. contains a rule pertaining to nonconsumer goods, it does not contain a rule for consumer goods (which are the type of collateral in this case), and instead allows state courts to formulate their own rules concerning the right to sue for a deficiency. Therefore, Repossession's ability to sue for a deficiency will be determined by the state's common law. [U.C.C. §9-626; *and see* §592] The debtor is also entitled to an explanation of how any deficiency was calculated, and if the creditor fails to provide it, the debtor may be entitled to punitive damages of $500 in addition to any actual damages. [U.C.C. §§9-616, 9-625(e); *and see* §591]

Table of Citations

CITATIONS TO UNIFORM COMMERCIAL CODE
(All Article 9 Citations are to the Revised 1999 Article 9)

U.C.C. Section	Text Reference	U.C.C. Section	Text Reference	U.C.C. Section	Text Reference
1-102(3)	§173	3-305	§521	9-102(a)(52)	§§309, 311
1-201	§246	3-419	§3	9-102(a)(53)	§290
1-201(9)	§423	3-605	§3	9-102(a)(54)	§290
1-201(15)	§63	5-114(c)	§221	9-102(a)(56)	§328
1-201(19)	§516	5-116	§240	9-102(a)(59)	§48
1-201(32)	§§247, 289	6-102(1)	§424	9-102(a)(61)	§75
1-201(33)	§§247, 289	7-403	§24	9-102(a)(64)(E)	§375
1-201(36)	§148	7-403(3)	§163	9-102(a)(67)	§290
1-201(37)	§§19, 44, 45, 78, 82	7-501	§435	9-102(a)(68)	§§146, 432
1-201(37)(a)	§80	7-505	§435	9-102(a)(69)	§127
1-201(37)(b)	§80	8-102(a)(18)	§215	9-102(a)(73)	§46
1-201(37)(c)	§80	8-106(a)	§214	9-102(a)(77)	§205
1-201(37)(d)	§81	8-106(b)	§214	9-102(a)(78)	§64
1-201(38)	§555	8-106(c)	§215	9-102(a)(79)	§292
1-201(44)	§146	8-108(d)	§216	9-102(a)(80)	§283
1-203	§514	8-110	§239	9-103	§184
1-205	§417	8-301(b)	§215	9-103(a)(2)	§185
1-205(4)	§417	8-303	§435	9-103(b)	§184
1-208	§§513, 514	9-102	§§54, 57, 58, 59	9-103(d)	§346
1-209	§110	9-102(a)(1)	§360	9-103(e)	§194
2-105	§51	9-102(a)(2)	§§68, 69	9-103(e)(2)	§195
2-208	§526	9-102(a)(5)	§99	9-103(e)(3)	§195
2-208(3)	§417	9-102(a)(7)	§127	9-103(f)	§194
2-209(5)	§526	9-102(a)(9)	§381	9-103(g)	§194
2-312	§§427, 600	9-102(a)(11)	§64	9-103(h)	§195
2-401(1)	§19	9-102(a)(13)	§72	9-104(a)	§219
2-402(2)	§7	9-102(a)(20)	§89	9-104(b)	§219
2-403(a)	§461	9-102(a)(23)	§§55, 187	9-105	§222
2-501	§151	9-102(a)(27)	§291	9-107	§220
2-602	§456	9-102(a)(28)	§48	9-108	§§129, 134, 275
2-608	§§456, 458	9-102(a)(29)	§71	9-108(b)	§130
2-702	§§20, 459, 460, 463, 465	9-102(a)(30)	§63	9-108(c)	§132
		9-102(a)(31)	§64	9-108(e)	§131
2-706	§§457, 458	9-102(a)(40)	§352	9-109	§94
2-711(3)	§§456, 458	9-102(a)(41)	§349	9-109(a)	§49
2A-308(3)	§8	9-102(a)(42)	§§73, 74	9-109(a)(3)	§104
3-104(2)	§61	9-102(a)(44)	§§51, 52, 53	9-109(b)	§111
3-104(3)	§61	9-102(a)(48)	§56	9-109(c)	§436
3-116	§3	9-102(a)(49)	§66	9-109(c)(1)	§94
3-302	§435	9-102(a)(51)	§70	9-109(d)(1)	§§97, 436

U.C.C. Section	Text Reference	U.C.C. Section	Text Reference	U.C.C. Section	Text Reference
9-109(d)(2)	§§98, 436	9-307	§228	9-316(c)	§252
9-109(d)(3)	§102	9-307(a)	§231	9-316(d)	§254
9-109(d)(4)	§105	9-307(b)(1)	§232	9-316(e)	§255
9-109(d)(5)	§106	9-307(b)(2)	§239	9-316(f)	§244
9-109(d)(6)	§107	9-307(b)(3)	§230	9-317	§§154, 489
9-109(d)(7)	§108	9-307(c)	§234	9-317(a)(2)	§§320, 452
9-109(d)(8)	§103	9-307(e)	§229	9-317(b)	§322
9-109(d)(11)	§§64, 97, 111	9-307(h)	§233	9-317(d)	§322
9-109(d)(13)	§§71, 103	9-308(a)	§224	9-320	§420
9-110	§458	9-308(c)	§225	9-320(a)	§§323, 389, 390,
9-201	§114	9-308(d)	§§111, 205		398, 420, 421, 423,
9-202	§§19, 149	9-308(e)	§245		430, 458
9-203	§§119, 126, 144,	9-309	§201	9-320(b)	§433
	186, 312	9-309(1)	§§182, 184, 190, 250	9-320(e)	§428
9-203(a)	§120	9-309(2)	§198	9-322(a)(1)	§§325, 387
9-203(b)(1)	§146	9-309(3)	§204	9-322(a)(2)	§318
9-203(b)(2)	§147	9-309(4)	§204	9-322(a)(3)	§317
9-203(b)(3)(A)	§§125, 128	9-309(13)	§197	9-323	§§404, 409
9-203(b)(3)(B)	§123	9-310	§§157, 203	9-323(b)	§§451, 453
9-203(b)(3)(D)	§124	9-310(b)(6)	§197	9-323(b)(2)	§453
9-203(d)	§328	9-311(a)	§190	9-323(d)	§§431, 451
9-203(e)	§328	9-311(a)(1)	§282	9-323(e)	§431
9-203(f)(3)(B)	§123	9-311(b)	§433	9-324	§§346, 406
9-203(g)	§111	9-311(d)	§190	9-324(a)	§§331, 333
9-204	§136	9-312	§206	9-324(b)	§388
9-204(a)	§§135, 142	9-312(a)	§435	9-324(b)(1)	§338
9-204(b)(1)	§136	9-312(b)(1)	§218	9-324(b)(2)	§339
9-204(b)(2)	§137	9-312(b)(2)	§220	9-324(b)(3)	§341
9-204(c)	§404	9-312(c)	§§163, 165	9-324(b)(4)	§340
9-205	§§34, 142, 371	9-312(d)	§166	9-324(d)	§345
9-207	§548	9-312(e)	§207	9-324(g)	§347
9-207(a)	§§170, 177	9-312(f)	§§209, 225	9-325	§328
9-207(b)(1)	§174	9-312(g)	§210	9-326(b)	§329
9-207(b)(2)	§176	9-313	§158	9-327(1)	§402
9-207(b)(4)	§180	9-313(a)	§160	9-327(3)	§402
9-207(c)	§175	9-313(b)	§160	9-327(4)	§402
9-207(c)(3)	§179	9-313(c)	§167	9-328	§212
9-208	§610	9-313(d)	§168	9-328(1)	§212
9-209	§611	9-313(f)	§167	9-328(3)	§217
9-210	§299	9-315	§§382, 420	9-329	§403
9-210(f)	§302	9-315(a)	§§376, 377	9-329(2)	§403
9-301	§226	9-315(a)(1)	§§415, 429	9-330	§§396, 399
9-301(1)	§227	9-315(a)(2)(c)	§378	9-330(a)	§390
9-301(2)	§235	9-315(b)(2)	§382	9-330(b)	§391
9-301(3)	§§235, 242	9-315(d)	§398	9-330(c)	§§395, 397, 399
9-301(4)	§236	9-315(d)(1)	§380	9-330(d)	§435
9-302	§241	9-315(d)(1)(C)	§381	9-330(f)	§392
9-303	§237	9-315(d)(2)	§382	9-331	§434
9-303(a)	§192	9-315(e)	§381	9-333	§§321, 436, 437,
9-303(b)	§191	9-316	§256		438
9-303(c)	§254	9-316(a)(1)	§249	9-333(b)	§441
9-304	§238	9-316(a)(2)	§243	9-334	§§359, 628
9-305	§239	9-316(a)(3)	§251	9-334(a)	§349
9-306	§240	9-316(b)	§§245, 246	9-334(c)	§357

U.C.C. Section	Text Reference	U.C.C. Section	Text Reference	U.C.C. Section	Text Reference
9-334(e)(1)	§358	9-513(b)	§293	9-610(d)	§600
9-334(e)(2)	§350	9-514	§§202, 297, 298	9-610(e)	§600
9-334(e)(3)	§359	9-515(a)	§287	9-610(f)	§600
9-334(f)	§356	9-515(b)	§290	9-611	§543
9-334(h)	§355	9-515(c)	§§288, 289	9-611(c)	§572
9-335(b)	§361	9-515(d)	§291	9-611(c)(2)	§571
9-335(c)	§362	9-516	§§261, 262, 269	9-611(d)	§§563, 573
9-335(d)	§363	9-516(a)	§284	9-612(a)	§§576, 578
9-335(e)	§626	9-516(b)	§263	9-612(b)	§577
9-335(f)	§627	9-516(d)	§262	9-613	§§564, 566
9-336(a)	§364	9-517	§286	9-614	§§565, 566
9-336(b)	§365	9-518	§296	9-615	§§581, 586
9-336(c)	§365	9-519	§285	9-615(a)(1)	§582
9-336(d)	§365	9-519(f)	§263	9-615(a)(2)	§583
9-336(f)(1)	§368	9-519(g)	§264	9-615(a)(3)(A)	§584
9-336(f)(2)	§366	9-521	§259	9-615(e)	§595
9-337	§257	9-523	§265	9-615(f)	§590
9-339	§110	9-523(e)	§263	9-615(g)	§§585, 598
9-340	§383	9-601	§510	9-616	§591
9-401(b)	§152	9-601(a)	§528	9-616(b)(1)	§613
9-403	§519	9-601(a)(2)	§529	9-616(b)(2)	§§591, 613
9-403(c)	§521	9-601(c)	§527	9-617	§598
9-403(d)	§525	9-601(e)	§601	9-617(b)	§599
9-403(e)	§522	9-602	§§569, 606, 615, 622	9-620	§§528, 550, 557, 558, 618
9-501	§281				
9-501(a)(1)(B)	§352	9-602(5)	§616	9-620(b)	§561
9-501(b)	§283	9-602(7)	§617	9-620(e)	§551
9-502	§§261, 266	9-602(10)	§§556, 618	9-620(g)	§558
9-502(b)	§§278, 352	9-602(11)	§619	9-621	§§528, 554
9-502(b)(4)	§354	9-602(13)	§621	9-622	§528
9-503(a)(4)	§273	9-603	§§547, 549, 615	9-623	§§603, 604, 605, 619
9-503(c)	§272	9-604	§530	9-624	§§553, 570
9-503(d)	§270	9-604(b)	§628	9-624(c)	§620
9-504	§§133, 275	9-604(c)	§626	9-625	§§296, 575, 609, 621
9-504(2)	§276	9-604(d)	§627	9-625(a)	§607
9-504(4)	§596	9-604(e)	§625	9-625(b)	§§292, 301, 591, 608
9-505	§§87, 92	9-607	§145		
9-506	§267	9-607(a)	§624	9-625(c)	§§551, 608
9-506(a)	§267	9-607(a)(1)	§34	9-625(c)(2)	§594
9-506(c)	§268	9-607(d)	§624	9-625(d)	§608
9-507(c)	§274	9-609	§531	9-625(e)	§591
9-508(a)	§328	9-609(a)(2)	§546	9-625(e)(4)	§292
9-508(b)	§274	9-609(b)	§532	9-625(f)	§301
9-509	§296	9-609(c)	§545	9-625(g)	§301
9-509(a)	§§266, 612	9-610	§§528, 559, 598, 600	9-626	§592
9-509(b)	§266			9-626(a)(2)	§§560, 592
9-510(a)	§296	9-610(b)	§560	9-626(a)(5)	§590
9-512	§§279, 295	9-610(c)(1)	§579	9-627(a)	§588
9-513(a)	§612	9-610(c)(2)	§580	9-627(c)	§602

Table of Cases

A

Aetna Insurance Co. v. Texas Thermal Industries, Inc. - **§445**

Allen, *In re* - **§359**

Architectural Woods, Inc. v. Washington - **§201**

Atlantic Stud Welding Co., *In re* - **§138**

B

Baker Products Credit Association v. Long Creek Meat Co. - **§418**

Balon v. Cadillac Automobile Co. - **§189**

Bank of North America v. Kruger - **§442**

Bank of Utica v. Smith Richfield Springs, Inc. - **§277**

Benedict v. Ratner - **§§32, 370, 394**

Bengtson, *In re* - **§269**

Black v. Peoples Bank - **§517**

Border State Bank of Greenbush v. Bagley Livestock Exchange, Inc. - **§149**

Brodheim v. Chase Manhattan Bank - **§173**

Brown v. Avemco Investment Corp. - **§513**

Burlington National Bank v. Strauss - **§269**

C

Certified Packaging, Inc., *In re* - **§73**

Chris-Don, Inc., *In re* - **§73**

Chrysler Credit Corp. v. Malone - **§425**

Clark Equipment Co. v. Armstrong Equipment Co. - **§545**

Clovis National Bank v. Thomas - **§414**

Commercial Credit Equipment Co. v. Carter - **§189**

Commercial Discount Corp. v. Milwaukee Western Bank - **§379**

Consolidated Film Industries v. United States - **§200**

Corn Exchange National Bank & Trust Co. v. Klauder - **§33**

Cox v. Galigher - **§539**

Coxall v. Clover Commercial Corp. - **§§564, 578, 588, 593, 594**

DE

Davenport v. Chrysler Credit Corp. - **§537**

Dynalectron Corp. v. Jack Richards Aircraft Co. - **§562**

F

Farm Credit Bank of St. Paul v. F & A Dairy - **§422**

Farmers State Bank v. Otten - **§561**

Filtercorp, Inc., *In re* - **§139**

Fontane v. Industrial National Bank - **§544**

Food Service Equipment Co. v. First National Bank - **§186**

Ford Motor Credit Co. v. Byrd - **§539**

Ford Motor Credit Co. v. Cole - **§§535, 549**

Fred Kraus & Sons, Inc. v. United States - **§446**

G

General Motors Acceptance Corp. v. Colwell Diesel Service & Garage - **§440**

Grace v. Sterling Grace & Co. - **§170**

Guzman v. Western State Bank - **§544**

H

Hill, *In re* - **§272**

I

I.T.T. Industrial Credit Co. v. H. & K. Machine Service - **§429**

In re - *See* name of party

Indianapolis Morris Plan Corp. v. Karlen - **§606**

International Harvester Co. v. Glendenning - **§426**

J

Jones v. General Motors Acceptance Corp. - **§549**

K

Klingbiel v. Commercial Credit Corp. - **§542**
Kruse, Kruse & Miklosko, Inc. v. Beedy - **§553**
Kubota Tractor Corp. v. Citizens & Southern National Bank - **§140**

L

Layne v. Bank One, Ky., N.A. - **§§172, 573**
Leger Mill Co. v. Kleen-Leen, Inc. - **§437**
Ludwigh v. American Woolen Co. - **§91**

M

Marshall, *In re* - **§250**
Masters, *In re* - **§286**
Moe v. John Deere - **§526**
Moore v. Bay - **§484**
Moran v. Holman - **§561**
Morris v. First National Bank - **§534**

N

National Bank v. Bergeron Cadillac, Inc. - **§439**
Nelson v. Monarch Investment Plan - **§574**
Nightway Transportation Co., *In re* - **§140**
Noble Co. v. Mack Financial Corp. - **§334**
Norton v. National Bank of Commerce - **§574**

O

Olsen v. Valley National Bank - **§528**

PQ

Pankratz Implement Co. v. Citizens Natonal Bank - **§268**
Pelletier, *In re* - **§151**
Philko Aviation, Inc. v. Shacket - **§94**

R

R & J of Tennessee, Inc. v. Blankenship-Melton Real Estate, Inc. - **§566**
Raffa v. Dania Bank - **§538**
Reed v. Central National Bank - **§170**

(Richards through Robinson)

Richards, *In re* - **§275**
Robertson v. Andrus - **§6**
Robinson v. Jefferson Corp. - **§605**

S

St. Paul Mercury Insurance Co. v. Merchants & Marine Bank - **§326**
Salem Trust Co. v. Manufacturer's Financial Co. - **§29**
Sams v. New Kensington City Redevelopment Authority - **§445**
Samuels & Co., *In re* - **§§460, 461**
Schabler v. Indianapolis Morris Plan - **§587**
Security Pacific National Bank v. Goodman - **§427**
Sierra Financial Corp. v. Brooks-Farrer Co. - **§§76, 588**
Stone Machinery Co. v. Kessler - **§536**
Street v. Commercial Credit Corp. - **§605**

T

Tanbro Fabrics v. Deering Milliken - **§428**
Transport Equipment Co. v. Guaranty State Bank - **§162**
Twyne's Case - **§5**

U

Unico v. Owen - **§520**
United States v. Antenna Systems, Inc. - **§73**
United States v. Gleaners & Farmers Cooperative Elevator Co. - **§305**
United States v. Kimbell Foods - **§95**
United States v. Orrego - **§296**
United States Fidelity & Guaranty Co. v. First State Bank - **§109**
Urdang v. Muse - **§605**

V

Van Horn v. Van De Wol, Inc. - **§516**
Vasques v. Superior Court - **§524**

WXYZ

Wabasso State Bank v. Caldwell Packing Co. - **§416**
Weiss v. Northwest Acceptance - **§562**
Wollin, *In re* - **§411**

Index

Subject	U.C.C. Section	Text Section
A		
ACCELERATION CLAUSE		
default and	1-208	513
effect on right of redemption. *See also* Remedies, debtor's		605
good faith requirement	1-208	513, 515-516
in security agreement		153
validity of	1-208	153
ACCESSIONS		
default rules	9-335(e); 9-604(c)	626-627
defined	9-102(a)(1)	360
perfection continues	9-335(b)	361
removal of upon default	9-335(f); 9-604(d)	626-627
usual priority rules	9-335(c)	362-363
motor vehicle exception	9-335(d)	363
ACCOUNT DEBTOR		
collection against upon default	9-209; 9-607(a), (d)	611, 623-625
nonnotification of assignments		28, 623
ACCOUNTING		
for rents, issues, and profits	9-207(c)	175
for surplus or deficiency	9-602(5); 9-616	591, 616
notice of, failure to send	9-625(b), (e)	591
ACCOUNTS		
Article 9 applied to	1-201(37); 9-102(a)(2), (3); 9-310	45, 49, 65, 68-69, 104, 198, 203
as inventory proceeds, priority of	9-322(a)(1)	386-387
assignment of. *See also* Assignment		
exempt from filing	9-309(2)	198-201
nonfinancing arrangements excluded	9-109(d)(4) - (7)	104-108
bank accounts, tracing into	9-315; 9-340	382-383
chattel paper compared		65, 388
default rules. *See also* Default	9-604(e); 9-607(a), (d)	623-625
deficiencies and surplus	9-604(e); 9-615(e)	595, 625
defined	9-102(a)(2)	65, 68-69
deposit accounts. *See* Deposit accounts		
intangible collateral	9-102(a)	50, 68-69
proceeds of inventory. *See also* Proceeds	9-322(a)(1)	386-387
"receivables" in general		
background		28-34
defined	9-102(a)(2)	68-69
health care insurance receivables as	9-102(a)(2)	69
sale of	1-201(37); 9-109(a)(3); 9-109(d)(4); 9-310	45, 104-105, 203, 595

Subject	U.C.C. Section	Text Section
securities or commodities	8-108(d); 9-328(3)	216-217
statement of, request for. *See also* Remedies, debtor's	9-210	299-305
surplus and deficiency rule	9-604(e); 9-615(e)	595, 625
ACTION FOR DEBT	9-601(a), (e)	528, 601-602
ADDRESS ON FINANCING STATEMENT	9-516	261, 269-271
See also Debtor's location; Financing statement		
ADVANCE		
future. *See* "Pursuant to commitment"		
AFTER-ACQUIRED PROPERTY		
See also Attachment of security interest; Security interest		
automatic attachment	9-204(a)	135
bankruptcy effect on security interest		507-509
commercial tort claims	9-204(b)(2)	137
consumer goods limitation	9-204(b)(1)	136
Credit Practices Rule		136
defined	9-204(a)	135
description of in financing statement		
fixtures		277
description of in security agreement. *See also*		
Security Agreement		138-140
accounts and farm equipment		140
inventory		139
effect of federal tax liens on security interest		449
financing statement and		277
in general	9-204(a)	135
purchase money holder's priority over	9-324(b)	336-341
time interest in attaches	9-204(a), (b)(1), (b)(2)	135-137
vs. consignments of inventory	9-103(d); 9-324	346
AGREEMENT		
See Security agreement; Subordination agreements		
AMENDED FINANCING STATEMENT		
See Financing statement		
ANTECEDENT DEBT		
transfer for as voidable preference		491-492, 504-505
ARTICLE 2		
See Sales Article		
ARTICLE 9		
See also Security Devices, pre-Code		
exclusions from	1-209; 9-109(c)-d; 9-339	77, 91, 93-110
in general		35-36
scope of	9-109(a)	49
when excluded	9-109(d)(4)-(7)	104-108
ASSIGNEE		
See also Default		
defenses against, waiver of	9-403	518-525
ASSIGNMENT		
accounts receivable		
nonnotification of		
pre-Code		28-33
present law	9-205; 9-607(a)(1)	34
not for financing purposes		104-108

Subject	U.C.C. Section	Text Section
coupled with delegation of performance	9-109(d)(6)	107
excluded from Article 9		104
for collection	9-109(d)(5)	106
payment of prior debts	9-109(d)(7)	108
sale of business, as part of	9-109(d)(4)	105
beneficial interest in decedent's estate	9-309(13)	197
by amending financing statement	9-514	202, 297-298
default rules. *See also* Default	9-604(e); 9-607(a), (d)	623-625
exempt from filing		198-203
assignments of accounts distinguished	9-310	203
"significant portion" of accounts	9-309(2)	198-201
"one shot"	9-109(d)(4)-(7)	104-108
sales of excluded from Article 9		104-108
statement of	9-514	202
waiver of defenses against assignees. *See also* Default	9-403	518-525
ASSIGNMENT OF CLAIMS ACT		94
ATTACHMENT OF SECURITY INTEREST		
after-acquired property		135-140
agreement to delay		120-121
coexistence	9-203(a)	120, 137
defined	9-203	118
proceeds. *See also* Proceeds of collateral	9-315	378-379
requisites for. *See also* Security agreement;		
Value; "Rights in collateral,"		
debtors	9-203	119-121
AUTHENTICATE	9-102(a)(7); 9-203(b)(3)	122-127
See also Security agreement		
AUTOMATIC PERFECTION		
See Perfection, automatic		
AUTOMATIC PERFECTION, TEMPORARY		
See Temporary perfection		
AUTOMOBILES		
See Motor vehicles		
B		
BAILMENTS	9-312	164-167
See also Perfection by possession		
BANKRUPTCY		
See also Insolvency, debtor's		
after-acquired property		507-509
automatic stay		479
contract rights	9-205; 9-607(a)(1)	34
early law		32-33
effect on priority		463-465
effect on secured party's rights		479
floating liens		143, 507-509
general creditors		477
in general		466
nonnotification financing	9-205; 9-607(a)(1)	31-34
preferential transfer prior to. *See* Voidable preference		

Subject	U.C.C. Section	Text Section
present law		34
proceedings		467-478
appeals		467
discharge		467, 478
distribution of assets		472-477
distribution of proceeds		475-477
exempt property		473
priority creditors		476
unsecured creditors		477
petition		468-469
property subject to security interest or liens		474
trustees		470-471
purchase money security interests		504-505
reclamation of goods by seller	2-702	463-465
special creditors		476
trustee's powers		311, 471, 481-489, 503
as hypothetical lien creditor	9-102(a)(52)	311
"fraud" defined		485-488
presumption of		487
Uniform Fraudulent Transfer Act		486
fraudulent interests set aside		482-488
strong arm clause		489
title and rights in debtor's property		471, 481
voidable preference		31-34, 143, 490-501
excused preferences		497-499
contemporaneous exchange		498
routine payments		499
floating liens		143
fully secured creditors, nonpreferential payments to		493
insolvency required		494-496
defined		496
preference defined		491
result of finding		492
time of transfer determinative		495-499
grace period for transfers of purchase money security interests		504-506
all creditors—10 days		506
PMSIs		504-505
hypothetical creditor or purchaser		503
transfers to insider		500-501
when voidable		491
***BENEDICT v. RATNER*,** **RULE OF**		370, 394
BENEFICIAL INTEREST IN DECEDENT'S ESTATE, **ASSIGNMENT OF**	9-309(13)	197
BILL OF LADING *See* Documents		
BREACH OF THE PEACE *See also* Remedies upon default, secured party's	9-609(b)	532-540
BREAKING AND ENTERING *See also* Remedies upon default, secured party's		537
BUYER *See also* Priorities; Third party Article 2 claimants to collateral		

Subject	U.C.C. Section	Text Section
bankruptcy of	2-702	463-465
insolvent buyer	2-702	459-465
possessory interests similar to Article 9 interests	2-602; 2-608; 2-711(3)	456
recognition by Article 9	9-110	458
priorities	9-110	458-465
buying consumer goods from consumer	9-320(b)	433
chattel paper	9-331	434-435
farm products	9-320(a)	421-422
in ordinary course of business	1-201(a); 9-320(a)	423, 428
of collateral	9-315(a)(1); 9-317(b), (d); 9-320(a); 9-504(4); 9-610(e), (f)	316, 322-323, 419, 421-429, 596-600
of inventory	9-320(a)	323, 419-420, 423-428
other than in ordinary course of business	9-320(6); 9-323(d) - (e); 9-331	430-435
pursuant to default, rights	9-504(4); 9-615(f); 9-617	590, 596-600
resale warranties	9-610(e), (f)	600
without knowledge	9-323(d) - (e)	426, 431, 433, 435

C

CAR DEALERS
See Motor Vehicles

CARE
See Reasonable care, duty of

CASH SALE	2-403(a); 9-324(b)	388, 461-462

CERTIFICATE OF TITLE IN MULTISTATE TRANSACTIONS	9-303, 9-316	190-192, 237, 254-257

CHATTEL MORTGAGE		13-15

CHATTEL PAPER
accounts distinguished		65
Article 9 applied to	9-102(a); 9-109(a)	45, 49, 62, 64
as proceeds	9-320(a); 9-330	388-393, 397-399
assignment of	9-109(d)	104-108
buyers of	9-331	434-435
buyers vs. inventory financers	9-330(c)	399
default rules	9-604(e); 9-607(a)	623-625
deficiency and surplus rules	9-604(e); 9-615(e)	595, 625
defined	9-102(a)(11), (31), (78)	64
electronic	9-102(a)(31)	64
instruments compared		62
instruments coupled with an interest as	9-102(a)(11)	62
inventory sold for	9-324(b); 9-330(a)	388, 390
multistate transaction	9-301(2) - (3)	235, 242-243
perfection of security interest in without filing	9-313(a) - (b)	160
place for perfection	9-301(2) - (3)	235
priority of purchaser of	9-317(d); 9-324(b); 9-331	322, 388, 434-435
reperfection	9-315(d)	398
sale of	1-201(37); 9-109(d)(8), (13); 9-604(e); 9-615(e)	45, 104
tangible	9-102(a)(31), (78)	62, 64
third party rights in	9-315(d); 9-330(c)	397-398

CLAIMANTS
See Priority

Subject	U.C.C. Section	Text Section
COLLATERAL		
See also Description of collateral		
accounting for rents, profits	9-207(c)	175
after-acquired. *See* After-acquired property		
alienability of debtor's rights in	9-401(b)	152
conflicting security interest in. *See* Conflicting security interests in same collateral		
debtor's right to redeem. *See also* Remedies, debtor's	9-623	603-606, 619-620
description of. *See* Description of collateral		
disposal by secured party. *See* Remedies upon default, secured party's		
documents of title	1-201(15); 9-102(a)(30); 9-601(a)(2)	63, 529
fixtures as. *See also* Fixtures	9-102(a)(41); 9-334(a)	193, 348-350
goods	2-105; 9-102	51-59
held by secured party. *See* Possession; Possession as means of perfection		
insurance on	9-207(a)	177-178
intangible		67-75
accounts	9-102(a)(2)	68-69
health care insurance receivables as		69
commercial tort claims	9-102(a)(13)	72
deposit accounts	9–102(a)(29)	71
general intangibles	9-102(a)(42)	73-75
payment intangibles	9-102(a)(61)	75
software	9-102(a)(42)	74
letters of credit	9-102(a)(51)	70
liquor license		73
list of, request for	9-210	299-305
"new" debtors	9-102(a)(56); 9-203(d)-(e); 9-326(b); 9-508(a)	327-329
proceeds of. *See* Proceeds of collateral		
profits on as additional security	9-207(c)	175
purchasers of. *See* Buyer; Third party		
quasi-tangibles		60-66
chattel paper	9-102(a)(31), (78)	64-65
defined		60
documents	1-201(15); 9-102(a)(30)	63
instruments	3-104(2) - (3)	61-62
investment property	9-102(a)(49)	66
real estate leases as	9-109(d)(1)	64
real property	9-604	64, 530
release of	9-512	295
right to use	9-207(b)(4)	180
removal of. *See* Fixtures; Removal of collateral interstate		
repledge of	9-207(c)(3)	179
retention of by defaulting debtor	9-601(e)	601
"rights in." *See* Rights in collateral, debtor's		
right to transfer	9-401(b)	152-153
risk of loss	9-207(b)(2)	176-178
Sale of. *See* Remedies upon default, secured party's		
secured party's rights to upon default	9-620	550-558
tangible	2-105; 9-102(a)(44)	51-59
computer software	9-102(a)(44)	53

Subject	U.C.C. Section	Text Section
defined	2-105; 9-102(a)(44)	51-53
goods, types of		54-59
consumer	9-102(a)(23)	55
equipment	9-102(a)(33)	58
farm products	9-102(a)(34)	57
inventory	9-102(a)(48)	56
title to irrelevant	9-202	19, 149
types		50-75

COLLECTION

assignment for	9-109(d)(5)	100
rights of secured party	9-607(a), (d)	623-625

"COMMERCIAL REASONABLENESS" STANDARD — 9-610(b); 9-626(a)(2) — 500-562
See also Remedies upon default, secured party's

COMMERCIAL TORT CLAIMS

after-acquired property exclusion	9-204(b)(2)	137
Article 9 applied to	9-102(a)(13)	72, 101
as collateral	9-102(a)(13)	72, 101
structured settlements		75, 101

COMMINGLED GOODS

defined	9-336(a)	364
priorities in. See also Priority	9-336	364-368

CONDITIONAL SALE — — 16-20, 46, 184
See also Purchase money security interest

**CONFLICTING SECURITY INTERESTS IN SAME
        COLLATERAL**
See also Priority; Protection against perfected security
                interest

between chattel paper purchaser and inventory financer	9-324(b)	336, 388
interests in crops	9-320(a)	421-422
nonperfected interest holders	9-317(d); 9-322(a); 9-333	317-323
perfected interest holders	9-203(d) - (e); 9-322(a)(1); 9-508(a)	324-329

CONSENT CLAUSES — 9-315(a)(1) — 413-418

CONSIGNMENT

Article 9 applied to	9-102(a)(20)	89-90
as PMSI in inventory	9-103(d); 9-324	90, 346
common law—when applicable		91
protective filing	9-505	92
true vs. inventory financing	9-102(a)(20)	90

CONSTRUCTION MORTGAGE
See Fixtures; Mortgage

CONSTRUCTIVE FORCE — — 530
See also Remedies upon default, secured
                party's

CONSUMER GOODS

and waiver of defenses	9-403(e)	522-525
as after-acquired property	9-204(b)(1)	136
automatic perfection	9-309(1)	182
buyer's priority	9-320(b)	433
defined	9-102(a)(23)	55, 187-193
fixtures as. See also Fixtures		193

Subject	U.C.C. Section	Text Section
notation on certificate required for motor vehicles. *See*		
also Motor vehicles	9-309(1); 9-311(d)	190-192
PMSI in	9-309(1)	182-196
purchased from other consumers	9-320(b)	433
retention of as satisfaction of debt. *See also* Remedies		
upon default, secured party's	9-620(e); 9-625(c)	551-553
termination statement	9-513(b)	293

CONSUMER PROTECTION STATUTES — 112-113, 136, 412, 422, 511, 522-525

CONTINUATION STATEMENT — 9-102(a)(27); 9-515(c), (d) — 288, 291

CONTRACT
- rights — 9-102(a)(49); 9-203 — 66, 144
- rights, sale of — 9-615(e) — 583
- security agreement as — 117, 144

CONTRACT RIGHTS
See Contract

CREATION OF A SECURITY INTEREST
See Attachment of security interest; Security interest

CREDIT PRACTICES RULE — 136

CREDITORS
- consignments — 9-102(a)(2) — 88-92
- general. *See* Unsecured creditors
- goals of — 2
- lien. *See* Lien creditor
- perfected and secured — 313
- secured — 9-203 — 312
- security agreement effective against — 9-201 — 114
- unsecured. *See* Unsecured creditors

CROPS
See Farm products

D

DEALERS, AUTOMOBILE
See Motor vehicles

DEBT, ACTION FOR
See Action for debt

DEBTOR
- alienability of rights — 9-401(b) — 152-153
- authentication. *See* Authenticate
- change of address. *See* Debtor's location
- change of identity — 9-316(a)(3) — 251
- change of name. *See also* Financing statement — 9-507(c); 9-508(b) — 274
- default of. *See* Default
- defined — 9-102(a)(28) — 48, 307
- "double debtor." *See also* Priority, among
-     perfected creditors — 9-102(a)(56) — 327-329
- foreign — 9-307(c) — 234
- goals of — 1
- liability for deficiency upon sale of collateral — 9-615 — 586
- name and address on financing statement — 9-503(a)(4), (c) — 260-261, 268, 271-274

Subject	U.C.C. Section	Text Section
indexed under name		260
notice of resale of collateral. *See also* Remedies upon default, secured party's	9-611(d)	563-578
obligor	9-102(a)(26)	48, 307
rights		
See also Remedies, debtor's		
to redeem collateral	9-602(11); 9-623	603-606, 619
to request statement of account or list of collateral	9-210, 9-625(b), (f)	299-301
upon default. *See* Default		
upon termination of security interest	9-102(a)(79); 9-625(b), (e)(4)	292-298
"rights in collateral." *See* "Rights in collateral," debtor's		
"seriously misleading" rule	9-507(c); 9-508(b)	274
trade names	9-503(c)	272
waiver by. *See* Waiver		

DEBTOR'S LOCATION

Subject	U.C.C. Section	Text Section
See also Place, perfection		
change in, effect of	9-316(a)(1)-(2), (b), (e)(2), (f)	243-250
judicial liens	1-201(32)	247-248
determinative law	9-307	227-234

DEFAULT

Subject	U.C.C. Section	Text Section
See also Liability; Remedies, debtor's; Remedies upon default, secured party's		
acceleration clauses	1-208	513
accessions	9-335(e); 9-604(c)	620
accounts		623-625
assignees, waiver of defenses against	9-403	518-525
consumer goods limitation	9-403(e)	522-525
federal statutes' prohibition	9-413(d)	525
most states prohibit waiver		524
good faith required		520
purpose		518
real defenses not waived	3-305; 9-403(c)	521
validity	9-403	519-521
attorney's fees		614
chattel paper		623-625
consumer transactions and common law		511
consumers and Article 9		511
creditor's rights in general. *See also* Remedies upon default, secured party's		527-528
damages for noncompliance. *See also* Remedies, debtor's	9-625	608-613
debtor's right of redemption	9-623	603-606
debtor's rights. *See also* Remedies, debtor's	9-602; 9-623; 9-625	603-622
failure under security agreement		510, 512
fixtures		626-628
damages caused by removal	9-335(f); 9-604(d)	627
foreclosure by other parties	9-604(b)	628
right of removal	9-335(e); 9-604(c)	626
insecurity clauses	1-203; 1-208	514-517
"good faith" defined	1-201(19)	515-517
intangibles	9-607	623-625
no right to surplus or deficiency	9-604(e)	625
right of secured party to notify	9-607(a), (d)	624
notice. *See* Notice; Remedies, debtor's		

Subject	U.C.C. Section	Text Section
occurrence of		512-517
retention of collateral by debtor	9-601(e); 9-627(c)	601-602
right of possession by secured party. *See* Remedies upon default, secured party's		
strict foreclosure	9-620	550-558
"time is of the essence" clause		526
waivers. *See* Remedies, debtor's; Waiver		
DEFENSES		
against assignee	9-403	518-525
waiver of	9-602; 9-603; 9-624	518-525, 544, 553, 556, 569-570, 606, 615-622
DEFICIENCY, SECURED PARTY'S RIGHT TO RECOVER	9-615	586-595
See also Remedies upon default, secured party's		
DEPOSIT ACCOUNT		
as proceeds from disposition of collateral	9-315(d)(2)	71, 103, 381-383
consumer deposit accounts excluded from Article 9	9-109(d)(8), (13)	103
defined	9-102(a)(29)	71
perfection by control	9-312(b)(1)	218-219
priority. *See also* Priority		400-402
reperfection	9-316(f)	244
setoff against	9-327(3) - (4); 9-340	383, 402
DESCRIPTION OF COLLATERAL		
in financing statement		
after-acquired property		277
amendments		279-280
compared to description in security agreement	9-108; 9-504	128-133, 275-276
fixtures	9-102(a)(40); 9-501(a)(1)(B); 9-502(b)	278, 352-354
minerals and timber to be cut	9-502(b)	278
proceeds of collateral	9-315(a), (d)(1)	376, 378, 380
reasonable identification rule	9-108; 9-504	275-278
supergeneric descriptions	9-504(2)	132, 276
requirement of	9-108; 9-504	261
sufficiency of in general	9-108; 9-504(2)	275-276
in security agreement		
after-acquired property	9-204	135-140
compared to description in financing statement	9-108; 9-504	133, 275
error in		134
floating lien		141-143
proceeds of collateral	9-315(a)(2)(c), (d)(1)	378, 380
requirement of	9-203(b)(3)(A)	128
sufficiency of	9-108	129-133
DISABLING OF EQUIPMENT	9-609(a)(2)	546-547
DISPOSITION OF COLLATERAL		
See Remedies upon default, secured party's		
DOCUMENTS		
Article 9 applied to	9-109(a)	49
bill of lading		63, 165
defined	1-201(15); 9-102(a)(30)	63
default, remedy against	9-601(a)(2)	529
issuance of to perfect security interest	9-312(c)	163-166

Subject	U.C.C. Section	Text Section
of title	7-403; 9-312(c), (d)	63, 163, 165-166
perfection of security interest in by possession	9-312(c) - (d), (f)	162-167, 209
protection of purchasers of	7-501; 7-505; 9-331	435
temporary perfection of security interest in	9-312(e) - (g)	206-209
warehouse receipt	7-403; 9-312(c)	63, 163, 166

DRAGNET CLAUSE

		410-412

DUTIES

filing officer's		
financing statement	9-516; 9-519; 9-523	262-265, 285-286
secured party's		
accounting	9-207(c); 9-602(5); 9-616	175, 581, 603
possession of collateral	9-207	169-173, 175, 177
profits on collateral	9-207(c)	175
reasonable care	9-207(a)	170-173
request for statement of account or list of collateral	9-210; 9-625	299-305
retention of collateral after default	9-602(10); 9-620(e); 9-621	551-556
sale of collateral		559-578
termination of security interest	9-102(a)(79); 9-513(b)	292-296
to insure	9-207(a)	177

E

ELIZABETH, STATUTE OF

		5

EQUIPMENT

definition	9-102	58
disabling of	9-609(a)(2)	546-547

ERRONEOUS FILING

See Filing, erroneous

ERRORS IN DESCRIPTION OF COLLATERAL

		134

ESTATES

See Beneficial interest in decedent's estate,
              assignment of

EXCULPATORY CLAUSE

	1-102(3)	173

See also Waiver

EXPENSES

acceleration clauses		605
attorney's fees		614
collection against underlying obligor, pursuant to	9-607(d)	624
priority of payment	9-615	581-582
sale of collateral, pursuant to	9-615(a)(1), 9-616	582, 591
secured party's when in possession of collateral	9-207(b)(1)	174
statement for request of account, re	9-210(f)	302

F

FACTOR'S ACTS

		25-27

FARM PRODUCTS

buyer protected	9-320(a)	421-422
defined	9-102	57
lien on	9-102(a)(5)	99
place for filing	9-501	281

Subject	U.C.C. Section	Text Section
PMSI in livestock	9-324(d)	345
FEDERAL AVIATION ACT		94
FEDERAL FILING ACTS	9-311(a)(1)	282
FEDERAL FOOD SECURITY ACT		422
FEDERAL LOANS		94
FEDERAL STATUTES	9-109(c)(1)	94-96, 136, 282, 422, 525
FEDERAL TAX LIEN		
creation of		314, 444
priorities		445-451
after-acquired property		449
future advances		450-451
in general		445
perfected security interest		447
subsequent PMSIs		448
unperfected security interests		446
scope of		443
FEDERAL TRADE COMMISSION	9-403(d)	525
FEES		
See also Expenses		
filing	9-516(a)	284
FIELD WAREHOUSING	7-403	24, 163
FILING		
assignment	9-514	297
bogus filings	9-510(a)	296
collateral, release of	9-572	295
consigned goods	9-515	89-92
continuation statement	9-102(a)(27); 9-515(d)	291
duration of. *See also* Financing statement	9-515	287-291
continuation statement	9-102(a)(27); 9-515(d)	291
effect of lapse	9-515(c)	288-289
five-year rule	9-515(a)	287-288
manufactured home, transaction	9-102(a)(53) - (54); 9-515(b)	290
public finance transaction	9-102(a)(67); 9-515(b)	290
electronically	9-509(b)	122, 125, 266
erroneous	9-517	286
federal filings	9-311(a)(1)	282
financing statement. *See* Financing statement		
fixture. *See* Fixture filings		
goods covered by certificate of title exemption	9-303(c); 9-316(d) - (e); 9-337	254-257
indexing	9-519	117, 260, 285-286
judicial liens		289
lapsed	9-515(c)	288-289
leased goods		77, 87
mechanics of		284-298
not required for perfection. *See* Perfection, automatic		
not required under field warehousing	9-312(c) - (d), (f)	163-167
officer, duties of	9-517; 9-519	284-286
perfecting security interest		156, 258
place. *See* Place for filing		
protective	9-505	87, 92, 253
termination statement. *See also* Termination statement	9-102(a)(79)	292-296

Subject	U.C.C. Section	Text Section
transmitting utilities		289
when effective	9-516(a)	284
without perfection, effect on priority	9-322(a)(1)	325

FINANCING STATEMENT

See also Filing

Subject	U.C.C. Section	Text Section
amendments to	9-512	279
collateral added, effect of	9-512	279-280
effect on original security interests	9-512	279
floating lien distinguished. *See also* Liens		280
as fixture filing	9-102(a)(40); 9-501(a)(1)(B); 9-502(b)	352
assignment of rights	9-514	297-298
assignments of rights under	9-514	297-298
authorization by debtor required	9-509(a) - (b)	266
commingled goods	9-336(b) - (d)	365-367
consigned goods	9-505	88-92
continuation statement	9-102(a)(27); 9-515(d)	291
creating security interest		116
debtor's name and address	9-503	261, 271-274
change of name	9-507(c); 9-508(1)	274
partnerships	9-503(a)(4)	273
trade names	9-503(c)	272
defined		116, 156-157
description of collateral in. *See* Description of collateral		
duration of	9-515(a) - (d)	287-291
continuation statement	9-102(a)(27); 9-515(d)	291
effect of lapse	9-515(c)	288-289
five-year rule	9-515(a), (c)	287-288
manufactured home transaction	9-102(a)(53) - (54); 9-515(b)	290
public finance transaction	9-102(a)(67); 9-515(b)	290
electronic filing	9-509(b)	266
errors in, effect of	9-506(a), (c); 9-517	267-268, 286
extension of. *See* Continuation statement		
filing requirement in general		117, 156-157, 258
form of	9-521	259
indexing	9-519	117, 260, 285-286
investment property		211
lapse	9-515(c)	288-289
leased goods	9-505	77, 87
mechanics of filing		284-298
See also Filing		
notice function		117, 258, 275
"open drawer" concept	9-519(f)	263
proceeds	9-315(a), (d)(1)	376, 378-380
purpose of		117, 254
required contents	9-502; 9-516	261-266
copies	9-523	265
one-year retention	9-519(g)	264
wrongful rejection of	9-516(d)	262
secured party's name and address	9-516	261, 269-270
representative's name	9-503(d)	270
"seriously misleading" rule	9-507(c); 9-508(b)	274
sufficiency of	9-506	267-280

Subject	U.C.C. Section	Text Section
errors in debtor's name	9-506(c)	268
substantial compliance	9-506(a)	267
termination statement. *See also* Termination statement	9-102(a)(79); 9-513(b)	292-296
trade names	9-503(c)	272
when effective	9-516(a), 9-517	284-286
where to file		281-285
federal filing acts	9-311(a)(1)	282
general rules	9-501	281
utilities	9-102(a)(80); 9-501(b)	283
"FIRST TO ATTACH RULE"	9-322(a)(3)	317
"FIRST TO FILE OR PERFECT RULE"	9-322(a)(1)	325, 385-387
FIXTURE FILINGS		
defined	9-102(a)(40); 9-501(a)(1)(B)	352
description of collateral	9-502(b)	261-274
description of realty		353
place for	9-102(a)(40)	352
priority of. *See* Fixtures		
required contents of	9-502(b)	352-354
FIXTURES		
Article 9 applied to	9-102(1)	348
as consumer goods	9-102(a)(41); 9-334(a)	193, 349-350
building materials excluded	9-102(a)(41)	349
defined	9-102(a)(41); 9-334(a)	349-350
factory or office machines, easily removable		350
filing. *See* Fixture filings		
mobile homes		350
non-purchase money security interest in		357-359
vs. prior recorded realty interests	9-334(c)	357
vs. subsequent lien creditors	9-334(e)(3)	359
vs. subsequent realty interests	9-334(e)(1)	358
prefabricated buildings		350
priority among perfected creditors	9-334	343-353
property law		352
purchase money security interest in	9-334(f), (h)	351-356
construction mortgage priority	9-334(h)	355-356
subordination agreement	9-334(f)	356
fixture filing required		351
removable consumer goods, replacements for	9-334(e)(2)	350
removal of upon default	9-335(e) - (f); 9-604(b) - (d)	626-628
"FOUR MONTH RULE"	9-316; 9-337	243-245, 255-257
See also Motor vehicles		
FRAUDS, STATUTE OF	9-203; 9-310(b)	122-126, 159
FRAUDULENT CONVEYANCES		
as real defense	3-305; 9-403(c)	521
history of		5-9
insolvent buyer on credit	2-702	459
retention of proceeds	9-205	370-371
risks in retention of goods		9
sale and leaseback distinguished		8
set aside in bankruptcy		482-489
"fraud" defined		485-486

Subject	U.C.C. Section	Text Section
presumption of		487
Uniform Fraudulent Transfer Act		486
Statute of Elizabeth		5
U.C.C. provision	2-402(2)	7
FUTURE ADVANCES		
buyers' priority over	9-323(d) - (e)	430-432
clause in security agreement	9-204(c); 9-323	404
federal tax lien holder's priority over		450-451
judicial lien creditors' priority over	9-323(b)	453
lack of future advances clause		405-409
filing or possession limitation	9-323	405, 409
priority rules	9-324	406
protection for later creditor		408

G

GENERAL CREDITOR		
See Unsecured creditor		
GENERAL INTANGIBLES		
defined	9-102(a)(42)	73-75
place for perfection	5-116; 9-304; 9-306; 9-316(f)	238, 240, 244
GOOD FAITH		
acceleration of payment	1-208	513
and waiver	9-403	519-520
buyer of inventory		426
collusion with assignor		520
insecurity clauses	1-203; 1-208	514-517
objective test		517
subjective test		516
sale of collateral	9-610(b)	560
GOODS		
See also Perfection of security interest; Place, for perfection; Returned goods		
Article 9 applied to	9-102(a)(44)	51
as collateral. *See* Collateral		
as proceeds	9-330(c)	394-399
buyers of protected. *See* Protection against perfected security interest		
classifications of	9-102	50-59
consumer. *See* Consumer goods		
defined	9-102(a)(44)	52
in possession of bailee	9-312(c)-(d); 9-313(c), (f)	164-167
leased. *See* Lease		
multiple state transactions. *See* Multistate transactions, perfection in		
seller's retention of after fraudulent sale		9

H

HEALTH-CARE INSURANCE RECEIVABLES	9-102(a)(2)	69, 103
HOLDER IN DUE COURSE		
defenses good against	3-305; 9-403(c)	521

Subject	U.C.C. Section	Text Section
rights of	3-302; 9-330(d)	434-435

I

Subject	U.C.C. Section	Text Section
IDENTIFICATION OF COLLATERAL	2-501	151
INDEXING		
See Filing		
INSECURITY CLAUSES	1-203; 1-208	514-517
See also Default; Good faith		
INSOLVENCY, DEBTOR'S		
See also Bankruptcy		
and proceeds. *See* Proceeds of collateral		
bankruptcy definition		496
effect of Article 2	2-702	459-465
judicial liens	9-102(a)(52)	309-311
priority rule		459-465
seller's right to reclaim goods on	2-702	459-465
INSTRUMENTS		
See also Negotiable instruments		
Article 9 applied to	3-104(2) - (3); 9-109(a)	49, 61
as proceeds	9-324(b)	388
defined	3-104(2) - (3)	61
perfection of security interest in	9-309(3) - (4); 9-312(e) - (g); 9-313(a) - (b)	160, 204, 206-210
priority of purchaser of	9-331	434-435
protection of purchasers of	9-324(b); 9-331	388, 434-435
temporary automatic protection	9-312(e) - (g)	206-210
INSURANCE POLICY, EXCLUDED FROM ARTICLE 9		103
INSURANCE PROCEEDS		178
INTANGIBLES		
See also General intangibles		
defined	9-102(a)	67
special default rules	9-604(e); 9-607(a), (d)	623-625
INTERSTATE TRANSFER OF COLLATERAL		
See Removal of collateral interstate		
INVENTORY		
accounts as proceeds of	9-322(a)(1)	386-387
after-acquired property clause implied		139, 336
buyers of	9-320(a)	323, 419-429
chattel paper as proceeds of	9-324(b); 9-330(a)	388-390, 393
consignments	9-103(d); 9-324	346
defined	9-102(a)(48)	56
financer vs. chattel paper purchaser	9-330	399
means of taking possession	7-403(3); 9-312(c)	163
priority of purchase money security interest	9-320(a); 9-324(b), (d)	336-346
INVESTMENT PROPERTY		
control, effect of on priority	8-106; 9-328	211-217
defined	9-102(a)(49)	66
financing statement		211
reasonable care	9-207(a)	170-173
reperfection	9-316(F)	244

Subject	U.C.C. Section	Text Section
JK		
JUDGMENTS, EXCLUDED FROM ARTICLE 9		100
JUDICIAL LIEN		
See Lien, judicial		
JUNK PILE TEST		
See Lease, as security transaction		
JURISDICTION		
See Multistate transactions, perfection in		
L		
LANDLORD'S LIEN		
See Lien, landlord's excluded		
LAPSE	9-316(a)(1); 9-515(c)	249, 288-289
LEASE		
as secured transaction	1-201(37)	77-87
junk pile test	1-201(37)(a)-(c)	80
option to purchase under	1-201(37)(d)	81
termination clause	1-201(37)	78
filing financing statement pursuant to, effect of		77
protective filing	9-505	87
LIABILITY		
debtor's		
deficiency upon sale of collateral	9-615; 9-626	586, 592
secured party's. *See also* Remedies, debtor's		
disclaimer of	9-602(13)	621
failure to comply with request for account	9-602(5); 9-625(b), (f) - (g)	301, 616
improper notice re sale of collateral	9-602	569, 617
noncompliance with default procedure	9-602(13)	621
pursuant to removal of fixtures	9-335(f); 9-604(d)	627
LIEN		
agricultural	9-102(a)(5)	99
artisan's excluded	9-109(d)(2)	98
consensual		41, 442
creditor. *See* Lien creditor		
defined		38
floating		
after-acquired inventory		344, 507-509
bankruptcy and		143
defined	9-204(a)	141
dealer's inventory	9-320(a)	420
financing statement amendment distinguished		280
inventory liens, protection of		344
not preferential in bankruptcy		508
security agreement description		141-142
judicial		
defined	9-102(a)(52)	39, 309
in bankruptcy		474, 503
lapsed perfection, effect on		247-248
motor vehicles transferred interstate		247-248

Subject	U.C.C. Section	Text Section
time of lien	9-102(a)(52)	310-311
vs. future advances	9-323(b)	453
vs. perfected creditor	9-317(a)(2)	452
vs. unperfected creditor	9-317(a)(2)	320
landlord's excluded	9-109(d)(1), (11)	97
mechanic's excluded	9-109(d)(2)	98
statutory		
defined		40, 314-315
priority		436-441
Article 9 exclusions	9-109(c), (d)(1) - (2)	436
consensual lien compared		442
possessory liens only	9-333	436-442
consent irrelevant		440
general rule	9-333	438-440
liens covered		439
statutory priority exception	9-333(b)	441

LIEN CREDITOR
See also Lien, judicial; Lien, statutory

defined	9-102(a)(52)	309
"hypothetical" trustee in bankruptcy as		489
judicial. *See also* Lien, judicial	9-102(9)(52); 9-314(a)(2); 9-323(b)	309-311, 452-453
rights of		
against perfected security interest	9-317(a)(2); 9-333	436-441, 452-453
re advances made by secured party	9-323(b)	441
statutory	9-333	314-315
vs. nonpurchase money security interests	9-334(e)(3)	359

LIST OF COLLATERAL, REQUEST FOR
See Collateral, list of, request for

LOANS, FEDERAL		95

LOCATION OF COLLATERAL	9-301(2) - (3)	235, 242, 254

See also Removal of collateral interstate

M

MARKET SLUMP		172

See also Investment property

MECHANIC'S LIEN
See Lien, mechanic's

MECHANICS OF FILING
See Filing

MINERALS

place for filing	9-301(4)	236

MOBILE HOMES
See Fixtures; Motor Vehicles

MONEY

perfection of security interest in	9-313(a) - (b)	160
received from collateral	9-207(c)	175

MORTGAGE
chattel. *See* Chattel mortgage
construction

Subject	U.C.C. Section	Text Section
defined		355
priority of. *See also* Fixtures	9-334(f), (h)	355-356

MOTOR VEHICLES

accessions, priority of	9-335(d)	363
dealers	9-309(1); 9-311(a), (d); 9-337	190, 257
four-month grace period	9-316(e)	255-257
innocent buyers	9-337	256-257
interstate transfer of	9-303(c); 9-316(d); 9-337	254-257
judicial lienors	9-316	256
notation on certificate required	9-303; 9-309(1); 9-311(a), (d)	190-192, 237
perfection of security interest in	9-303	190-192, 237
"recognized market"		574
repossession and sale		574-575

MULTISTATE TRANSACTIONS, PERFECTION IN

See also Place, for perfection; Removal of collateral
        interstate

agricultural liens	9-302	241
automobiles	9-303; 9-309(1); 9-311(a), (d)	190-192, 237, 254-257
collateral transferred interstate	9-301(3); 9-316(c)	242, 252
conflict of laws general rule	9-301	226-227
debtor's identity, change of	9-316(a)(3)	251
debtor's location, change of	9-316(a)(2)	243-251
deposit accounts	9-304; 9-316(f)	238, 244
electronic chattel paper	9-316(a)(3)	222
fixtures	9-301(2) - (3)	193, 235
"four-month rule"	9-303(c); 9-316(a)(2), (d)	243-250, 255
general rule	9-301(1)	227
goods covered by certificate of title	9-303	190-192, 237, 254-257
goods intended for use in another jurisdiction	9-301(1)	226-227
investment property	8-110; 9-305; 9-316(f)	239, 244
letter of credit rights	9-306; 9-316(f)	240, 244
minerals	9-301(4)	236
possessory security interests	9-301(2) - (3); 9-316(c)	235, 252
relation back	9-308(c); 9-316(b)	225, 245-246
reperfection	9-316(a)(1) - (2), (b), (f)	225, 243-250
timber	9-301(2) - (3)	235

N

NAME ON FINANCING STATEMENT

See also Financing statement

change of	9-507(c); 9-508(b)	274
debtor	9-503(c)	271-274
partnership	9-503(a)(4)	273
secured party	9-502	269
trade name	9-503(c)	272

NEGOTIABLE INSTRUMENTS

See also Instruments

as proceeds, priority of	9-324(b)	343, 388
perfection of security interest in	9-312(e) - (f); 9-313(a) - (b)	160, 165, 207-210
secured party's possession where held by bailee	9-312(c)	165

NEW PERFECTION

Subject	U.C.C. Section	Text Section
See Removal of collateral interstate		
NONNOTIFICATION FINANCING		28-29, 623-625
NON-PURCHASE MONEY SECURITY INTERESTS		
vs. prior recorded interest in realty	9-334(c)	357
vs. subsequent interests in realty	9-334(e)(1)	358-359
vs. subsequent lien creditors	9-334(e)(3)	359
NOTICE		
See also Remedies upon default, secured party's; Waiver		
account debtor upon default	9-607(a)	624
conflicting security interest in inventory	9-324(b)	339-342
consignor's	9-103(d); 9-324	346
deficiency or waiver of	9-616(b)(1) - (2)	591, 613
failure to give pursuant to sale of collateral	9-602(7); 9-624	570, 617
resale. *See* Remedies upon default, secured party's		
retaining collateral in satisfaction of debt	9-602(10); 9-621	554-556
sale of collateral upon default	9-611(d); 9-612; 9-614	543; 563-578
security agreement, required by		542
strict foreclosure	9-602(10); 9-621	554-556
waiver of	9-602; 9-624	553, 556, 570, 606, 617
NOTICE FILING	9-502; 9-516	258-261

O		
OBLIGOR		
See Debtor		
"ONE-SHOT" ASSIGNMENTS	9-109(d)(4) - (7)	104-108
See also Assignments		
OPTION		
to purchase under lease	1-201(37)(d)	81
to renew lease		84

P		
PEACE, BREACH OF		
See Breach of peace		
PERFECTION, AUTOMATIC		
See also Perfection of security interest		
assignment of accounts and payment intangibles	9-309(2)	198-203
assignment of security interest distinguished	9-310; 9-514	202-203
"significant portion" limitation		199-201
assignment of beneficial interest in decedent's estate	9-309(13)	197
attachment sufficient		181
collateral moved to new state. *See also* Multistate transactions, perfection of		250
consumer goods purchase money security interests	9-309(1)	182-196
"consumer good" defined	9-102(a)(23)	187
primary use test		188
fixtures exception		193
motor vehicle exception		188-192
purchase money security interest described	9-103	184

Subject	U.C.C. Section	Text Section
security agreement required	9-203	186
who may be secured party	9-103(a)(2)	185
sales of promissory notes	9-309(3) - (4)	204
supporting obligations	9-102(a)(77); 9-308(d)	205
temporary. *See also* Perfection, temporary	9-312	206-210

PERFECTION BY CONTROL

See also Perfection of security interest

Subject	U.C.C. Section	Text Section
deposit accounts, control over		218-219
methods of	9-104(a)	219
only means of perfection	9-312(b)(1)	218
electronic chattel paper, control over	9-105	222
investment property, control over		211-217
alternative to filing		211
certificated securities	8-106(a) - (b)	214
priority	9-328(1)	212
securities intermediary creditor	9-328(3)	217
securities or commodity accounts	8-108(d)	216
uncertificated securities	8-106(c); 8-301(1)	215
letter of credit rights, control over	9-107; 9-312(b)(2)	220-221
oral agreement sufficient	9-203(b)(3)(D)	124
priority		400-403
deposit accounts	9-327	401-402
investment property	9-328	212
letter of credit rights	9-329	403
protective filings	9-505	87, 92, 253
rights and duties of party with control		223

PERFECTION BY POSSESSION

See also Perfection of security interest

Subject	U.C.C. Section	Text Section
benefits of		159
collateral moved to new state	9-316(c)	252
duration	9-313(d)	168
duties and rights of secured party. *See also* Secured party		169-180
accounting of profits	9-207(c)	175
expense reimbursement	9-207(b)(1)	174
insurance on collateral	9-207(a)	177
insurance proceeds		178
liability waivers void	1-102(3)	173
notice to debtor		171
reasonable care	9-207(a)	170
right to repledge	9-207(c)(3)	179
user of collateral	9-207(b)(4)	180
field warehousing	7-403(3); 9-312(c)	163
means of taking possession		162-167
goods held by bailee		164-167
negotiable document of title	9-312(c)	165
no document of title	9-313(c), (f)	167
nonnegotiable document of title	9-312(d)	166
inventory	7-403(3); 9-312(c)	163
oral agreement sufficient	9-203(b)(3)(B)	123, 159
perfection assured	9-310(b)(6)	159
pledge		158
pledge transaction	9-313	121, 157
"possession" defined		162

Subject	U.C.C. Section	Text Section
property covered	9-313(a) - (b)	160-161
repledge of collateral	9-207(c)(3)	179
rights pursuant. *See also* Secured party	9-207	169-180
risk of loss	9-207(b)(2)	176-178
substitute for filing		160
when perfection occurs	9-313	158

PERFECTION OF SECURITY INTEREST

See also Filing; Perfection, automatic; Perfection by
control; Perfection by possession;
Place, for perfection; Priority

Subject	U.C.C. Section	Text Section
accessions	9-335(b)	361
accounts	9-310	157
assignment of	9-309(2)	198-203
Article 2 security interests similar		454-465
assignments of security interests	9-309; 9-514	198-203
automatic. *See* Perfection, automatic		
commingled goods	9-336(b) - (d), (f)	364-368
consigned goods	9-505	88-92
consumer goods	9-309(1)	182-196
control as. *See* Perfection by control		
defined		154
deposit accounts	9-104(a); 9-312(b)(1)	218-219
documents	9-312(c) - (g)	160, 162-166, 206-210
duration of filing	9-515	287-291
effect of in general	9-317	154
electronic chattel paper	9-105	222
filing as	9-310	116-117, 155-157
"first to file or perfect" rule	9-322(a)	317, 325, 385
foreign debtors	9-307(c)	234
goods covered by documents of title. *See also* Motor vehicles	9-303	190-192, 237
goods held by bailee	9-312(c) - (d); 9-313(c), (f)	164-167
instruments	9-312	160, 206-210
investment property	8-106; 9-328	211-217
lapse	9-316(a)(1); 9-515(c)	246-249, 288-289
leased goods	9-505	87
methods of in general. *See also* Attachment of security interest; Filing; Perfection, automatic; Perfection by control; Perfection by possession		155
multiple state transaction. *See* Multistate transactions, perfection in		
place. *See* Place, for perfection		
possession as. *See* Perfection by possession		
priorities. *See* Priority		
proceeds	9-309; 9-315; 9-322(a)(1)	203-204, 386-388
processed goods	9-336(a) - (d), (f)(1)	364-368
reperfection. *See* Removal of collateral interstate		
returned goods	9-330(c)	395-396
supporting obligations	9-102(a)(77); 9-308(d)	205
temporary. *See* Temporary perfection		
time of	9-308(a), (c)	224, 280

PERFECTION, TEMPORARY

Subject	U.C.C. Section	Text Section
See Temporary perfection		
PERFECTION WITHOUT FILING		
See Perfection, automatic; Perfection by control; Perfection by possession; Temporary perfection		
PERSONAL PROPERTY		
See Security interest		
PLACE		
for filing		
central state office generally	9-501	281
collateral related to realty	9-501	281
fixtures	9-102(a)(40); 9-501(a)(1)(B); 9-502(b)	352
under Federal Filing Acts	9-311(a)(1)	282
utilities	9-501(b)	283
for perfection. *See also* Multistate transactions, perfection of	9-301	226
change of collateral's location	9-316(c)	252
change of debtor's location (four month rule)		243-251
automatic perfection exception		250
change of debtor's identity (one year rule)	9-316(a)(3)	251
failure to reperfect	9-316(b)	246-248
judicial liens		247-248
lapse of perfection	9-316(a)(1)	249
relation back	9-308(e); 9-316(b)	245
reperfection required	9-316(a), (2), (f)	243-244
conflict of laws general rule	9-301(1)	227
debtor's location	9-307	227-234
corporations and registered organizations	9-307(e)	229
federal government	9-307(h)	233
foreign debtors	9-307(c)	234
individuals	9-307(b)(1)	232
other organizations	9-307(a), (b)(2) - (3)	230-231
exceptions to general rule		235-241
agricultural liens	9-302	241
certificate of title goods	9-303	237
deposit accounts	9-304	238
fixtures	9-102(a)(40); 9-501(a)(1)(B)	235, 352
investment property perfected by control	8-110; 9-305	239
letter of credit rights	5-116; 9-306	240
minerals	9-301(4)	236
possessory security interests	9-301(2) - (3)	235
timber		235
general rule—debtor's location governs	9-301(1)	227
effect of perfection and priority—collateral's location governs	9-301(3)	242
PLEDGE		10-12, 43
See also Perfection by possession		
PLEDGEABILITY	9-313(a)-(b)	160-161
POSSESSION		
after default. *See also* Remedies upon default, secured party's	9-609; 9-620	531, 550-558
bailee's	9-312	164-167

Subject	U.C.C. Section	Text Section
debtor's, effect on security interest.	1-201(36); 9-203(b)(2); 9-205;	148, 369-379
See also Proceeds of collateral	9-315(a)(2)(c)	
defined		162
field warehouse		24, 165-167
lien holder's	9-333	436-442
perfecting security interest. *See* Perfection by possession		
pledge	9-313	10-12, 158, 179
PREEXISTING DEBT, ASSIGNMENT OF	9-109(d)(7)	108
PREFERENCE		
See Voidable preference		
PRIORITY		
See also Conflicting security interests in same		
collateral; Protection against		
perfected security interest		
accessions. *See also* accessions	9-335(c) - (e)	360-363, 626
among nonperfected interests	9-322(a)(3)	317
among perfected interests, in general	9-322(a)(1)	324-329
First to file or perfect rule	9-322(a)(1)	325
new debtor, merger into	9-203(d) - (e); 9-508(a)	327-329
newly acquired collateral	9-326(b)	329
Knowledge or attachment not determinative		326
Article 2 claimants vs. Article 9 security interests		454-465
automatic Article 2 security interest	2-602; 2-608; 2-706; 2-711(3)	455-457
claimant's possession gives priority	9-110	458
insolvent buyer rule	2-702	459-465
Article 9 creditor prevails	2-702	460
buyer's bankruptcy		463-465
cash sales	2-403(a)	461
livestock exception		462
buyers of collateral vs. perfected security interests		419-435
consumer goods purchased from consumer	9-320(b)	433
farm products	9-320(a)	421-422
Federal Food Security Act		422
general rule		419
in ordinary course of business	9-320(a)	420-429
inventory only		420
"ordinary course of business" requirements		423-429
secured party in possession priority	9-320(e)	428
noninventory collateral	9-315(a)(1)	429
not in ordinary course of business—future advances	9-323(d)-(e)	430-432
quasi-tangible collateral		434-435
general rule	9-331	434
holders in due course	9-330(d)	435
buyers of collateral vs. unperfected security interests	9-317(b)	322, 419
chattel paper	9-317(d); 9-324(b); 9-331	322
commingled goods	9-336	364-368
competing security interests		366-368
proportionate interests	9-336(f)(2)	366
unperfected interests junior	9-336(f)(1)	368
ultimate product, interests in	9-336(b) - (d)	365
consent clauses		
and waiver of interests	9-315(a)(1)	413-418
consignor's	9-103(d); 9-324	90-92, 346

Subject	U.C.C. Section	Text Section
creditors perfected by control	9-327(3)-(4); 9-328; 9-329	212, 400-403
delay in perfection, effect of	9-322(a)(1)	325
disposition of proceeds on resale of collateral	9-615	581-585
federal tax liens. *See also* Federal tax liens		445-451
fixtures. *See also* Fixtures	9-334	351-359, 626
future advances. *See* Future advances		
judicial lien creditors. *See also* Liens, judicial	9-317(a)(2); 9-334(e)(3)	248, 320, 359, 452-453
knowledge of conflicting interest, effect of		326, 334, 339, 420
over lapsed interest	9-515(c)	288
over unperfected interest		317-323
proceeds. *See also* Proceeds of collateral		385-393
purchase money security interests. *See also* Purchase money security interests	9-324	330-347
purchase money security interests in inventory. *See also* Purchase money security interests	9-324	330, 333-344, 346-347
purchase money security interests in livestock. *See also* Purchase money security interests	9-324(d)	345
purchaser. *See* Buyer		
purchaser of chattel paper	9-320; 9-324(b); 9-330	388-393, 434
purchaser of negotiable instrument	9-324(b), 9-331	388, 434
returned goods	9-330(c)	394-399
security agreement affecting creditor's priority		404-418
consent clauses and waiver of interests		413-418
conditional consent theory		418
"course of dealing" theory	1-205(4); 2-208(3)	416-417
waiver by secured party	9-315(a)(1)	413-415
dragnet clauses		410-412
defined		410
state consumer laws		412
validity	9-204	411
future advances	9-204(c); 9-323	404-409
statutory lien holders. *See also* Liens, statutory	9-333	436-442
subordination agreements	1-209; 9-334(f); 9-339	110, 356
unperfected creditors		317-323
first to attach rule	9-322(a)(3)	317
priority among	9-322(a)(3)	317
vs. buyer	9-317(b)	322-323
accounts, electronic chattel paper, or investment property	9-317(d)	322
inventory, purchase of	9-320(a)	323
vs. judicial lien creditor	9-317(a)(2)	320
vs. perfected creditor	9-317(a)(2)	318-319
vs. statutory lien holder	9-333	321
PROCEEDS OF COLLATERAL		
application of from sale upon default. *See also* Remedies upon default, secured party's	9-615	581-600
attachment and perfection	9-315	378-384
chattel paper, sale of as		388-393
consumer buyer, effect of	9-320(a)	389
inventory financer protection		393
new value and possession vs. inventory proceeds	9-330(b)	390
notice of assignment on	9-330(f)	392
vs. noninventory security interest	9-330(b)	391

Subject	U.C.C. Section	Text Section
defined		369, 373-375
description of in security agreement	9-315(a)	376
insurance as	9-102(a)(64)(E)	375
inventory. *See* Inventory		
operation of law, arise by	9-315(a)	376
option between proceeds or collateral	9-315(a)	377
priority of security interests in		
accounts as proceeds of inventory	9-322(a)(1)	386-388
"first to file or perfect" general rule	9-322(a)(1)	385
inventory purchase money security interests	9-324(b)	343
livestock purchase money security interests	9-324(d)	345
proceeds of cash proceeds	9-315(d)(1)(c); (e)	381-383
purchase money security interest in	9-324(b)	343, 388
pursuant to insolvency. *See* Insolvency, debtor's		
returned goods as		394-399
general rule—interest continues	9-330(c)	395-396
inventory financer vs. chattel paper	9-330(c)	399
perfection of		395
perfection required	9-315(d)	398
repossessed goods	9-330	396
third-party rights	9-330(c)	397-398
secured party's right to	9-315(a)	377
temporary automatic perfection	9-315(d)(1)(C), (e)	381
tort claims as	9-102(a)(64)(E)	375
PROFITS, ACCOUNTING FOR	9-207(c)	175
PROMISSORY NOTES	9-104(3); 9-309(3) - (4)	61, 204, 388
PROTECTION AGAINST PERFECTED SECURITY		
INTEREST IN		
buyer in ordinary course of business	9-320(a)	420-429
buyer not in ordinary course of business	9-323(d) - (e)	430-433
holder in due course	9-331	434-435
holder in lien implied by law	9-333	436-441
purchaser of consumer goods from consumers	9-320(b)	433
purchaser of nonnegotiable instruments	9-324(b)	388
PURCHASE MONEY SECURITY INTERESTS		
automatic perfection	9-309(1)	182
bankruptcy, grace period for		504-505
change in purchase money security interest debt, effect of	9-103(e) - (g)	194-196
combined with other security interests	9-103(e) - (h)	194-196
application of payments	9-103(a)(2) - (3)	195
consumer debts—no U.C.C. rule		196
dual status rule	9-103(e) - (g)	194
nonconsumer debt	9-103(e) - (g)	194
consignment as	9-103(d); 9-324	90, 346
consumer goods. *See also* Perfection, automatic	9-309(1)	182-196
defined	9-103	184-185
federal tax liens		448
fixtures	9-334	351-356
construction mortgage priority	9-334(h)	355-356
filing required	9-102(a)(40); 9-501(a)(1)(B); 9-502(b)	351-354
inventory	9-324(b)	336-347

Subject	U.C.C. Section	Text Section
after-acquired and existing		336
consignments treated as inventory purchase money		
security interests	9-103(d); 9-324	90, 346
floating lien creditors		344
livestock and proceeds of	9-324(d)	345
notice requirement	9-324(b)(2) - (4)	339-341
contents	9-324(b)(4)	340
duration	9-324(b)(3)	341
time of	9-324(b)(3)	341
perfection requirement	9-324(b)(1)	338
proceeds covered		343
multiple purchase money security interest creditors	9-324(g)	347
non-inventory, non-livestock	9-324(a)	331-335
proceeds of	9-324(b); 9-330(b)	388-391
security agreement requirement	9-203	186
super-priority of		330
who can obtain	9-103(a)(2)	185

PURCHASER
See Buyer

"PURSUANT TO COMMITMENT"	9-102(a)(68); 9-323(d)-(e)	431-432

Q

QUASI-TANGIBLE COLLATERAL
See also Collateral

buyers of	9-331	434-435

R

REAL ESTATE
See also Fixtures; Fixture filings

collateral description	9-502; 9-516	261
debtor's default re	9-604	530
financing statement	9-501	281
interest in, excluded from Article 9	9-109(d)(1), (11); 9-334(e)(1)	97, 358
rent from, excluded from Article 9	9-109(d)(1), (11)	97
timber and minerals on	9-502(b)	278

REALIZING UPON THE COLLATERAL
See also Remedies upon default, secured party's

disposition by sale	9-610	559-580
judicial sale	9-627(c)	602
strict foreclosure	9-620	550-558
suing on the debt	9-601(e)	601-602

REASONABLE CARE, DUTY OF	9-207(a)	170
RECEIVER	9-102(a)(52)	309-311
"RECOGNIZED MARKET"	9-611(d)	573-575
REDEMPTION OF COLLATERAL, DEBTOR'S **RIGHT OF**	9-623	603-606

See also Remedies, debtor's

REIMBURSEMENT	9-207(b)(1)	174
RELATION BACK	9-308(c)	225, 279

Subject	U.C.C. Section	Text Section
RELEASE OF COLLATERAL	9-512	295
REMEDIES, DEBTOR'S		
actual damages	9-625(b), (d)	608
attorney's fees		614
compulsory disposition of collateral (60% rule)	9-620(e); 9-625(c)	551-552
judicial remedy or damages	9-625(a)	607
noncomplying resale penalties	9-626	592
nonwaivable rights	9-602; 9-603	615-622
accounting for surplus	9-602(5)	616
compliance with default provisions	9-602(13)	621
discharge upon creditor's retention of collateral	9-602(10)	618
guarantor rights	9-602	622
notice requirements	9-607(7)	617
right of redemption	9-602(11)	620
punitive damages	9-625	609-613
bogus filing	9-509(a)	612
failure to relinquish control	9-208	610
improper payments from account debtors	9-209	611
notice of accounting	9-625(b), (e)	613
statement of account, failure to send	9-625(g)	301
termination statement, failure to send	9-513(a), (c)	612
waiver of accounting	9-625(b), (e)	301
redemption, right of	9-623	603-606
acceleration clause, effect of		605
tender of entire debt		604
waiver prior to default	9-602	603
statement of account or list of collateral	9-210	299-305
REMEDIES UPON DEFAULT, SECURED PARTY'S		
action on debt	9-601(e); 9-627(c)	601-602
debtor's right of redemption. *See also* Remedies, debtor's	9-623	
disposition of collateral by sale		559-580
commercial reasonableness	9-610(b); 9-626(a)(2)	560-562
good faith		560
preparation for sale		562
time of sale		562
notice required	9-611(d); 9-612(a), (b)	563-578
contents	9-613; 9-614	564-566
consumer goods	9-614	565, 578
safe harbor forms	9-613; 9-614	566
improper notice		567
perishable goods exception		563
persons to be notified	9-602; 9-611(c)	568-572
"recognized market" exception	9-611(d)	563, 573-575
nonconsumer transactions—safe harbor rule	9-612(b)	577
timing of	9-612(a)	576-578
consumer transactions	9-612(a)	578
other means of disposition	9-610	559
secured party's right to bid	9-610(c)	579-580
private sale	9-610(c)(2)	580
public sale	9-610(c)(1)	579
in general		527-530
basic remedies		528
cumulative	9-601(c)	527

Subject	U.C.C. Section	Text Section
documents or underlying goods	9-601(a)(2)	529
no election required	9-601(c)	527
real and personal property	9-604	530
partial satisfaction	9-620	558
proceeds from sale of collateral		581-600
debt defaulted on	9-615(a)(2)	583
expenses	9-615(a)(1)	582
junior creditors	9-615(a)(3), (g)	584-585
priority of application of sale proceeds	9-615	581
purchasers, rights of	9-504(4)	596-600
defective sale, effect of	9-617(b)	599
warranties on resale		600
surplus and deficiency	9-615	586-595
accounting to consumers	9-616; 9-625(b), (e)	591
accounts and chattel paper	9-615(e)	595
collusive sales	9-615(f); 9-626(a)(5)	589-594
consumer cases		593-594
computation of		587-591
debtor's liability for deficiency	9-615	586
noncompliance penalties	9-625(c)(2); 9-626	592, 594
payment intangibles and promissory notes	9-615(e)	595
removal of fixtures or accessions	9-335(e); 9-604(c)	626-628
repossession of collateral	9-609	531-549
breach of peace	9-609(b)	532-542
breaking and entering		537
constructive		536
debtor's protest		534-555
effect of		540
notice not required		541
simple trespass		538
trickery allowed		539
contrary security agreement provision		542
disabling equipment	9-609(a)(2)	546-547
duties of secured party	9-207; 9-603	548-549
in general	9-609	531
judicial process unnecessary		532
notice not required		541-543
right of assemblage of collateral provision	9-609(c)	545
retention of collateral—strict foreclosure	9-620	550
consumer goods exception		551-553
notice required	9-621	554-557
objection, effect of	9-620	557
no waiver	9-602(10)	556
sixty percent repayment rule	9-620(e); 9-625(c)	551-552

REMOVAL OF COLLATERAL INTERSTATE

See also Multistate Transactions, Perfection in

goods covered by certificate of title	9-303; 9-316(d), (e)	237, 254-257
possessory security interest in	9-301(2) - (3); 9-316(c)	235, 252
reperfection required	9-316(a)(1) - (3), (b), (f)	225, 243-250

RENTS

accounting for	9-207(c)	175
exclusion	9-109(d)(1), (11)	97

Subject	U.C.C. Section	Text Section
REPERFECTION		
See Removal of collateral interstate		
REPLEDGE OF COLLATERAL BY SECURED PARTY	9-207(c)(3)	179
REPOSSESSION OF COLLATERAL		
See Possession; Remedies upon default, secured party's		
RETENTION OF COLLATERAL		
See Possession; Remedies upon default, secured party's		
"RETURNED GOODS"	9-315(d); 9-330(c)	394-399
RIGHTS IN COLLATERAL, DEBTOR'S		
acceleration or insecurity clauses	1-203; 1-208	153, 513-517
after-acquired property, application to		135-143
alienability of	9-401(b)	152-153
defined	1-201(36)	148
identification of goods	2-501	151
requirement for attachment	9-203(b)(2)	119, 147
title irrelevant	9-202	149
when acquired		150-151
RISK OF LOSS	9-207(a), (b)(2)	176-178
S		
SALARY CLAIMS, EXCLUDED FROM ARTICLE 9	9-109(d)(3)	102
SALE		
See also Third party		
accounts	1-201(37); 9-109(a)(3); 9-309(3) - (4); 9-310	45, 49, 104, 204, 595, 623-625
chattel paper	9-109(a)(3), (d)(8), (d)(13); 9-604(e); 9-615(e)	45, 49, 104, 595, 623-625
collateral upon default. *See* Remedies upon default, secured party's		
conditional. *See* Conditional sale		
inventory, effect on priority	9-320; 9-322(a)(1); 9-324	336-337, 386-388, 419-428
public vs. private	9-610(c)(1), (2)	579-580
SALES ARTICLE, RELATION OF ARTICLE 9 TO		
conflicts with Article 9 interests. *See also* Priorities	2-702	454-465
identification of goods	2-501	151
insolvent debtor	2-702	459-465
security interest arising under	2-702; 9-110	455-465
SECURED PARTY		
assemblance of collateral, right to	9-609(c)	545
defined		47
duties of. *See* Duties		
liability of. *See* Liability		
protection against burdensome request	9-210(f)	302
remedies. *See* Remedies upon default, secured party's		
right to declare entire obligation due	1-208	513-517
rights and duties in possession	9-207	169-180
rights upon debtor's insolvency. *See* Insolvency, debtor's		
SECURITIES		
See Investment property		

Subject	U.C.C. Section	Text Section
SECURITY AGREEMENT		
acceleration clause in. *See also* Acceleration clause	1-208	153, 513
after-acquired property clause	9-204	135-140
accounts and farm equipment		140
commercial tort claims exception	9-204(b)(2)	137
consumer goods exception	9-204(b)(1)	136
Credit Practices Rule		136
inventory		139
specificity required		138
anti-waiver clause	2-208	526
as financing statement		258
authenticated record required, in general	9-203(b)(3)(A)	122, 125-143
effect of		126
electronic means or writing	9-102(a)(7), (69)	122, 127
no possession or control of collateral	9-302(b)(3)(A)	125
consumer protection statutes		112-113, 136, 412
creation of security interest	9-102(a)(73)	46
debtor's authentication	9-102(a)(7); 9-203(b)(3)(A)	125-127
default provisions	9-601	145, 510
defined	9-102(a)(73)	46, 117
description of collateral in. *See also* Description of collateral, in security agreement		
errors, effect of		134
financing statement distinguished		133
no supergeneric descriptions	9-108(c)	132
reasonably identifies collateral	9-108	129-133
when type alone insufficient	9-108(e)	131
dragnet clause in		410-412
exculpatory clause in	1-102(3)	173
floating liens	9-204(a); 9-205	141-143, 344, 420, 449, 507-509
bankruptcy problem		143, 507-509
defined		141
federal tax liens		449
inventory	9-320(a)	344, 420
governing default, in general		510, 512-526
insecurity clause in	1-208	514-517
good faith	1-201(19)	515-517
miscellaneous terms		144
oral agreement, when sufficient	9-203(b)(3)(B), (D)	123-124
proceeds obtained in violation of		379
prohibiting alienation of debtor's rights in collateral	9-401(b)	152-153
provision for collateral assemblage	9-609(c)	545
"time is of the essence" clause		526
unconscionability of		544
validity of, in general	9-203	122-127
waiver of defenses against assignee	9-403	518-525
consumer goods limitation	9-403(e)	522-525
federal statutes		525
good faith	9-403	519
validity of	9-403	519-521
SECURITY DEVICES, PRE-CODE		
chattel mortgage		13-15

Subject	U.C.C. Section	Text Section
conditional sales		16-20
U.C.C. provisions	9-202	19-20
factor's acts		25-27
field warehousing		24
fraudulent conveyances		5-9
early U.S. law		6
incorporation by U.C.C.	2-402(2)	7-8
Statute of Elizabeth		5
nonnotification assignment of accounts receivable		28-34
bankruptcy proceedings		31-34
pledge		10-12
trust receipt		21-23

SECURITY INTEREST

Subject	U.C.C. Section	Text Section
arising under Article 2		454-465
Article 9 priority and Article 2 rights. See also Priority, Article 2		
claimants vs. Article 9 security interests	9-110	458-465
assignment of	9-514	202-203
attachment of. See Attachment of security interest		
conflicting. See Conflicting security interest in same		
collateral		
creation of. See also Attachment of security interest		116-117
defined	1-201(37)	43-45
effect of bankruptcy upon	2-702	463-465, 474-477, 507-509
governed by U.S. statute	9-109(c)(1)	94
perfection of. See Perfection of security interest		
priority. See Priority		
purchase money. See Purchase money security interest		
termination of. See Termination of security interest;		
Termination statement		
U.C.C. policies		114-115
prevention of non-U.C.C. systems		115
protection of lenders	9-201	114
unperfected, in general. See also Priority		312-323
waiver. See also Waiver		413-418

SELF-HELP

See Remedies upon default, secured party's

Subject	U.C.C. Section	Text Section
SET-OFF, PRIORITY	9-327(3) - (4); 9-340	383, 402

Subject	U.C.C. Section	Text Section
SHIP MORTGAGE ACT		94, 282

SIGNATURE

Subject	U.C.C. Section	Text Section
as authentication of record	9-102(a)(7)	122, 126-127
prior requirement of		122, 127

Subject	U.C.C. Section	Text Section
"SIGNIFICANT PORTION" RULE	9-309(2)	198-201

See also Assignment

STATEMENT OF ACCOUNT, REQUEST FOR

Subject	U.C.C. Section	Text Section
STATEMENT OF ACCOUNT, REQUEST FOR	9-210	289-305
burdensome requests	9-210(f)	302
by debtor	9-210	299
by third party		303-305
estoppel and misstatements		305
information on file limitation		303
recourse of		304
failure to reply to	9-625(b), (f) - (g)	301

Subject	U.C.C. Section	Text Section
secured party's response		300
STATUTE OF ELIZABETH		5
STATUTES, FEDERAL		
See Federal statutes		
STATUTORY LIEN		
See Lien, statutory		
STATUTORY LIEN CREDITOR		
See Lien creditor		
STRICT FORECLOSURE	9-620	550-558
See also Remedies upon default; secured party's		
SUBORDINATION AGREEMENTS	1-209; 9-339	110
See also Priority, subordination agreements		
and construction mortgages	9-334(f)	356
defined	1-209	110
effect on priority	9-339	110
not a security interest	9-209	110
SUBROGATION RIGHTS		
See Sureties		
SUING ON THE DEBT		
See Action for debt		
SUIT		
See Action for debt		
SURETIES		
and Article 9		1, 3
entitled to notice	6-111(c)(2)	571
nonwaivable rights	9-602	622
subrogation rights not security interest		109
supporting obligations, perfection of	9-102(a)(77), 9-308(d)	205
SURPLUS		
See Deficiency, secured party's right to recover		
T		
TANGIBLE COLLATERAL		
See Collateral		
TAX LIEN		
See Federal tax lien		
TEMPORARY AUTOMATIC PERFECTION		
See Temporary perfection		
TEMPORARY PERFECTION		
See also Multistate transactions, perfection in		
debtor's change of identity	9-316(a)(3)	251
delivery of goods or negotiable documents	9-312(f)	209
delivery of instruments or certificated securities	9-312(g)	210
interstate transfer of collateral	9-316(a)(2), (b), (e)-(f)	243-245, 255-257
new value given for documents, certificated securities, or instruments	9-312(e)	207
proceeds	9-315(d) - (e)	381, 384
TENDER	9-623	604-605

Subject	U.C.C. Section	Text Section
See also Remedies, debtor's redemption		
TERMINATION CLAUSE		
See Lease		
TERMINATION OF SECURITY INTEREST		
See Termination statement		
TERMINATION STATEMENT		
as remedy for bogus filings	9-509	296
damages for noncompliance	9-625(b), (e)(4)	292
when necessary to send	9-102(a)(79)	292
written demand by debtor	9-513(b)	293-294
THIRD PARTY		
purchaser upon default, rights of	9-617	596-600
request for information re security interest		303-305
right to notice of sale of collateral	9-611(c)	571-572
security interest in returned goods	9-315(d); 9-330(c)	397-398
subordination of security interest to	1-209; 9-334(f); 9-339	110, 356
TIME FOR		
attachment	9-203	118-121
attachment in after-acquired property	9-204(a)	135
continuation statement	9-102(a)(27); 9-515(d)	286
disposal of collateral	9-610(b); 9-612(a)	561, 576-578
effectiveness of financing statement	9-515(a); 9-516(a)	284, 287-290
perfection	9-308(a), (c)	224-225
termination statement	9-102(a)(79); 9-625(b), (e)(4)	292-293
TITLE		
irrelevant under U.C.C.	9-202	19
TORT CLAIMS		
See Commercial tort claims		
TRADE NAMES	9-503(c)	272
TRANSACTIONS EXCLUDED FROM ARTICLE 9	9-109	93-113
artisan's liens	9-109(d)(2)	98
consumer deposit accounts	9-109(d)(13)	103
consumer protection statutes		112-113
federal statutes	9-109(c)(1)	94-96
insurance policies	9-109(d)(8)	103
judicial claims		72, 100-101
commercial tort claims exception		72
landlord's liens	9-109(d)(1), (11)	97
liens on real property	9-109(d)(11)	97
mechanic's liens	9-109(d)(2)	98
"one-shot" assignments	9-109(a)(3)	104-108
coupled with performance delegation	9-109(d)(6)	107
for collection	9-109(d)(5)	106
payment of prior debts	9-109(d)(7)	108
sale of business	9-109(d)(4)	105
rents		97
subordination agreements	1-209; 9-339	110
subsequent transactions included	9-109(b)	111
surety's subrogation rights		109
U.C.C. remedies		96
wage and salary claims	9-109(d)(3)	102

Subject	U.C.C. Section	Text Section
TRANSACTIONS SUBJECT TO ARTICLE 9	9-109(a)	76-92, 95
consignments		88-92
defined		88
protective filing	9-505	92
true consignments, when covered	9-102(a)(20)	89-91
federal loans		95
leases		77-87
protective filing	9-505	87
true lease vs. security interest		78-86
irrelevant terms		82-85
test	1-201(37)	78-86
TRESPASS		
See Breaking and entering		
TRUST RECEIPT		21-23
TRUSTEE IN BANKRUPTCY		
See Bankruptcy		
U		
ULTIMATE PRODUCT	9-336(b) - (d), (f)(1), (2)	365-368
See also Commingled goods		
UNCONSCIONABILITY		594
UNDERLYING TRANSACTIONS NOT WITHIN CODE	9-109(b)	111
UNIFORM FRAUDULENT TRANSFER ACT		486
UNIFORM TRUST RECEIPTS ACT		23
UNPERFECTED SECURITY INTEREST, EFFECT OF	9-322(a)	317-323
See also Priority		
UNSECURED CREDITOR		
bankruptcy, effect on		31-33, 477
generally		303, 483
USE OF COLLATERAL		
secured party in possession	9-207(b)(4)	180
V		
VALUE		
definition	1-201(44)	140
purchase money security interest	9-103(a)(2)	185
requirement of	9-203(b)(1)	119, 146
VOIDABLE PREFERENCE		
See also Bankruptcy		
excused preferences		497-499
contemporaneous exchange		498
routine payments		499
floating lien as		143, 507-508
generally		491-492
insolvency requirement		494-496
nonnotification financing as		31
nonpreferential payments		493
transfer of security interest as		490-492

Subject	U.C.C. Section	Text Section
WXYZ		
WAGE CLAIMS, EXCLUDED FROM ARTICLE 9	9-109(d)(3)	102
WAIVER		
See also Default; Remedies, debtor's		
accounting for surplus	9-602(5)	616
antiwaiver clause and late payments	2-208	526
debtor's right of compulsory disposition of collateral	9-624	553
defenses against assignee. *See also* Default, assignees		
consumer goods limitation	9-403(e)	518-525
"good faith"		520
in general	9-403	519
"real" defenses	3-305; 9-403(c)	521
validity of	9-403	519-521
discharge upon retention	9-602(10)	618
disclaimer of liability	1-102(3); 9-602	173, 601
due care of collateral	1-102(3)	173
foreclosure sale, right to	9-624	553
nonwaivable rights. *See* Remedies, debtor's		
notice of resale after default	9-602(7); 9-624	603, 617
notice of resale before default	9-602	569, 617
right of redemption after default	9-624(c)	620
right of redemption before default	9-602(11)	606, 619
secured party's right to deficiency	9-616(b)(1) - (2)	591, 613
security interest		413-418
WAREHOUSE RECEIPT	7-403; 9-312(c)	24, 63, 163, 165
See also Documents, warehouse receipt		
WARRANTIES FOR RESALE AFTER DEFAULT		600

Notes

Notes

Notes

Notes

Notes

Notes